The

ACT

of

LIVING

ALSO BY FRANK TALLIS

The Incurable Romantic: And Other Tales of Madness and Desire

Love Sick: Love as a Mental Illness

Hidden Minds: A History of the Unconscious

The
ACT
of
LIVING

WHAT THE GREAT
PSYCHOLOGISTS CAN TEACH US
ABOUT FINDING FULFILLMENT

FRANK TALLIS

BASIC BOOKS
New York

Basic Books
Hachette Book Group
1290 Avenue of the Americas, New York, NY 10104
www.basicbooks.com

Printed in the United States of America

First U.S. Edition: July 2020

Published by Basic Books, an imprint of Perseus Books, LLC, a subsidiary of Hachette Book Group, Inc. The Basic Books name and logo is a trademark of the Hachette Book Group.

The Hachette Speakers Bureau provides a wide range of authors for speaking events. To find out more, go to www.hachettespeakersbureau.com or call (866) 376-6591.

The publisher is not responsible for websites (or their content) that are not owned by the publisher.

Print book interior design by Amy Quinn.

Library of Congress Cataloging-in-Publication Data has been applied for.

ISBNs: 978-1-5416-7303-8 (hardcover), 978-1-5416-7304-5 (ebook)

LSC-C

10 9 8 7 6 5 4 3 2 1

In memory of Professor Walter Wells: academic, writer, teacher, editor, raconteur, role model, prizewinner, kindler of talents, polymath, bon viveur, accidental pugilist, gentleman, friend, American.

CONTENTS

INTRODUCTION

There is only one meaning of life: the act of living itself.

—Erich Fromm, *Escape from Freedom* (1941)

The average person has no difficulty naming five philosophers. Plato, Aristotle, Descartes, Nietzsche, and Sartre appear so frequently in our general reading that they are familiar to many of us. However, if this same person were asked to name five famous psychotherapists, he or she would probably find it more difficult—perhaps even impossible. Freud and Jung might spring to mind, but others would be slow to follow. Older respondents might remember R. D. Laing, who became something of a celebrity in the 1960s. That only brings the count to three. Most people have never even heard of figures like Fritz Perls, Wilhelm Reich, Donald Winnicott, or Albert Ellis. They certainly wouldn't be able to name any contemporary psychotherapists, such as Francine Shapiro or Steve Hayes.

Yet the major figures of psychotherapy have had much to say about the human condition. Viewed as a cohesive body of knowledge, psychotherapy is equal in ambition, scope, and utility to any other scholarly tradition. Even so, it is rarely perceived in this way. Instead, we think of it only in its narrowest sense: as a treatment for mental illness. Although the clinical provenance of

1

psychotherapy is important, its intellectual legacy has much wider relevance. It can offer original perspectives on the "big questions," the ones usually entrusted to philosophers and representatives of faith: Who am I? Why am I here? How should I live?

Although psychotherapy (in a limited sense) has existed for as long as doctors have been comforting and advising patients, it wasn't until the nineteenth century that cultural and scientific conditions favored the emergence of psychoanalysis, the first truly modern form of psychotherapy.

Sigmund Freud began his career studying nerve cells in a laboratory before becoming a neurologist and going on to develop psychoanalysis. Compared to his contemporaries, Freud was—perhaps with the single exception of the philosopher and psychologist Pierre Janet—by far the most ambitious theorist. Freud amalgamated French psychopathology, German psychophysics, and sexology to craft a flexible model of the mind that possessed enormous explanatory power. In due course, the compass of psychoanalysis expanded beyond purely medical considerations. Freud's new "science" afforded fresh insights into art, speculative prehistory, and religion. In the 1920s, Freud asserted that "psychoanalysis is not a medical specialty." He was concerned that psychoanalysis would be viewed only as a treatment method because he had become convinced that he had stumbled upon something closer to a "worldview." His clinical work was merely an entry point, a way into the mind that would ultimately lead to important nonmedical discoveries. Psychoanalysis could explain much more than hysteria and neurosis. It could explain love, desire, dreams, ghosts, violence, literature, and the behavior of crowds. One could even use psychoanalysis to peer into the minds of long-dead creative geniuses, such as Leonardo da Vinci and Michelangelo.

Freud compared psychoanalysis to electricity. Electricity is used in hospitals—for example, to make X-ray images—but electricity is not categorically "medical." Electricity powers radios, trams, and streetlights. Powering hospitals is only one of its many uses. Freud's electricity analogy works not just for psychoanalysis, but for all of psychotherapy. Ideas generated by psychotherapists can be used to treat mental illness, but they can also be used to show how the mind functions, how minds relate to each other, and how minds operate within cultures. They can also be used to answer questions concerning ideal ways to live (the so-called good life, or eudaimonia) that have been debated since ancient times.

If psychotherapy is a tradition that can inform and instruct beyond medical settings, why don't we, as a society, consult the psychotherapy literature more often when grappling with the problems of living? After all, the problems of living are its core concern. The principal reason is that the interested layperson is immediately confronted with impenetrable language. What might we expect to gain by acquainting ourselves with the basic tenets of Gestalt therapy or logotherapy? We can easily guess what a specialty like heart surgery involves, because we all know what a heart is. But what's so primal about primal therapy, and what kind of transaction takes place in transactional analysis? The nomenclature of psychotherapy is so opaque it usually discourages further inquiry.

Even the word "psychotherapy" is frequently used in ways that breed confusion. In some hospitals, for example, the psychotherapy department offers treatments strongly associated with Freud and psychoanalysis. Psychological treatments unrelated to the Freudian tradition might be offered elsewhere in the same hospital. This gives the impression that some forms of psychological treatment are called psychotherapy and others aren't; however, all forms of psychological (as opposed to pharmacological) treatment can be accurately described as psychotherapy.

Nearly all psychotherapies have conversation and a confiding relationship in common.* They also share a common goal: reducing distress, even if this means facing up to difficult truths and realities in the short term. Techniques vary according to what theory is guiding the treatment process. Some approaches are exploratory, while others are directive; some seek to recover inaccessible memories, others aim to modify unhelpful beliefs; some encourage deeper self-understanding, some focus on the acquisition of coping skills. And so on. Freudian psychoanalysis is the most famous and established form of psychotherapy. We are all familiar with the cliché: a bearded therapist sitting behind a reclining patient. But this popular image of Freudian psychotherapy is actually misguided. It suggests that psychoanalysis is unitary and fixed. In fact, Freud was constantly revising psychoanalysis and it continued to evolve after his death.

The numerous types of psychotherapy that exist today fall into three main groups: psychoanalytic, humanistic-existential, and cognitive-behavioral. Psychoanalysis emphasizes the recovery of unconscious memories and the management of tensions that arise when primitive desires come into conflict with moral and social expectations. The humanistic-existential school stresses the importance of autonomy and authenticity: making choices, accepting

---

* There are exceptions, insofar as some interventions are automated and delivered by telephone or over the Internet. There are also apps designed to help people manage problems such as anxiety, depression, and posttraumatic stress disorder. Nevertheless, the vast majority of psychotherapy involves dialogue and face-to-face contact, and the nature of these conversations and the therapeutic significance of the relationship will differ according to the kind of psychotherapy being practiced.

responsibility, finding meaning, and achieving personal growth. And the cognitive-behavioral school connects distress with aversive learning experiences, inaccurate thinking, and the formation of dysfunctional beliefs. These are highly reductive summary descriptions that will be elaborated in subsequent chapters.

From Freud's time onward, the history of psychotherapy has been one of continuous argument. There has always been animosity within schools and between schools, giving the impression of fragmentation. There doesn't seem to be much of a "tradition" to consult. Although there *are* differences between schools of psychotherapy, there are also very many areas of agreement. The schools of psychotherapy resemble an archipelago. Above the water, we see disconnected islands, but if we dive beneath the surface, we find that these individual columns of rock are rooted in the same landmass. The deeper we go, the more obvious it becomes that all the islands are supported by similar (or even the same) bedrock.

Apart from Freud and psychoanalysis, the intellectual legacy of psychotherapy remains relatively inaccessible. Indeed, it is encountered almost exclusively in consulting rooms and academia. Magazines and websites include abundant quantities of pop psychology, but typically, the key ideas of significant psychotherapists are either misrepresented or oversimplified. This is unfortunate, because we have never been in greater need of real psychological knowledge.

Compared to previous generations, we have unprecedented access to information, increased personal freedom, more material comforts, more possessions, and longer life expectancy. Yet a very significant number of people are depressed, anxious, or dissatisfied. Mental "health" statistics demonstrate that as life gets better, we (and our children) are becoming increasingly sad, worried, and lonely. In the United Kingdom, the first "minister for loneliness" was appointed in January 2018. While pundits warn of impending catastrophes—rising sea levels, robots taking our jobs, collapsing financial markets, bacterial resistance to antibiotics, collision with an asteroid—another disaster has already arrived. The number of people currently suffering from mental illness is unprecedented. The World Health Organization reports that more lives are claimed globally by suicide than by war, murder, state execution, and terrorist attacks combined. The toll now amounts to approximately one million people every year.[1] Someone, somewhere, chooses to die—often violently—every forty seconds. For these individuals, just being conscious has become intolerably painful. In the developed world, self-harm is the main cause of death for people between the ages of fifteen and forty-nine. It has overtaken heart disease and cancer.

The incidence of mental illness is so high that the provision of proper treatment and care for all those affected is no longer possible. Politicians have only recently acknowledged the financial impact of this developing crisis. "Subjective well-being" is now construed as a form of capital, and psychological health has been afforded special significance in "happiness economics." This new approach to fiscal governance is predicated on the idea that eventually, all unhappy countries become poor countries. Mental illness is costly. Psychological problems are the most common reason people take time off work; the loss of productive workdays in modern economies is calculated to be on the order of hundreds of billions of dollars. The economic burden of depression alone on the US economy is estimated at $210 billion a year—a figure in excess of the combined gross domestic product (GDP) of several smaller countries. There are direct or "visible costs" (such as medication, psychotherapy, hospitalization, etc.) and indirect or "invisible costs" (such as reduced productivity and early retirement). Based on data from 2010, the European Molecular Biology Organization published a report in 2016 in which the global direct and indirect economic cost of mental illness was calculated to be $2.5 trillion.

According to the World Health Organization, half of those affected by mental illness exhibit symptoms before reaching the age of fourteen. Various indices of severity have doubled or even quadrupled in recent years. For example, the National Health Service Adult Psychiatric Morbidity Survey in the United Kingdom found that rates of self-harm among English adults had doubled between 2000 and 2014. A 2019 study published in *The Lancet* reported that the prevalence of nonsuicidal self-harm in English women and girls aged sixteen to twenty-four had risen from 6.5 percent in 2000 to 19.7 percent in 2014. Prescription drug use for psychological problems has shown a roughly proportional increase. National Health Service digital figures recorded 70.9 million prescriptions for antidepressant medications in England during 2018, almost double the number dispensed in 2008. Presumably, if pharmacological treatments—which are relatively inexpensive and can be delivered easily—were not available, the situation would be considerably worse. Globally, one in nine people suffer from an anxiety disorder in any given year. Seven million of those sufferers are in the United Kingdom, and 35 million in the United States.[2]

Some have suggested that contemporary mental health statistics should be treated with caution because they do not reflect a "real" trend. Reduced stigma has encouraged more people to report symptoms, diagnostic manuals have become thicker, and better professional training has improved detection rates. Arguments of this kind are not compelling, because however we choose to qualify our interpretation of mental health statistics, the fact remains that they describe a society in crisis.

It is difficult to specify when ordinary sadness becomes a clinical condition. Diagnostic criteria represent an attempt to differentiate normal sadness from abnormal sadness, but almost all diagnostic systems are imperfect and to a greater or lesser extent arbitrary. There are no definitive biological tests—like a blood test—for mental illness. Current mental health statistics suggest that so many people are affected by psychological problems that what we have previously called abnormal is becoming increasingly typical. Behind the very high numbers of people who meet diagnostic criteria stand those who, although not "ill," are not functioning optimally. Life doesn't feel quite right—something is missing—they are beset by doubts about purpose and want more. "Is this all there is?" The relative contributions of biological and psychological factors to mental illness can vary from person to person; however, given that the brain hasn't changed at all in the last ten thousand years, it is very likely that rising levels of mental illness and dissatisfaction are largely attributable to modern life.

Modernity, as we now think of it, refers to technological and social changes arising after the industrial revolution. The American physician George Beard introduced the psychiatric diagnosis of neurasthenia in 1869, a symptom cluster characterized by nervous exhaustion and malaise, which he attributed to the fast pace of urban living. The relationship between modernity and mental illness was explored again by Freud in *Civilization and Its Discontents*. This extended essay, published in 1930, is probably the most famous exposition of a recurring thesis: living in the modern world creates stresses and strains that have a detrimental effect on the psychological health of human beings. In *Freud and Man's Soul*, the psychoanalyst Bruno Bettelheim suggested that *Civilization and Its Discontents* is a misleading translation of Freud's original German title: *Das Unbehagen in der Kultur*. A more accurate rendition in English would be *The Uneasiness Inherent in Culture*. Freud's German title does not include the word "and"—a connective that implies that there is a thing called "civilization," and among the civilized there are some who are "discontent." (Freud didn't like "discontent"; he preferred "malaise" or "discomfort.") Bettelheim pointed out that in the German title, "uneasiness" and "culture" are inseparable. If you live in the modern world, you will be—at least to some extent—uncomfortable and unhappy. This is inevitable.

Freud's position is entirely consistent with that of evolutionary psychology. We have evolved to live in one environment but live in another, and the faster our environment changes, the more our brains get left behind, unable to adapt and adjust to new demands. We now spend much of our lives in an entirely novel environment: cyberspace. There is nothing inherently wrong with the Internet, but a great deal of discomfort and malaise seems to have arisen because of our limited capacity to make swift, healthy adaptations—particularly so with respect to social media. Mental illness, especially in the young, has been linked with screen time. There are significant problems with existing research: poorly defined variables, a dearth of direct causal data, and selective reporting intended to support critical arguments.[3] However, yearly surveys conducted in the United States of over a million young respondents show a sudden decrease in psychological well-being (self-esteem, life satisfaction, happiness) after 2012. Experts have concluded that the most plausible explanation for this decline is the rapid adoption of smartphones by adolescents.[4] It is easy to characterize critics of the Internet as Luddites or alarmists, but among those critics we must count Tim Berners-Lee—the man who invented the Internet. "Humanity," says Berners-Lee, "connected by technology on the web is functioning in a dystopian way."[5]

The first ever best-selling self-help book was called, somewhat literally, *Self-Help*. It was written by Samuel Smiles and published in 1859, the same year as Darwin's *On the Origin of Species*. The self-help industry has been growing ever since—and it continues to balloon. Sales for self-help books in the United Kingdom climbed by 20 percent in 2018.[6] Shelves sag under the weight of these books. Many offer ideas for living derived from alternative cultural perspectives, the works of celebrated writers and historical figures, philosophical schools, or pop psychology. Others summarize the thoughts and reflections of various celebrity gurus. Sometimes, a self-help agenda is found in unexpected places. A recent and highly acclaimed best seller was marketed as a work that could potentially deepen the reader's understanding of life by means of chopping, stacking, and drying wood. Reviewers found within its pages (probably contrary to the author's intention) instructions for transcendence and well-being. People are clearly desperate for answers. Although charismatic figures are reassuring, and inspirational slogans can raise one's mood and provide motivation, the beneficial effects of such remedies are likely to be short-lived. Recalibration with reality is accompanied by the painful recognition that nothing has really changed. When we wake up in the middle of the night and stare into darkness, the existential absolutes still weigh heavily upon us.

The frenetic level of activity that characterizes modern life suggests that many people are engaged in an ongoing and profitless search. We rush from one thing to another, seemingly caught up in endless rounds of gratification and frustration: money, diets, cosmetics, social media, cars, games, smartphones—trends, fashions, fads. Are all these things substitutes for something more substantial—something invisible but nevertheless real and attainable—or are they simply distractions, a means of avoiding feelings of emptiness that would otherwise overwhelm us?

When we ask ourselves big questions, we want answers that have credible rationales, answers that arise from within a coherent intellectual framework or can be confirmed through observation.

Freud and the post-Freudians scrutinized unhappiness and excavated the mind to discover its causes. They rejected religious dogma, along with philosophical abstraction, and developed theories from frequent and systematic study. They understood that human questions demand human answers and that, without understanding what it means to be human, there are no answers.

For over a hundred years, psychotherapists have been developing and refining models of the human mind. They have endeavored to alleviate distress, and they have offered help to people who want to make better life choices. Collectively, they have produced a body of work that has kept faith with Freud's lofty ambitions for psychoanalysis—his hope that psychoanalysis would eventually become widely acknowledged as more than a branch of medicine, something closer to a general frame of reference, something relevant and applicable beyond the treatment of psychiatric conditions.

When psychotherapists look at a person, they see a very different creature from the one that, say, a philosopher or a priest would see. Aspects of the human experience that seem trivial, irrelevant, or distasteful to other disciplines are often given special significance by psychotherapists. Freud was willing to consider aspects of being human that had barely been acknowledged before his time—for example, awareness of bowel movements, early memories, primitive urges, and our propensity to tell jokes. Psychotherapy has been relatively fearless in this respect. It has resisted aggrandizing the human condition and has always accepted the coarse realities of embodiment.

Leonardo da Vinci's famous pen-and-ink drawing *Vitruvian Man*—depicting the proportions of the human body according to the Roman architect Vitruvius—is frequently reproduced to represent the power of the human intellect and the preeminence of humankind. The symmetries and mathematical perfection of the human form are said to signal our cosmological significance. Freud and other major figures from psychotherapy reverse Vitruvian exceptionalism. They check our narcissistic tendencies, advising us to see ourselves as we really are, neither at the center of things nor dignified by expansive symbolism.

Human nature has been shaped by confluent evolutionary pressures. We have identical nervous systems, all experience basic emotions, and are motivated by the same "drives." Geneticists frequently remind us that we share 96 percent of our DNA with chimpanzees. If we are that closely related to our animal cousins, then the fundamental differences that distinguish us from each other must be very small indeed. Even people from entirely different parts of the world are more similar than they are different, and when people are raised in the same culture, their needs, desires, and dreams converge.

How we choose to live is highly individual, and what is right for one person might be wrong for his or her neighbor. But pain

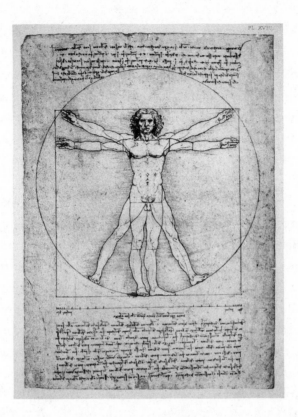

is always painful and pleasure is always pleasurable. We can be dissatisfied for different reasons, but the quality of that dissatisfaction, its felt essence, is a reliable constant.

So, if we grapple with the same problems of living, why is it that we rarely consult psychotherapy as a repository of ideas? Opaque nomenclature is one obstacle. Antagonism between schools of psychotherapy is another. Psychotherapy is also accused of intellectual impoverishment, absurdity, and charlatanry. When Alfred Adler, one of Freud's early associates, was scorned for espousing ideas that were really just common sense, he replied, "And what is wrong with common sense?" If the recommendations for living derived from psychotherapy are sometimes straightforward and correspond with experience, then surely that is desirable.

The charge of absurdity usually arises in the context of psychoanalysis. Freud's theory of sexual development, for example, which hinges on precocious sexual feelings and incestuous urges, has been outraging commentators since its inception. And yet, over the past thirty years, Freud's theory has gained at least partial support from several respectable sources, most decidedly neuroscience and evolutionary biology, and many significant scientists have expressed admiration for Freud's general accomplishments. In his 2012 book *The Age of Insight*, Eric Kandel (who received the Nobel Prize for his work on memory storage and the brain) wrote the following summation: "The consensus is that Freud's theory of mind is a monumental contribution to modern thought. Despite the obvious weakness of not being empirical, it still stands, a century later, as perhaps the most influential and coherent view of mental activity that we have."[7] A new discipline—neuropsychoanalysis—which seeks to discover the biological underpinnings of Freudian concepts, emerged in the 1990s. There is now an International Neuropsychoanalysis Society that publishes its own scientific journal.

Unfortunately, many of the major thinkers of psychotherapy have been exceptionally bad role models. Individuals like Otto Gross and Wilhelm Reich ended their lives ignominiously—the former destitute, the latter in jail. Disappointing anecdotes concerning the unorthodox behavior of counterculture heroes such as Fritz Perls and R. D. Laing are commonplace. Given their questionable conduct, we are tempted to conclude that their theories must be worthless. However, many of these figures were casualties as well as pioneers, victims of their own success. They tested their theories by experimenting with alternative lifestyles and altered states of consciousness; they followed their patients into madness; they were like explorers, venturing into the unknown. And inevitably, some of them paid a very high price. Gross and Reich paid with their sanity.

Psychotherapy, as a source of life lessons, is best appreciated as a totality. Adler's critic was not entirely misguided. Certain psychotherapeutic ideas, removed from their context, *can* appear simplistic, or even banal. Others seem far-fetched. Even so, if one steps back to see the bigger picture, if one sees psychotherapy not as a group of competing schools, but as a single tradition, then one begins to get a sense of how much is required to achieve fulfillment. The enormity of the task is daunting because we have numerous and complex needs. We need to talk, to be understood, to have a cohesive sense of self, to have insight, to be loved, to feel safe, to satisfy biological appetites, to resolve inner conflicts, to be accepted, to overcome adversity, to have purpose, to find meaning, and to accept our own mortality. Viewed in this way, it isn't at all surprising that so many people are unhappy and dissatisfied. Life is a lifetime's work.

The goals of psychotherapy are not so very different from the goals of everyday life. People want to be happy and optimize outcomes. Psychotherapy stands in stark opposition to quick fixes. The problems of living cannot be addressed by simply adopting a positive attitude, reciting mottos, or chopping wood. Fulfillment is *so* challenging, *so* contingent upon an incalculable number of processes and chance events, that it is necessary to establish priorities. Where do we start? In my view, this is what psychotherapy, as an intellectual tradition, has achieved. It has identified what is important. The major figures of psychotherapy, its greatest thinkers, spent every working day of their lives confronting the problems of the human condition in their most intense and distressing forms.

Psychotherapy is grounded in reality, unflinching and pragmatic. It poses questions that are particularly relevant to life as lived by conscious, embodied beings whose psychology has been shaped by evolution, childhood, and social context. It eschews rote answers and teaches us that a well-constructed and precisely aimed question is almost always more consequential than a nugget of received wisdom.

I trained in clinical psychology at what was once called the Institute of Psychiatry (now the Institute of Psychiatry, Psychology and Neuroscience) in London. It was essentially a research establishment attached to the Bethlem Royal and Maudsley Hospitals. Bethlem, a contraction of Bethlehem, is the etymological germ of the word "bedlam," which is routinely used to mean insanity, uproar, and chaos. Although the Bethlem Hospital was founded in 1247, the mad arrived about twenty years later, when Richard II closed a small hospital called Stone House because the noisy residents were disturbing his falcons.[8] The department of clinical psychology at the Institute of Psychiatry, with its oblique connections with medieval London, had its own (if somewhat shorter) historical legacy. It was at the Institute of Psychiatry that Hans Eysenck (and a small group of colleagues) established the United Kingdom's first course in clinical psychology. Eysenck rejected psychoanalysis and was a vociferous advocate of behavior therapy. He believed that psychological problems were best construed as instances of "bad" learning and that they could be unlearned using brief, simple procedures.

Eysenck was an enormously influential figure who became well-known for his pugnacious advocacy of scientific psychology. When I was a trainee clinician, he still—quite literally—loomed large. Before being accepted as a student at the institute, I had completed a doctorate at St. George's Hospital Medical School and Royal Holloway and Bedford New College. One of my supervisors was the eminent clinical cognitive psychologist Andrew Mathews. The other was Hans Eysenck's son, Michael, whose relaxed manner seemed to me to be a constant refutation of his father's genetic determinism.

Ultimately, it was because of Hans Eysenck that I served my clinical apprenticeship in an environment where all treatment methods other than behavioral or cognitive-behavioral therapy were considered unscientific, ineffective, and potentially harmful. Yet, back then, even without the benefit of what would eventually amount to twenty years of clinical experience, I was deeply suspicious of therapeutic fundamentalism. Why not keep an open mind? I joined a small supervision group run by Dr. Nicholas Temple, a future president of the British Psychoanalytic Society, and found the experience both stimulating and enriching. I had always been taught that psychoanalysis and behavioral therapy were antithetical, but I began to identify similarities.

I became increasingly impatient with territorial posturing and found it much more rewarding to reflect on how ostensibly oppositional schools of psychotherapy shared common ground. Moreover, I realized that many of the differences among the three main divisions of psychotherapy were exaggerated by the use of specialized vocabularies. Abandoning exclusive jargon immediately resolved many contradictions.

Eclecticism has its problems: it lacks purity, it can be unfocused, and, if taken to extremes, it can become incoherent. Nevertheless, I remain convinced that the benefits of judicious eclecticism vastly outweigh the potential costs.

A book of this kind—which is essentially a personal synthesis—is necessarily selective. Nevertheless, I have tried to reference most of the major personalities in psychotherapy and their key contributions. There are some notable omissions: Franz Alexander, Ludwig Binswanger, Erik Erikson, Karen Horney, Harry Stack Sullivan, Rollo May, Jacques Lacan, William Glasser, Anthony Ryle, Emmy van Deurzen, Marsha Linehan. This roll call could continue more or less indefinitely. My cast of great thinkers has been circumscribed not only by stature, but also by the topics I have chosen to explore (for example, identity, insight, or narcissism). This approach has narrowed the field. There is also a marked gender bias in my pantheon favoring men, although this is largely attributable to the social inequalities and prejudices that prevented women from becoming doctors—and then psychotherapists—for much of the twentieth century. The unacknowledged intellectual contribution of women to psychotherapy (particularly during Freud's lifetime) made by patients, family members, correspondents, associated professionals, and friends should never be underestimated.[9] Occasionally, I illustrate points using descriptions of men and women in therapy. These are real people, all former patients, and I have changed clinically irrelevant details to ensure anonymity.

Getting life right is hard. Psychotherapy has always recognized the magnitude of the task, and it doesn't make extravagant promises. Freud famously said that his method turned "misery" into "common unhappiness." It is impossible to transcend "the uneasiness inherent in culture," and there are no simple answers. You won't be reborn after reading a slogan on a tea towel. Freud's realism is superficially unattractive. It seems that he is offering us poor consolation: "common unhappiness." But modest assurances leave plenty of room for surprises. If we temper our expectations, happiness might catch us unawares more often.

1

TALKING

Leaving the Silent Theater

Some years ago, I attended a landmark Edward Hopper exhibition in London. Moving from canvas to canvas, I was repeatedly reminded of the artist's genius for capturing private moments. Hopper's work often shows ordinary men and women in sparsely furnished interiors, staring out of windows or gazing blankly into space. Even when he introduces several figures into his paintings, they are separate, inhabiting different universes.

One of Hopper's most affecting explorations of aloneness is *Automat*. The title refers to an early chain of self-service restaurants where meals were dispensed by vending machines, not delivered by people. Hopper's painting shows a young woman sitting at a table in such an establishment, about to raise a cup of coffee to her lips. The self-service restaurant immediately underscores her solitude. Even though her coat has fur trimmings and she is close to a radiator, she still needs more warmth. She has removed one of her gloves to absorb the heat of her coffee cup. The image is very realistic, but one detail is anachronous. On a shelf behind the young woman is a bowl piled high with fruit. Where did it come from? We are in New York, the season is cold, and it is the 1920s. At that time, out-of-season fruit wasn't available. Fruit like that shouldn't really be there. Hopper is inviting us to think symbolically. He is asking us to consider how the luscious, rounded forms in the bowl correspond with what Freud called "the larger hemispheres of the female body."

The young woman's coat is green (the color of innocence), unbuttoned and open, and we can see that she is wearing a red garment (the color of passion) underneath. Her neckline is low and her skirt has risen to reveal a pair of shapely legs. These erotic elements alert us to what she might be thinking. Above her head, the reflected ceiling lights of the automat recede into darkness; they resemble the "thought bubbles" of a cartoon strip. There are two lines of these bubbles, which means she must be of two minds. Will she? Won't she? The chair that she faces is conspicuously empty. She struggles to resolve a dilemma without companionship or support. Her aloneness is amplified by the infinite nothingness outside, which is mitigated only in part by the double row of reflected lights. Angular bannisters, just visible, suggest a descending staircase. It appears to be the only means by which she can leave. Like all of us, she has limited options.

The men and women in Hopper's paintings are almost invariably mute; even when they are depicted in conversation, they are sealed in, separated from us by an additional barrier, like the glass of a window. The absence of sound in Hopper's paintings (and particularly the absence of imagined voices) is discomfiting. Human beings are social animals and we crave conversation. When we talk to each other, we no longer feel so alone, and the black nothingness outside the automat window ceases to be quite so threatening.

I'd like to claim these observations as my own, but I'm paraphrasing Professor Walter Wells, an American academic who wrote a remarkable book titled *Silent Theater: The Art of Edward Hopper.* I was introduced to Walter at a dinner party in London, and we became friends. We used to meet up intermittently, just to chat. He was a brilliant conversationalist, insatiably curious, and knowledgeable across an impressive range of subjects: the language of business communication, aspects of medicine, Mark Twain, and the Hollywood novel, to name but a few. We would talk about pretty much anything. I can remember raising the question of whether Marvel and DC superheroes were the American equivalent of Greek gods. Walter politely pointed out that if I really wanted to put America on the couch, then I'd probably find genre fiction more illuminating. "America has come to terms with its past through the western, engages with the present through crime writing, and explores potential futures in science fiction."

Like many astute observations, it's blindingly obvious—but only in retrospect, once it's been said. Walter and I were never silent, not even for a few seconds.

The last time I met Walter for lunch was a sad occasion. His wife, who was some years younger than him, was dying. I did my best to avoid offering him platitudes, because he wasn't the kind of person to shrink from hard truths. He was unflinching in his intellectual honesty and possessed what one existentialist writer has described as a willingness to "stand naked in the storm of life."[1] Having already lost one wife to cancer, he understood that bad things happen, and when they do, we can't escape them. As the bill arrived, Walter reached for his wallet and said, "You pay next time." But there was no next time. A few months later his wife died. He traveled for a while, and then he died. His cancer diagnosis couldn't hide the fact that his end had been hastened by personal loss. Emotional pain really does break hearts. *Takotsubo*, or stress cardiomyopathy (also known as broken heart syndrome), is a recognized medical condition.

When Walter and I met, we tended to talk about ideas more than personal experiences. I was therefore somewhat surprised, maybe even astonished, to hear some of the things that were being said about him at his memorial service. This witty, charming, stylish man had been raised in very modest circumstances, and occasionally, evidence of his insalubrious youth would become apparent. He once knocked out a French restaurant proprietor whose unreasonable behavior (and it was unreasonable) had severely tested Walter's ability to tolerate provocation. Someone remarked, "You can take the boy out of Queens, but you can't take Queens out of the boy." It made me laugh to think of my mild-mannered friend slugging his way across the south of France.

I miss Walter. More so than I ever expected. I bitterly regret not having spent more time with him. Of course, I had my reasons. There was always something else that had to be done first. Now, I can't even remember what those pressing matters were. I want to continue our conversation. We weren't finished; there was so much more to be said.

A few years ago, I visited the Whitney Museum of American Art in New York City, Walter's hometown. I was keen to see the Hoppers. While browsing in the bookshop, I came across a copy of *Silent Theater.* I took it off the shelf and sighed. If a passing stranger had taken a photograph of me at that moment, the resulting image would have resembled an Edward Hopper: a man, standing apart, isolated by introspection. I slotted the book back into its place and went to find my wife and son.

"I just found Walter's book." With these words I broke the silence, and in doing so, I reconnected. Some critics have described Hopper's silences as deadly. This isn't hyperbole. It's a scientific fact.

Bertha Pappenheim, immortalized in the annals of psychiatry as Anna O., suffered from hysteria. She was treated by Josef Breuer in the 1880s using a method that was later developed by Breuer's junior colleague Sigmund Freud. The final form of that treatment is now called psychoanalysis, and it is the first major example of a formalized psychotherapy. The treatment of Anna O. is described in *Studies on Hysteria*, a pioneering work published by Breuer and Freud in 1895. If psychoanalysis is the first instance of psychotherapy, at least in a recognizably modern form, then Pappenheim is arguably the first psychotherapy patient. She invented a term to describe her treatment: the "talking cure." In doing so, she identified the key ingredient of psychotherapy, the principal means by which psychotherapy achieves its beneficial effects.

The evolutionary psychologist Robin Dunbar has suggested that talking evolved from grooming, the mutual hygiene maintenance behavior that our apelike ancestors practiced. This theory hasn't gained much traction among academics, but it has a certain intuitive appeal. In addition to having positive health consequences, grooming—in apes—strengthens social bonds. When we talk to each other meaningfully, we are, in a sense, experiencing something that feels like a form of primal intimacy. Words allow minds to touch. The evolutionary significance of talking is reflected in our neural preparedness. We are disposed to acquire language, and the learning process begins at the earliest opportunity.[2] Newborn babies will suck harder (a sign of recognition and interest) when they hear their mother tongue, as opposed to a foreign language. They have been eavesdropping from within the womb. Such accelerated learning is all the more remarkable given that fetal wakefulness is only present in the final trimester of pregnancy—and then for no more than two or three hours a day. The first flickering of consciousness is very probably accompanied by speech. We are made aware of ourselves by listening to others.

Talking isn't just about words. We adopt congruent postures; we smile, frown, gesticulate, and make eye contact; we read expressions and know exactly when to stop in order to let the other person respond. Once again, these are skills that we acquire early. As soon as a neonate is placed in its mother's arms, the mother will coo, tickle, gaze, and prompt simple turn-taking games. These "dialogues" serve as templates for more complex communication skills. Mother and child become attached, and the strength of this attachment is predictive of future social adjustment, emotional maturity, and resilience.[3]

Direct face-to-face communication is one of the most fundamental and earliest human needs, and yet we live in a world in which it is becoming increasingly rare. Mothers spend more time interacting with their electronic devices than with their children. An observational study published in the journal *Paediatrics* in 2014 found that forty out of fifty-five caregivers in a restaurant used devices during the course of their meal. Sixteen of these caregivers used their devices continuously, looking at their screens instead of their children. The social world has migrated to cyberspace. Emails, text messages, and communication via social media are preferred to talking on the telephone. For many, direct communication is becoming effortful, demanding, or even aversive. These trends will inevitably have consequences. In Japan, for example, information technology has been linked with a decline in intimacy and a dramatic drop in the national birthrate. Pessimists suggest that by 2060 the population of Japan could shrink by as much as 30 percent.[4] A 2019 study examining three National Surveys of Sexual Attitudes and Lifestyles in the United Kingdom concluded that frequency of intercourse among British couples is declining. Similar declines have been recorded in Australia, Finland, and America. The demands of modern living and information technology were implicated as causal factors: "Life in the digital age is considerably more complex than in previous eras, the boundary between private space and the public world outside is blurred, and the internet offers considerable scope for diversion."[5]

The Harvard Longitudinal Study, the oldest and most extended of its kind, began collecting data relevant to physical and mental health in 1938 and continues to the present day. The original cohort consisted of 268 young men, but in due course their children (about 1,300 of them) were also recruited. Results indicate that close relationships (i.e., the kind in which people communicate) keep people happy throughout the course of their lives (much more so, for example, than wealth or fame). Moreover, close relationships are associated with longevity. They are a better predictor of long-term health than social class, IQ, or genes. Not all forms of conversation are equivalent. Are some forms more likely to produce well-being than others? And if so, can psychotherapy—the talking cure—give us any useful indications as to what the characteristics of an optimal conversation might be?

People often look back on their teenage and young adult years with great fondness. This is an interesting phenomenon, almost a paradox, because those years are also associated with significant challenges: first loves, important decisions that will affect future prospects, the establishment of a sense of identity. When deconstructed, much of this nostalgia can be attributed to the formation of close friendships that thrived in an environment where frequent and long conversations were possible. As soon as we enter the workplace, take on responsibilities, and begin the struggle to meet the demands of modern life, opportunities for long, candid conversations are reduced. In some cases, they disappear altogether.

An interesting feature of teenage conversation is its lack of purpose and constraint. This is not a new development. In a quotation attributed to Socrates by Plato, the great philosopher criticizes the readiness of the young to "chatter." Teenagers just shoot the breeze, one thing leading to another, their idle talk moving the conversation forward: random observations, confidences, gossip, popular culture. And yet it is by having aimless conversations of this kind that they consolidate their sense of personhood, establish emotionally meaningful connections with their peers, and discover their values. Somehow, while talking about nothing in particular, they become mature adults. This process is so rewarding that most people recall the atmosphere, if not the precise content, of such conversations for the rest of their lives.

A fluid, improvisatory style of talking has much in common with Freud's technique of "free association." At the beginning of consultations, he asked his patients to say the first thing that came into their heads and then to carry on talking without restraint or censorship. He found that when patients talked in this way, adventitious associations led to interesting discoveries about the person. Significant and otherwise inaccessible memories seemed to ascend from hidden depths. By simply talking, we frequently discover what it is that we really need to say.

The English Romantic poet John Keats spoke of "negative capability" when he wished to describe the looseness of thought and openness of mind that make great artists and writers innovative. It is a view of creativity that has much in common with Aristotle's contention that producing works of genius requires a little madness (a mental state characterized by extreme loosening of associations). There are certainly many examples of wholly original ideas arising under conditions where consciousness is completely untethered—for example, when we are asleep. Albert Einstein was afforded valuable insights into relativity—and Mary Shelley was inspired to write *Frankenstein*—while dreaming. Others who have experienced revelatory dreams include Beethoven, Salvador Dalí, Charlotte Brontë, Dmitri Mendeleev (the periodic table), August Kekulé (the structure of benzene), and Niels Bohr (quantum theory).[6] In his 2017 book *Why We Sleep*, neuroscientist and psychologist Matthew Walker reports that when a person is awakened from a dream, the dreaming brain-state persists for a short duration, and he or she will perform better than usual on problem-solving tasks that require creative thinking.[7]

Studies of problem solving suggest that the best solutions are reached when focused thinking is preceded by a period of "brainstorming," during which ideas are generated but judgments about their value suspended. Counterintuitive solutions that might have been otherwise prematurely dismissed are given proper consideration at a later point. Prescriptions of this kind have much in common with free association. In addition to psychoanalysis, certain schools of existential and humanistic psychotherapy advocate uninhibited, free-ranging speech. Around 2,500 years ago, the Taoist master Lao Tzu suggested that "being a good listener spares one the burden of giving advice." In the same spirit, it is supposed that a therapist isn't obliged to supply patients with specific answers, because eventually, patients will discover their own answers.

The benefits of allowing thoughts to go where they will also has a historical precedent in the person of Michel de Montaigne, the sixteenth-century writer whose rambling and digressive essays stumble, in a roundabout way, upon answers to the problems of living. They may not be ultimate answers, but they are answers relevant to Montaigne's time and even our own. His writing technique, which was essentially letting his mind go into free fall, was extremely productive, and his wise words have been valued for generations. Reading Montaigne is a little like listening to a man reclining on Freud's couch, free-associating his way toward insightful observations.

Historically, film heroes have conformed to the cultural ideal of the strong, silent type. Such men do not speak unless they have something to say; they are doers, and "actions," we are assured, "speak louder than words." Hollywood has encouraged us to admire actors whose square jaws are firmly set in the face of adversity. The stereotypical British "stiff upper lip" signifies a related set of virtues: stoicism, bravery, courage. Recently, the strong, silent woman has also emerged as a recognizable character. She appears in many guises, although perhaps most frequently as the world-weary detective in crime dramas. Implicit in these portrayals is the notion that voluble people are weak and emotionally incontinent. Polarizations of this kind are wildly inaccurate. In fact, people who talk freely are generally less troubled than those who hold back. They have a cohesive sense of self and are more likely to generate creative solutions to problems. They feel less isolated and their secure attachments protect them from the effects of stress.

If we don't use language to communicate our thoughts and feelings, we cannot be known. Our inner lives will have fewer points of contact with the exterior world, and we will feel detached from others. Existential psychotherapists identify aloneness as one of the fundamental terrors of the human condition. This shouldn't be very surprising, because a solitary hominid would not have survived for very long in the ancestral environment. We have evolved to fear loneliness for a very good reason. Ultimately, when we're talking, we are also keeping the darkness in Edward Hopper's *Automat* on the other side of the glass.

A recurring idea endorsed by several schools of psychotherapy is that we should constantly strive to be genuine. We must say what we mean and mean what we say. Although this dictum may sound simple, it is difficult to put into practice. Human beings, either knowingly or unknowingly, frequently adopt "personas," or social masks, through which they speak their lines like actors in a Greek drama. The words they say do not reflect their inner needs, wants, and feelings.

Sometimes, the extent of our habitual dishonesty only becomes known to us when the truth "breaks through." This is what happens when we make a "Freudian slip," unintentionally saying something that expresses how we *really* feel. In response to a colleague's promotion, a disingenuous individual might intend to say, "I'm not envious," but what actually comes out is the opposite: "I'm envious." Freud attributed such errors to interference emanating from the unconscious, a division of the mind not overly concerned with social niceties. When we make a Freudian slip, what we are trying to conceal becomes embarrassingly obvious.

The Canadian psychiatrist Eric Berne pointed out that human beings often communicate using what he called "ulterior transactions." These are verbal exchanges that are dishonest, insofar as they conceal a hidden motive. Berne's guide to ulterior transactions, *Games People Play*, became a best seller in the 1960s. The outcome of a "game" usually involves some kind of payoff that makes subsequent repetitions more likely. The game that Berne called "See what you made me do" is a typical example of an ulterior transaction. A husband wants to be alone and engages in an immersive activity to escape domestic obligations. When he is interrupted by an intruder, his chisel, paintbrush, pen, or soldering iron slips and he cries, "See what you made me do!" It is not the intrusion that has caused the fumble, but his own irritability. The fumble provides him with an excellent excuse to dismiss his visitor. Consequently, he can continue avoiding any of the demands his wife or children might care to make on him.

The more games of this kind we play, the more unsatisfactory our relationships will be.

Games can become so well practiced that we play them automatically, with little or no insight into what is really happening. When they are maintained by regular, questionable payoffs, an individual might continue to reenact the same maneuvers and countermaneuvers until this style of relating to others becomes rigid and inflexible. One of the chief aims of "transactional analysis" is to help people recognize and acknowledge these games as well as other patterns of self-defeating behavior. The process usually involves gaining greater access to feelings that have been, to some extent, previously denied. Simply talking about ourselves can help us to reconnect with our feelings. This experience of reconnection can also be assisted by exploiting the subtle properties of language.

Whenever the air cools and the leaves begin to change color, I think of a sublimely beautiful Keats line: "Season of mists and mellow fruitfulness." We can express the exact same sentiment using different words. For example: "The time of year when you get a lot of fog and fruit becomes ripe." But it's not the same, is it? The mood is entirely different; something essential has been lost. Keats's poetry, although impressionistic, seems to say so much more. There is depth and richness to Keats's evocation—the stirring of memory, hints of bonfire smoke, and the still-sweet smell of decay. Edges blur, and a muted light plays on shades of russet and amber. We *feel* something.

Words come with associations, overtones, and emotional resonances. From the mid-nineteenth century to the late twentieth, experts believed that language was mediated by only two small areas of the brain. With the introduction of brain-scanning technology, it immediately became apparent to researchers that language involves a much more extensive network of interconnections, regions, and structures than they had previously thought.[8] If you think of the word "hammer," for instance, a part of the motor cortex lights up in readiness to strike a blow. And if you think of "autumn," the visual cortex flickers with ghostly impressions of mist and falling leaves. Metaphors produce congruent brain activity. For example, it has been found that reading the phrase "He had a rough day" produces more activity in cortical areas associated with feeling texture than reading the phrase "He had a bad day."[9]

Every word reverberates through the vastness of the brain's architecture, and when we substitute one word for another, we trigger varying patterns of spreading activation. These patterns are distinct and will have a differential effect on the availability of certain memories and feelings. Therefore, when we are talking about ourselves, our precise choice of words will influence the degree to which we are self-aware, and naturally, the more self-aware we are, the better able we are to make good life decisions.

One of the first psychotherapists to focus on the minutiae of speech and to experiment with the modification of language as a practice procedure was Fritz Perls. During the 1940s and 1950s, he was largely (although not solely) responsible for the creation and development of Gestalt therapy. *Gestalt* is the German word for "shape" or "form," but it also implies "wholeness." (The word was originally adopted by a group of experimental psychologists in the 1920s as the name for their particular school; however, the principal objective of these experimentalists was to discover the laws that govern visual perception. Although there are some interesting affinities between Gestalt therapy and Gestalt psychology, they should be viewed as separate.) In textbooks, chapters on Gestalt therapy frequently include a photograph of Perls as an old man sporting a long white beard. His portrait is typically contextualized by supplementary photographs of hippies, psychedelia, and flower-power. Perls's guru-like image was consolidated with the publication of his much-quoted "Gestalt prayer," a marginal exercise that nevertheless encapsulated something of the prevailing contemporary attitude: "I do my thing and you do your thing. I am not in this world to live up to your expectations, and you are not in this world to live up to mine. You are you and I am I, and if by chance we find each other, it's beautiful. If not, it can't be helped." One can almost hear The Doors playing in the background.

Perls produced cultural ripples that reached Hollywood. The 1969 Academy Award–nominated film *Bob & Carol & Ted & Alice* features a married couple who question social conventions after exposure to a type of therapy that encourages personal license and emotional honesty. They smoke marijuana, openly discuss affairs, and consider "wife-swapping." The inspiration for the film was a photograph published in *Time* magazine of Perls bathing naked in a hot tub with his novitiates at the Esalen Institute in California.[10] At that time, Esalen was the flagship of the human potential movement. In many ways, it still is.

Perls and his Esalen associates were employing psychotherapeutic methods to facilitate personal growth rather than to treat mental "illness." They were interested in how psychotherapeutic ideas could help people discover better ways of living. This approach has much in common with Freud's hope, expressed in the 1920s, that psychoanalysis would transcend medicine and be regarded as a more generally relevant discipline.

Perls drew attention to the fact that we often use impersonal or neutral language to interpose distance between ourselves and our painful feelings. This might reduce anxiety and discomfort in the short term, but in the long term we are failing to acknowledge our totality. Consequently, the decisions we make will not be based on all the information at our disposal.

Sometimes, when we say, "It feels bad," what we actually mean is, "I feel bad." By favoring the neutral third-person pronoun over the first person, we restrict the potential of the sentence to bring us fully into the here-and-now of the conversation. If a patient receiving Gestalt therapy says, "You know how it is, when people are in social situations they can get uptight," the therapist might ask him or her to repeat the sentence, but using less abstract and more direct language. For example, "When I'm with my friends, I usually feel very tense." This recalibrated sentence possesses quite different qualities. It is more personally meaningful and revealing. As with poetry and prose, identical content can produce different effects depending on how that content is worded. There are many ways in which modifying language can be beneficial. For example, sometimes we find ourselves in situations where we protest, "I can't do that," when perhaps it would be more accurate to say, "I won't do that." Here, the replacement of *can't* with *won't* admits the possibility of choice. There is an empowering shift from helplessness toward agency.

Words increase transparency and make us more available to others. The closeness that makes us happy and helps us live longer develops only when we speak truthfully. When we use language that interposes distance between ourselves and our own feelings, we are almost invariably introducing distance between ourselves and others. We are choosing to stand among Edward Hopper's figures, in rooms where the silences cut us off from the rest of humanity.

Perls was a great communicator. Born in the late nineteenth century, he studied medicine at the University of Berlin. When World War I broke out, he was classified as unfit for duty due to a heart abnormality, asthma, and a stoop. He continued his studies, but by 1916 the death toll had risen so steeply that the criteria for admission into the German army were relaxed. Perls volunteered and worked as a medical orderly in the trenches. One can easily picture him, a delicate young man, lungs aching, coughing into his clenched fist, surrounded by appalling horrors: exploding shells, gas attacks, and unspeakable carnage. He spent nine months in these hellish conditions and was later decorated for his bravery. After completing his medical studies, Perls practiced as a neuropsychiatrist and then trained as a psychoanalyst. In 1933, forced to leave Germany when his name appeared on a Nazi blacklist, he traveled to South Africa to practice in Johannesburg.

Three years later, Perls returned to Europe to attend a conference. He decided to pay Freud a somewhat presumptuous social call in Vienna. The door opened and Freud peered out. Perls explained that he had come all the way from South Africa. Freud was unimpressed. ("And when are you going back?" he asked.) There was some desultory conversation, and Perls was obliged to leave.[11] The memory of this humiliation rankled, and embarrassment became rancor. Thereafter, he never missed an opportunity to insult his former master.

After World War II (and another stint of voluntary service, this time for the Allies), Perls settled in the United States. He read volumes of Eastern mysticism and worked closely with Paul Goodman developing Gestalt therapy, and in 1964, moved to Esalen, where he remained until 1969. During the last decade of his life, Perls acquired his messianic appearance and became a counterculture hero, dispensing witty aphorisms such as "Lose your mind and come to your senses." He was adored by his disciples and frequently demonstrated his therapeutic skills onstage, performing to large audiences. He participated in debates with fashionable mystics such as Baba Ram Dass and the Maharishi Mahesh Yogi. If the twenty-three-year-old soldier had leapt forward in time and come face-to-face with the seventy-three-year-old guru, he would never have guessed who he was looking at. The early and late incarnations of Fritz Perls were from different planets.

In his final year, Perls purchased an old motel in Canada, where he intended to establish a Gestalt community. He died before this dream was realized, on March 14, 1970, of a heart attack. His funeral service in San Francisco was attended by over a thousand people.

Talking freely and frankly improves the quality of our relationships, and meaningful close relationships are associated with happiness and longevity—but the opposite is also true. When we are guarded and disingenuous, our relationships become impoverished; impoverished relationships make us unhappy and increase our vulnerability to illness.

Psychotherapists have always understood that keeping secrets can affect the mind and the body. In Freud and Breuer's earliest publications on hysteria (a condition associated with an almost infinite number of physical symptoms), they identified repressed memories as the primary cause. In a sense, repression is the ultimate form of secrecy, because the secret is being kept not only from others, but even from the person to whom the secret belongs.

Repressed memories are buried so deep in the unconscious that they are no longer accessible; however, they can still produce symptoms, and there is often a symbolic connection between repressed memories and the symptoms they cause. For example, a person who has witnessed something traumatic might repress the memory, but thereafter experience episodes of blindness. A physical symptom has been substituted for a thought: "I've seen enough and I don't want to see any more." Secrets can have a pervasive detrimental effect because they must be guarded, and the constant demands of keeping them safe depletes energy that might have been used for other purposes. Although Freud's thinking about internal energies is vulnerable to criticism (the notion of psychic energy has figurative utility, but it cannot be quantified like physical energy), the basic notion that secrecy can have harmful effects on our health has found much scientific support.

Concealing an uncomfortable truth has immediate physical consequences. When we are duplicitous, stress hormones are released, activating a division of the autonomic nervous system, and we start to perspire. (A lie detector works by measuring the electrical conductance of the skin, which varies according to how much moisture our sweat glands are secreting.) Over time, a closely guarded secret will engender a chronic state of arousal, and the biochemical changes this state causes can compromise bodily defenses, impact the cardiovascular system, and alter neurotransmitter levels in the brain. The renowned experimental psychologist James Pennebaker has concluded that excessive withholding of thoughts and feelings increases the risk of developing both major and minor diseases. In an early study reported in his 1990 book *Opening Up: The Healing Power of Expressing Emotions*, he found that individuals who had not previously disclosed their traumatic experiences were much more likely than others to suffer from a range of health problems, including cancer, high blood pressure, ulcers, flu, headaches, and even earaches. The precise nature of the trauma (be it sexual abuse or a death in the family) was inconsequential: "The only distinguishing feature," he wrote, "was that the trauma had not been talked about to others."[12] Repression is not always the cause of illness—and certainly not the only cause—but it represents an important risk factor. Holding back is essentially a defensive strategy. We repress, suppress, and lie to protect ourselves. But these forms of self-protection are often inefficient and tend to make matters worse rather than better.

Attempts to bury thoughts and memories in the unconscious frequently fail and cause a rebound effect. They return and trigger episodes of rumination and worry. Indeed, the paradoxical consequences of thought suppression might be responsible for turning some thoughts and memories into distressing obsessions.[13] Individuals who keep secrets are more distractible and experience lower levels of well-being than those who speak more freely.[14] When we go to bed and switch off the lights, there are no competing demands, and it is then that secrets can become a torment, keeping us awake, pricking conscience. Sleep, when it finally comes, isn't necessarily restorative, because repressed material tends to influence the content of dreams—particularly the emotional content.[15] We are then more likely to wake up from nightmares. Extended periods of disturbed and fragmented sleep will almost certainly exacerbate any preexisting physical or mental health risks.

Sharing secrets is strongly associated with the notion of unburdening, a perception that becomes manifest in certain figures of speech—such as "I just need to get something off my chest." Once the weight is removed, we can breathe more easily. It is a very apposite turn of phrase, because it implicates the most important life sign: respiration. If we're not sure whether a person is dead or alive, we check, as if by reflex, that they are breathing. Anything that affects breathing is a threat to be taken very seriously. When individuals who have been unfaithful are asked to estimate the energy and effort required to undertake physical tasks, such as carrying shopping up a flight of stairs, those who admit to feeling burdened by their hypocrisy tend to overestimate the challenge.[16] The weight of their secret is not merely metaphorical. It weighs them down. It robs them of breath. Life seems altogether harder.

The more we learn about the universe and the natural world, the more we appreciate the importance of interconnectedness. Trees thrive most when they exist in groups. The reason is that they are in constant conversation. They "talk" to each other by releasing chemical compounds and electrical impulses via intersecting root systems, and these messages are almost invariably altruistic.[17] Nutrients and water are distributed so that each member of the wider community can achieve its full potential. A lonely tree is rarely a healthy tree. The benefits of interconnectedness are subtle. When we talk, a great deal is happening invisibly. The dendritic branches of our nervous system are "reaching out," gleaning information and absorbing nourishment.

For a social animal, being alone is a distressing experience. It signals existential threats that have their ultimate provenance in prehistory. We need the tribe and the huddle of bodies to keep us warm and safe. A sophisticated ape might find itself sitting in an automat, but it will still be aware of the darkness outside, pressing against the glass, and it will still want to be groomed and comforted by the communicative ministrations of a companion's fingers.

The physical presence of others is not a panacea. A crowded room can still be a very lonely place. In the 1970s, Robert Weiss made a useful distinction between social and emotional isolation.[18] An individual can be isolated because he or she has a restricted social life (few friends), or because of the absence of close relationships (few good friends). Social and emotional isolation are not wholly independent concepts (people with no friends won't have *any* good friends); even so, it is possible to evaluate the differential effects of these situations. Research conducted by Philip Hyland and colleagues, published in the journal *Social Psychiatry and Psychiatric Epidemiology* in 2018, shows that with respect to mental health, the number of relationships we have is less important than their quality.

This same principle applies to social media—which can easily become another lonely, crowded room. Joining an online support group can be comforting; however, even the most sympathetic Internet chat rooms cannot compete with the power of eye contact, a familiar voice, responsive body language, and the warmth of a solicitous hand. The more we try to connect through tablets and smartphones, the more we are likely to experience the frustration of emotional needs, because the principal means by which human beings combat loneliness and maintain mental health is face-to-face communication. A common defense of online interaction is that it provides a social outlet for those who find face-to face communicating difficult; however, socializing online can easily become counterproductive. Anxious individuals rob themselves of opportunities to practice their social skills in "real-life" situations, skills that could potentially facilitate the development of meaningful (and ultimately therapeutic) intimate relationships.

Loneliness is associated with poor sleep, high blood pressure, cognitive and immune decline, depression, and early death.[19] The current director of the Harvard Longitudinal Study, Professor Robert Waldinger, has said, "Loneliness kills. It's as powerful as smoking or alcoholism." In 2016, the social neuroscientist John Cacioppo told *The Guardian* that "chronic loneliness increases the odds of an early death by 20%."

Almost all the great thinkers who emerged from the tradition of inquiry that began with the "talking cure" had enormous faith in the power of words. In this respect, they were very different from Edward Hopper, who mistrusted words, and whose most striking feature was his "gigantic resistance to speech." Perhaps this explains why he experienced episodes of melancholy and was unable to communicate with his wife. One of her 1946 diary entries reads, "Any talk with me sends his eyes to the clock." Because they couldn't exchange words, they exchanged blows instead.[20]

Many of Hopper's masterpieces create an impression of sustained tension that would instantly be relieved by the introduction of sound. But the silence can never be broken; the tension is preserved in perpetuity. It is an unassailable silence, a distillation of our existential terror. If only someone would speak. Fortunately, we are not locked into ourselves like Hopper's figures. We can leave the automat. We can open our mouths.

2

SECURITY

Primal Needs

Abraham Maslow was born in New York in 1908, the son of Jewish immigrant parents who had fled Czarist Russia to escape political upheavals. He was the eldest of eleven children and, in his words, "a slum boy." His father repaired barrels and earned barely enough money to feed his wife and children. Despite these inauspicious beginnings, Maslow graduated from the University of Wisconsin and was later mentored by Alfred Adler, one of Freud's earliest associates.

When Maslow was being educated, behaviorism and psychoanalysis dominated academic psychology. He found the former superficial and the latter bleak. In addition, behaviorism and psychoanalysis had very little to say about some aspects of human existence, and Maslow chose to examine these neglected and largely positive aspects of human psychology more closely. Today, he is recognized as one of the founders of humanistic psychology, the school that overlaps with the existential branch of psychoanalysis.

At the time of his death in 1970, Maslow was regarded as an exceptionally wise man. Yet throughout the preceding decade, he had resisted being typecast as a 1960s guru. He dressed conventionally and his speech was modest and unaffected. Unlike Freud, whose account of mental life gives special emphasis to primitive urges, Maslow espoused a more benign view of humanity. Human beings love, experience moments of transcendence, evolve as individuals, search for meaning, are transported by music, and produce works of art. For Freud, all these states and behaviors are secondary to basic instincts, the incidental consequences of redirected desires and energies, displacements. But for Maslow, they are all significant and reflect different aspects of the whole person. Self-actualization (the goal of personal fulfillment) can only be reached after various classes of need are satisfied, at least partially, in a specific ascending order. He illustrated this progression with a diagram that has since become iconic and is now referred to as "Maslow's hierarchy of needs."

An equilateral triangle is divided into five horizontal bands. The lowest band is labeled "Physiological"—which refers to necessities like air, food, and drink—and from the base to the apex the narrowing bands read "Safety," "Love and Belonging," "Esteem," and "Self-actualization." The hierarchy is sometimes presented with additional upper divisions—the need for knowledge, aesthetic needs, spiritual needs.

Some needs are more fundamental than others, and we are motivated to satisfy these basic needs before our discretionary needs. We are not inclined, for example, to consider complex philosophical issues when we are cold and hungry. Heat and food take precedence. If we are in a dangerous situation, we seek safety, not approval.

If a human being is to ascend the slope of Maslow's hierarchy and conquer the summit, then, assuming physical needs are met, safety is the next priority. Our sense of safety as adults, our sense of inner security, is profoundly influenced by the degree to which we were made to feel safe as children. The satisfaction of safety needs, particularly in infancy, facilitates our climb to the next level of Maslow's hierarchy, love and belonging. Safety in infancy will influence our capacity to give and receive love as adults. Indeed, safety is a precondition of love, the fertile ground in which love flourishes.

What does it mean to feel safe? And how does safety nourish our capacity to love?

Psychotherapists have always been interested in safety, because the first duty of a psychotherapist is to create a safe space, a situation where difficult and sometimes dangerous truths can be articulated and explored without fear of judgment, rejection, or condemnation—a place where patients can break down, or even break up, and subsequently experiment with different ways of putting themselves back together again.

Our need for safety is conspicuous, and the psychotherapists who reflected on its role in emotional development produced bold theories about the origins of love and the sources of pain. These theories also inform childrearing practices.

It is possible that feelings of safety begin to develop very early, perhaps even before birth. Feeling safe in the world is so fundamental that it can be viewed as the foundation of identity. The solidity of our psychological foundation is as important as the physical foundation of a building. If our foundations are insecure, we will likely be insecure too.

No one appreciated this more than Otto Rank. His family was poor and his childhood was profoundly unhappy. He was sickly, anxious, and the entries in the journal he kept from the age of eighteen suggest that he may have been sexually molested. After enrolling at a technical college, he trained as a machinist and worked in a factory. At fifteen, he began to discover writers like Ibsen, Stendhal, Dostoevsky, Nietzsche, and Darwin; this proved transformative. When he was twenty-one, Rank introduced himself to Freud by sharing a manuscript titled *The Artist: Approach to a Sexual Psychology*. The work demonstrated such a comprehensive grasp of psychoanalysis that he was immediately invited to join Freud's circle. Freud hired Rank as the secretary of what became the Vienna Psychoanalytic Society, offered him intermittent financial assistance, and encouraged him to continue his education. Eventually, Rank was awarded a doctorate by the University of Vienna.

Rank joined the Freud family for dinner every Wednesday and sat at Freud's side during meetings. He was extremely deferential. He fetched glasses of water for Freud and was always on hand to light the great man's cigars. Freud (who was five feet seven inches tall) was in the habit of calling his meek, biddable, and slightly shorter devotee "Little Rank." It was inevitable that Freud's condescension would become irksome, and that Rank would disavow pet names and crave independence. In 1915, Rank was drafted into the army, and when he returned to Vienna he was a changed man. He had toughened up and was less compliant. Ernest Jones, Freud's principal British advocate and biographer, described Rank as having acquired a "masterful air."

It is ironic that Rank's ultimate split from Freud was largely precipitated by Rank's 1924 book *The Trauma of Birth*, because it develops an idea proposed some years earlier by Freud himself. Freud had suggested that anxiety might have its origins in the experience of being born. This idea was never very important to Freud, but it became central to Rank's thinking. He believed that fetuses are conscious of being safe in the womb and supposed that the warmth and pleasurable sensations they experience there prefigure sensuality. Birth, therefore, is always experienced as traumatic, a wrenching, painful separation, and unconscious memories of this trauma make us emotionally sensitive to subsequent separations for the rest of our lives. Rank wrote that love between adults, consummated by sexual union, is partially motivated by a desire to "re-establish the primal situation between mother and child."

The peristaltic crush of the birth canal, sudden blinding light, the severing of the umbilical cord, and the excoriating fire of air in raw lungs: Rank's willingness to empathize, to imagine what it is like to experience the symbiotic bliss of the womb, followed by expulsion, represents not only an impressive act of identification but also an early example of the raised consciousness that mobilized the campaign for natural childbirth in the 1970s and ultimately made obstetrics a more humane profession.

Rank's assertion that unconscious memories of the womb and traumatic birth continue to exert an influence throughout the course of an adult's life is contentious; however, in his 1999 book *The Scientification of Love*, the distinguished French obstetrician Michel Odent (a pioneer of birthing rooms and birthing pools) argues that there is in fact a considerable body of research linking what he calls the primal period (gestation, birth, and the first year of life) with subsequent physical and psychological health. He goes on to say that pre- and perinatal experience appear to affect the long-term emotional adjustment of children (particularly the capacity to love) more than postnatal experience. Thus, the mental state of a mother-to-be during pregnancy will influence her child's emotional development more than her mental state throughout the first year of her child's life.[1]

Birth complications are frequently documented in the medical records of individuals who suffer from mental illness.[2] This association is probably mediated in most cases by subtle forms of brain injury; however, some studies suggest that the link *can* be psychological. For example, one 1987 investigation authored by Bertil Jacobson and colleagues, published in the journal *Acta Psychiatrica Scandinavica*, discovered very specific symbolic connections between suicidal behavior and traumatic birth. Suicide by asphyxiation was found to be associated with asphyxiation during delivery, whereas suicide by violent mechanical means was found to be associated with other forms of birth trauma. Otto Rank's disciple Stanislav Grof, a Czech psychiatrist and psychoanalyst, used LSD to help his patients reexperience their traumatic births and noted many correspondences between recovered memories and contemporaneous medical and parental reports.[3] More recently, a large-scale 2019 investigation conducted by Marina Mendonça and colleagues at the University of Warwick in the United Kingdom, involving a meta-analysis of 21 studies with 4.4 million participants, discovered that adults born preterm or with low birth weight were significantly less likely than their full-term peers to experience romantic relationships, sexual intercourse, or parenthood. Those adults born earliest were 67 percent less likely to be in a romantic relationship. The authors suggest that both biological and environmental (including psychosocial) factors should be taken into account when considering possible explanations.[4] Rank's theory also predicts a link between prematurity and emotional problems in later life, because the fetus isn't ready—if readiness can be considered meaningful in this context—to be born. Precipitate births will be correspondingly more traumatic, and the long-term psychological consequences more apparent.

That birth trauma can have long-term consequences mediated by brain damage is incontestable; however, the assertion that "experiences" in the womb and the birth canal are major influences on later psychological development remains problematic for skeptics. Why should these experiences be so influential compared to subsequent experiences? Is it enough to suggest that the human mind is particularly impressionable when the nervous system is between seven and nine months old? By contrast, there is almost universal agreement concerning the importance of postnatal experience—even *very early* postnatal experience—in subsequent psychological development. We owe this consensus to research conducted by the British psychiatrist and psychoanalyst John Bowlby, whose "attachment theory" has become a cornerstone of modern psychology.

Edward John Mostyn Bowlby was the son of a British baronet. As was customary for someone of his class, he was raised mainly by a nanny and nursemaids. He usually saw his mother for only one hour a day. At the age of seven, he was packed off to a boarding school that was so unpleasant he later confided to his wife that he wouldn't have sent a dog there. The remoteness of his family and the inaccessibility of his mother must have affected him deeply, because he spent most of his professional life cataloging the long-term effects of maternal deprivation.

Unlike Rank, whose focus was on the distress experienced during birth itself, Bowlby was interested in the distress experienced during the early postpartum period. Bowlby concluded that the absence of maternal love in the first seven years of life increased the likelihood of mental illness developing at some later point. If, as children, our basic need for security is badly met, we are more likely to become vulnerable adults.

Young children typically pass through three stages when they are separated from their mothers or other primary caregivers: protest, despair, and detachment. First, they cry. Then they become miserable. Finally, they become emotionally numb. The pain of separation is unbearable and they suppress their feelings. I have often seen these stages reproduced in adults living through a crisis: anger and wretchedness followed by a kind of fatalistic indifference. The voice becomes a robotic monotone and the eyes acquire a glazed, soulless vacancy. When we feel unsafe, we can easily regress.

Bowlby was one of the first psychoanalysts to recognize that psychological theories are more persuasive if they can be aligned with evolutionary narratives. He recognized that in the ancestral environment, if a child was separated from its mother, it made sense for the child to cry in order to attract its mother's attention. However, if the child was too far away to be heard, then continuing to cry would simply waste energy and alert predators. Crying, followed by misery and withdrawal, was an optimal strategy for survival. The final paralysis of fatalistic indifference turns a lively child into an inanimate object—something less conspicuous against the static backdrop of the ancestral savanna.

According to Bowlby, a secure attachment gives a child confidence to explore. He or she can be independent, make discoveries, satisfy curiosity, and acquire skills. If something goes wrong, or the child gets frightened, he or she knows that the attachment figure will be there, waiting—a reliable source of comfort and protection: a secure base. When the danger has passed, the child can carry on exploring. Bowlby pointed out that this process is ongoing, that we spend the whole of our lives making exploratory excursions and returning home to be with our attachment figures. Paradoxically, the more securely attached we are, the farther we can travel. Close bonds do not constrain us. They free us. This principle is also applicable beyond the physical. Close bonds allow us to travel to remote destinations intellectually and emotionally, to become the best person we can be.

After Bowlby conducted his research, he explained his results in terms of psychological constructs that he called "working models." These are thematically organized memories and dispositions that influence how events are interpreted and the kind of responses that follow. The most important determinant of a working model is early social learning. Through repeated exchanges, we consolidate an inner representation of ourselves, of our parents, and of the relationship we have with our parents.

In *A Secure Base: Clinical Applications of Attachment Theory*, first published in 1988, Bowlby provided a succinct description of how working models develop: "Once built, evidence suggests, these models of a parent and self in interaction tend to persist and are so taken for granted that they come to operate at an unconscious level. As a securely attached child grows older and his parents treat him differently, a gradual up-dating of models occurs. This means that, though there is always a time-lag, his current operative models continue to be reasonably good simulations of himself and his parents in interaction." These simulations are likely to bias our expectations of other close relationships at a later stage.[5]

A securely attached child internalizes its loving caregiver. Moreover, the working model of the secure child's self is of a person worthy of being loved. The opposite is true of an insecurely attached child. His or her internalized caregiver is unreliable. Or even worse, there is no internalized primary caregiver, because he or she was absent. The world is then perceived as dangerous and the people who populate it are treated with caution. The child feels unlovable and erects defenses that distort experience and interfere with the formation of new relationships. Over time, destabilizing stresses accumulate and exacerbate underlying feelings of insecurity.

Love makes us stronger, more daring, and more resilient. It makes us receptive to new experiences. And most important of all: love makes us lovable.

Society is competitive, and academic accomplishments are positively correlated with income and opportunity. It is customary for parents to encourage their children to do well at school; however, excessive emphasis on intellectual development can sometimes lead to a corresponding neglect of emotional development. Nurseries and universities are places of learning, but they are also social environments. Mentoring is predicated on a personal relationship, and the rewards we expect education to deliver are usually contextualized by family and friends. Excellence is desirable, but qualifications and advantages are much more likely to be converted into happiness when there is a secure base.

Matthew and Susanna had been married for seven years. At first, they were very happy together and emotionally close. But when Mike, their first son, was born, things began to change. Susanna put all her energy into creating a stimulating environment and filled Mike's bedroom with educational toys. When Andy, their second son, was born, she became even more single-minded.

"Why," she asked, "wouldn't you want the very best for your children?" Matthew and Susanna spent less time talking. Susanna was increasingly preoccupied and emotionally unavailable, and the couple became less intimate. Matthew had hoped that having a second child would repair their relationship. But after Andy's arrival, a brief thaw was followed by a return to bickering and chilly silences. Matthew felt angry and let down.

"What do you argue about?" I asked.

"Everything," Matthew replied. "But mostly the boys: Susie can be very critical."

Matthew and Susanna never held hands in these sessions. It was as if they didn't want to be reminded of what they'd lost. Once, I saw them touch accidentally. They both recoiled, as if their fingers had been burned on a hotplate.

"He just doesn't take being a parent seriously," said Susanna, turning her head away from her husband; the swiftness of the movement suggested dismissal, contempt. "He *wanted* children. It wasn't just me. But he doesn't want to put the time in, the work. He doesn't make any effort."

"Why do you say that?" I asked.

"All he wants to do is sit in front of the TV with the boys and watch football. That's his idea of being a good parent."

"Is that true?" I asked Matthew.

He looked tired: too tired to be anything but honest. "Yeah," he said. His expression recapitulated a history of recrimination and defeat. "I watch a lot of football with the kids."

"If I go out," Susanna continued, "even for just a few minutes, I know exactly what I'll find when I get back." She turned to Matthew. "Would it really hurt to do something with them, something useful, something constructive? Get some paper and pencils out of the drawer? Make something?"

"I guess not," Matthew replied.

Susanna turned to face me. "They need the attention."

"Look, I get that . . ." Matthew objected.

"Then why don't you act more responsibly?" Susanna grumbled. "It's important. Isn't it?"

"Yes," Matthew replied. "But they like it . . . watching TV."

"Of course they do," Susanna responded. "They're kids. That's why *we* have to make the right decisions for them."

"They're still really small. I think . . ." Matthew dared to finish his sentence. "I think you push them too hard."

"Well, you would say that." Matthew shrugged and Susanna continued: "If I'd left it all up to you, how do you think that would have worked out? How well do you think they'd be doing at school right now?"

"I know," Matthew replied. "You do a lot for them. And yes— you do all the hard stuff. And maybe I don't think about what's good for them as much as I should." He fell silent, but I extended my hand, encouraging him to continue. He shook his head and looked a little confused. "We sit on the sofa, cuddle up. I put my arms around them, one either side." Being close to his children felt good. It felt safe.

Things feel good for a reason. Evolutionary pressures have made them feel good, because at some point in the history of our species, those things increased the chances of survival, and therefore reproduction. The fact that holding our children feels *very* good says much about the importance of love. When a parent cuddles a child—or looks into the child's eyes, or gives the child a smile, or strokes his hair, or kisses her head—there are extraordinary consequences.

The orbitofrontal cortex is one of several brain areas that underlie "emotional intelligence" (our ability to recognize and manage our own emotions and to identify and respond to the emotions of others). It is a region that develops almost entirely after birth. This growth is not preordained. The quality of a child's social and emotional experiences will determine the degree to which his or her orbitofrontal cortex can serve its designated purpose.[6] When a parent looks lovingly at a child, endogenous opioids like beta-endorphin and the neurotransmitter dopamine are released. These will trigger reactions—such as the uptake of glucose—that promote neuronal growth. Pleasurable, affectionate interactions between parent and child are largely responsible for "wiring" the prefrontal cortex. Without a fully functioning orbitofrontal cortex, a child will suffer profound social and emotional handicaps. Neurological patients with orbitofrontal damage have diminished empathy and poor control of aggressive impulses.[7]

Susanna wasn't wrong. Children must acquire knowledge and skills, and she wanted what we all want: the best for our children. But by focusing on hothousing her sons she was neglecting something essential. Matthew was watching TV, but he was also enjoying the proximity of his children, their warmth and the snugness of their small bodies in his safe embrace. He was pulling them close—chatting to them about the game, ruffling their hair, catching their eyes, and smiling. From Susanna's point of view, Matthew appeared to be doing nothing, but actually, he was doing a great deal. He was building "being loved" into two working models.

One of the most unlikely poems to become treasured by a nation is "This Be the Verse" by the English poet Philip Larkin. The first two lines are frequently quoted:

> *They fuck you up, your mum and dad.*
> *They may not mean to, but they do.*

The expletive is shocking, funny, and most of all, poignant, because the comedy isn't quite enough to dull the effect of the subsequent tragic observation. Very few parents set out to harm their children, but it happens. This, I suspect, is why Larkin's caustic little poem is so popular. In the opening lines, Larkin separates us from the crowd with the second-person pronoun and we immediately feel that the poem is personally relevant. We are reminded of *our* parents, our mother's flaws, our father's shortcomings, and, if we have children of our own, we reflect on our experiences of being a less-than-perfect parent. History has a habit of repeating itself, and when in the final verse of the poem Larkin remarks, "Man hands on misery to man," he seems to be voicing an immortal truth.

Larkin composed "This Be the Verse" in 1971, a year after the publication of Arthur Janov's *The Primal Scream*. Janov, an American psychotherapist who died in 2017, suggested that all neurotic illnesses and addictions can be traced back to a common origin: primal pain caused by dysfunctional or deficient parenting. His book earned him instant international celebrity. I can remember watching Janov being interviewed on TV when I was about thirteen years old. He must have made a big impression on me, because I can't remember any comparable interviews. What captured my attention initially was a portentous introduction, which promised the British public a man touched by greatness. Janov had, as I recall, an interesting manner; he managed to be laid-back and very intense at the same time. I wonder if Philip Larkin also saw that interview, because "This Be the Verse" is a distillation of Janov's psychology.

The Primal Scream begins with a passage that blends clinical memoir with psychological thriller: "Some years ago, I heard something that was to change the course of my professional life and the lives of my patients. What I heard may change the nature of psychotherapy as it is now known—an eerie scream welling up from the depths of a young man lying on the floor during a therapy session."[8] It could be a voice-over at the start of a movie: psychoanalytic *noir*. Janov's patient was a withdrawn, twenty-two-year-old student who had been encouraged to call out for his mother and father. Cries of "Mommy!" and "Daddy!" were immediately accompanied by signs of distress, and the student was soon writhing on the floor in agony. Convulsions preceded the release of a scream that "rattled the walls." The entire episode lasted only a few minutes, but when the young man had recovered his composure, he claimed that he was no longer suffering from emotional anesthesia. He could *feel* again. Repetitions of the same procedure and similarly favorable outcomes led Janov to construct a theoretical framework that connected the scream with very early experiences of neglect, criticism, or rejection.

My own copy of *The Primal Scream* is a 1970s paperback edition, a well-thumbed volume with discolored pages that I found in a secondhand bookshop about twenty years ago. The art department of the publishing house chose a literal but perfect cover

image: *The Scream* by Edvard Munch. Few comparable examples of modernism are so well-known—it has its own emoji—but what explains its enormous popularity?

Many critics have theorized about the meaning of Munch's masterpiece, but the sinister central figure is often identified as a personification of death. Sickness and mortality are certainly recurring themes in Munch's oeuvre. However, the restless background, with its undulations and curves, evokes the feminine and the organic. The blood-red sky is like twisted muscle tissue, and the blue waters of the fjord resemble a birth canal. Munch said the inspiration for the painting was a great "scream of nature" he heard one day while out walking with friends.* What kind of associations does the word "nature" suggest? Mother Earth, fertility, abundance, fruitfulness? Perhaps Munch's painting isn't about death at all. Perhaps it's about birth: a universal experience. The first thing we do is scream.**

When a basic infantile need is not satisfied, the experience is painful. If the need continues to go unsatisfied, it will be suppressed, but it will not diminish or disappear. Indeed, it will continue to motivate behaviors, the purpose of which will be to secure substitute gratifications. An unsatisfied infantile need can influence desires and choices for a lifetime.

The pains of infancy are not necessarily the result of what would ordinarily be described as traumatic experiences (such as physical or sexual abuse). Small but regular acts of parental insensitivity, including harsh reprimands, inattention, or aloofness, can have equally damaging effects. When these effects are severe, they acquire the status of symptoms, and the affected person is described as suffering from a neurotic illness.

The principal reason why parents fail to satisfy the infantile needs of their children is that they are too busy trying to satisfy their own infantile needs. They are psychologically and emotionally absent, always pursuing the false promise of substitute gratifications. The relationship between a substitute gratification and a

---

* Some art critics assert that the central figure in *The Scream* isn't screaming, but "reacting" to the scream of nature; however, for me at least, the wide-open mouth and terrified expression are strongly suggestive of a scream.

** Munch would have been a very suitable candidate for primal therapy. His mother died when he was very young, and his father raised him in an atmosphere of stultifying piety. As an adult he chased after many substitute gratifications (alcohol, fame, sex), and at the age of forty-six he suffered a nervous breakdown.

primal need is symbolically meaningful. For example, a child who has been repeatedly humiliated and made to feel "small" might become an adult preoccupied with maintaining an outward appearance of importance; an overweight woman might constantly eat comfort foods because she is seeking the security she never had in infancy; a man may feel compelled to fill every pause in a conversation with inconsequential chatter because his parents never listened to him.

But substitute gratifications cannot satisfy infantile needs, and consequently, neurotic individuals become trapped in endless cycles of craving and disappointment. The infant is predisposed to pursue things that it *does* need—warmth, safety, and love—whereas the neurotic adult pursues things that he or she *doesn't* need: alcohol, pornography, drugs, designer clothes, expensive restaurants.

Pursuing substitute gratifications creates a false sense of identity—an "unreal self." As more and more control is ceded to this sham identity, the "real self"—with its unmet infantile needs—becomes increasingly numb and silent. The unreal self is really a finely coordinated defense system, insofar as its pursuits and activities distract the individual from reflections that would ultimately revive memories of infantile pain. As with all defense mechanisms, the unreal self maintains an unsatisfactory compromise in which anxiety is warded off by dulling insight and distorting perception. The neurotic is alive—but not fully alive.

Sometimes, the unreal self is prevented from engaging in its well-practiced diversionary tactics, and the real self—and intimations of deeper needs—impinge upon consciousness. When this happens, a person might feel disoriented, strange, or stirred up. It is most likely to occur when routines and habits are interrupted, as might happen on a vacation. Removed from their regular world of superficial stimulants and pacifiers, people are often discomfited by unnerving dissociations. The life they have been living doesn't feel familiar anymore; in fact, it feels more like someone else's life. Suddenly, they're not sure who they are or what they want. It is a common and powerful experience.

Primal therapy works by breaking down defenses, recovering early memories, and, most importantly, facilitating the reexperiencing of primal pain. This reexperiencing is so overwhelming that patients typically scream. It is not the scream, however, that is curative, but the pain. The scream is simply an accompanying phenomenon. Although the scream is often preceded by sobs, cries, and other vocalizations, Janov assures us that the authentic article is unmistakable.

Janov's book is full of clinical case studies, affecting accounts of ordinary people, who, when immersed in memory, become desperate, unhappy children: "Daddy, don't hurt me anymore!"—"Mama, I'm afraid." They writhe and groan and beg ghosts for the things they never had. They face hard truths: Mummy doesn't love me; I can't depend on Daddy; I am alone. And finally, they recognize their deepest needs and feel the pain they have been circling all their lives. They become reacquainted with their real selves. The experience is distressing, but it is also a renewal of sorts. One could even describe it as a rebirth.

Arthur Janov wasn't feted for very long. He arrived a little too late to take full advantage of the revolutionary zeal of the 1960s. Even so, people still flocked to his Primal Institute for training and treatment. His most famous patient was John Lennon. Janov's influence is evident in post-Beatles songs like "Mother," which begins with Lennon confessing that his mother had him—but he never had her. The coda is extended by repeated pleas for mamma not to go and daddy to come home. With each repetition these entreaties become increasingly like inarticulate howls of pain.

Primal therapy is something of a historical curiosity and it is difficult to understand why its initial appearance was invested with so much significance. It was lauded as radical, daring, new, and a bold challenge to classical Freudianism. Yet Janov strayed no further from psychoanalytic orthodoxy (if such a thing ever really existed) than many of his rebellious predecessors, and in some ways, less so. The release of suppressed emotion was understood to be therapeutic by Freud and Breuer before the end of the nineteenth century. What distinguishes Janov from earlier dissenters is his procedure.

The claims that Janov made for his therapy were, without doubt, exaggerated. He asserted that primal therapy wasn't just the *best* cure for neuroses, but the *only* cure. He once boasted that in a few years primal therapy would become *the* therapy.[9] This was hubris, because his procedure never came close to being the universal panacea he wanted the world to embrace. Even after extensive psychological preparation, there is no guarantee that patients will reexperience primal pain. Indeed, many patients fail to achieve the desired regression and recovery of feeling. After the initial media fanfare, Janov sank out of general view, and primal therapy started to look more and more like a disreputable fad.

Yet Janov's opinions about the importance of early parenting, love, and substitute gratifications, although not wholly original, were coherent, plausible, and well argued. His "revolutionary" procedure was simply an attempt to facilitate the discovery and release of embodied emotions—deep, visceral feelings that are resistant to reactivation by simply having a conversation. Fritz Perls had already reached the limits of what might be achieved by manipulating language. He had shown that by rephrasing sentences, a person might become more emotionally available and present. The purpose of Janov's procedure was to make even more of the person available and present, particularly those primal, inarticulate parts of the person that aren't easily persuaded to come out of hiding by conventional talking cures. This was a perfectly reasonable therapeutic objective. And we shouldn't let Janov's grandiosity bury the fact that many people have been helped by primal therapy. One can support Janov with a circular but acceptable defense: primal therapy works for the kind of person for whom primal therapy works.

But how many of us would feel comfortable lying on a floor and calling out to our mothers and fathers? Is the idea unappealing because we already know that it would be embarrassing, that we would feel foolish—or is it because we fear what might happen? The recovery of memories—tears—primal pain? "They fuck you up, your mum and dad." Most of us don't want to find out how much.

After reading Rank, Freud, and Janov, would-be parents might have second thoughts about starting a family. Children have traumatic births, they wrestle with anxieties, and their primal needs are easily frustrated. Problems arise, and mothers and fathers are forced to examine their consciences. Am I to blame? Is it my fault? But the great virtue of psychoanalysis is its willingness to examine aspects of the human condition that other intellectual traditions either ignore or refuse to acknowledge. We are being offered a corrective to the Victorian domestic ideal, the shallow fantasy of rosy-cheeked children playing with kittens by the fireside and basking in the love of impossibly benign parents who have been united for eternity by the will of God. Psychoanalysis reminds us that such chocolate-box caricatures of family life, though reassuring, are ultimately dishonest.

Natural selection should have ensured that parents are equipped to satisfy their children's primal needs. Parents should be predisposed to do everything required to raise socially intelligent, resilient, emotionally stable offspring, because, endowed with those qualities, children will be more likely to survive, find a mate, and reproduce. Unfortunately, natural selection's agenda doesn't correspond exactly with ours. It has one overriding purpose: to transfer genes from one generation to the next. Everything else is incidental. Natural selection is not "blind" to the benefits of good parenting, but some dispositions are selected preferentially because they are more likely than others to result in successful reproduction. Sexual desire, for example, is indispensable; parental attentiveness, less so. The fact that we want sex doesn't always mean that we also want to have children. Or that we will make good parents. Thousands, or even millions, of years ago, our parenting skills were probably more fit for the purpose. Successful parenting was less demanding, because, except for encountering a predator, there was much less that could go wrong. In the middle Pleistocene epoch of the Cenozoic era, there weren't many opportunities for unhappy progeny to seek substitute gratifications. We were less free to turn unhappiness into patterns of self-destructive behavior.

Even though natural selection doesn't ensure that we will be perfect parents, that doesn't mean that we're hopeless. The idea of being a "good enough" parent was introduced by the British pediatrician and psychoanalyst Donald Winnicott. Everyone makes mistakes; however, even if these mistakes are harmful, negative consequences can be mitigated if children are made to feel secure when they are at their most dependent—that is, in the very earliest weeks, months, and years of life. This is achieved by demonstrations of affection and empathy, and the creation of an environment in which the infant feels protected from danger. Winnicott referred to the provision of care as "holding." An infant can be held both physically and metaphorically—in one's arms and in one's mind.

Winnicott was more forgiving than Janov, but he never romanticized the bond between parents and children; he was suspicious of sentimentality, which he viewed as a form of overcompensation for the kinds of thought and feeling that we habitually disown. Children can be testing, exhausting, provocative, demanding, and narcissistic. They are not "little angels," and mothers and fathers are not blessed with saintly detachment. Sometimes, we resent our children, because we have to make sacrifices for them; we have to

accept that we can no longer enjoy all the freedoms we took for granted before their arrival; we are weighed down by new responsibilities. A "good enough" parent does not have to be completely selfless or beyond reproach.

Winnicott referred with modest deference to the "ordinary devoted mother." His use of the word "ordinary" underscored his mistrust of academic interference in the nursery. If he were alive today, he would be truly horrified by the modern child-care industry: the armies of experts, the mountains of books—regimens, hothousing, gadgets, gimmicks, and apps. Winnicott believed that mothers, left to their own devices, will—on the whole—do what is right for their children. The care they provide might not be perfect, but it is probably a great deal better than programmatic alternatives.

There are many past instances of psychological theories being rigidly and inappropriately applied to child care. John Watson, for example, who established American behaviorism, published an influential book in 1928 titled *Psychological Care of Infant and Child*. His advice, based on a framework informed by Pavlovian conditioning, was to avoid hugging, kissing, and the stimulation of "love" responses. This Spartan system, he believed, would produce a self-reliant child: "Shake hands with them in the morning. Give them a pat on the head if they have made an extraordinarily good job of a difficult task." Both of Watson's sons suffered from depression as adults. One committed suicide, and the other attempted suicide. The surviving son blamed his father's childrearing practices.

From the 1940s to the 1960s, Winnicott delivered a series of radio lectures that were broadcast by the BBC. His voice (pitched in a kindly, high register) is measured and comforting.

He offers his observations with great humility and in simple, easy-to-understand language; he "holds" the listener in much the same way that he urged mothers to "hold" their children. He is also subtly suggesting that we should all "hold" each other.

It is interesting that Winnicott rarely employed the word "love," because, most of the time, this is what he's really talking about. He tells us—sometimes directly, sometimes indirectly—that providing we love, or simply attempt to love, we can transcend our imperfections, and when we love our children, we are making the world an infinitely better and safer place. He connected the private, intimate world of the playroom with the success or failure of democratic processes. Emotionally secure children grow into emotionally secure adults; they create stable family units, which in turn are the basis of a stable society. Stability is necessary for elections—the replacement of leaders by free vote, the peaceful transfer of power. Winnicott placed the entire fate of civilization in the hands of ordinary devoted mothers. They are superheroes, whose secret power is that they are unexceptional.

Safety doesn't feature very much in high romance. Star-crossed lovers are passionate and elemental; love is an adventure. Safety is somewhat dull in comparison, a condition we associate with routines and domesticity. In the context of romance, safety might even acquire negative connotations, because if we feel too safe, our relationship could potentially become boring and predictable. And yet, we should probably judge the quality of love, its depth and durability, by the extent to which it makes us feel secure. Are we being held? Do we feel protected? Is our relationship a place that we can return to after undertaking exploratory voyages? Is it a thing of permanence that we trust will still be there, even if our explorations take us far and wide?

Love is not an adventure. But it makes adventures possible.

The reasons why people fall in love with each other are too numerous to identify. When asked to explain partner choice, people frequently volunteer vague justifications, such as "It felt right." References to "chemistry" are also commonplace. In all probability, this sense of rightness, of pieces falling into place, of complementarity—all of these nebulous generalities—are different ways of describing safety. When talking about our partners, we rarely say they make us "feel safe." For heterosexual women, such a statement might imply disempowerment, and for heterosexual men, weakness. Gender politics and cultural baggage confuse the issue. Love is necessarily a state of dependency. It recollects the state of childhood dependency and perhaps even the ultimate dependency of prenatal symbiosis.

When we make our children feel safe, we are preparing them, in spite of our shortcomings, to give and receive love. We are giving them the ability to form bonds—not restraining bonds, but bonds that liberate. Our children are then free to fulfill their evolutionary destiny.

The International Mate Selection Project, a survey of over nine thousand people, from thirty-three countries located across six continents, found in 1990 that the most valued attributes in a prospective partner were kindness and understanding.

Safety is anything but dull. Safety is sexy.

3

INSIGHT

The Heart Has Its Reasons

Freud's most significant contribution to psychological knowledge was his insistence that we have little insight into our own behavior. We can generate explanations, but these are post hoc justifications and frequently wrong. Much of what we do is prompted by unconscious memories or stimuli that register in the brain but which we are not aware of. Although the importance of unconscious mental life has been periodically questioned, converging evidence from a number of related disciplines has confirmed Freud's general position.

Because our insight is poor, we frequently repeat self-defeating patterns of behavior. Escape from these unhappy cycles can be achieved by acquiring better self-understanding, but the unconscious does not yield its secrets on request. Insight is effortful. Talking without inhibition and the habit of self-reflection are essential if buried memories are to be recovered. Only then can the connections among past events, thoughts, feelings, and behavior be fully understood.

It is widely acknowledged that Freud's account of humanity is unflattering. Aristotle defined man as a "rational animal." Freud, in contrast, saw human behavior as mostly irrational. The idea that behavior could be influenced by unconscious memories had already appeared long before Freud's early publications. (For example, the seventeenth-century mathematician Blaise Pascal remarked, with poetic economy, "The heart has its reasons, which reason does not know.") Freud, however, goes one step further. Human beings are irrational, certainly. But even rational (or apparently rational) behavior can be rooted in the murky depths of the unconscious.

How does the unconscious influence our thoughts and behavior?

Freud suggested that memories, ideas, and feelings can cluster together in the unconscious and produce systematic perceptual and behavioral biases when we find ourselves in certain situations. It was in fact Jung, rather than Freud, who first employed the term "complex" to describe such assemblies. In *A Review of the Complex Theory*, published in 1934, Jung suggested that a complex is like a "fragmentary personality," a largely autonomous part of the mind that, in a sense, intermittently takes possession of us. Thus, when a complex is "active," we are functioning under conditions of "diminished responsibility." We are largely unaware of our complexes, and their presence can only be inferred by observing their effects.

The lynchpin of psychoanalysis is the Oedipus complex (named after a character in Greek mythology). It is often summarized in the following way: boys want to have sex with their mothers and kill their fathers. When blunt language of this kind is employed, most people find the idea preposterous and actually quite offensive. But the concept deserves more measured consideration.

Oedipal themes surface in Western art and literature with extraordinary frequency. From Sophocles and Shakespeare to *Psycho* and *Star Wars*, the tortured dynamics of the basic family triad (mother-father-child) have provided countless plotlines with their vital, propulsive energies. Conspicuous regularities of this kind are usually the outcome of evolutionary pressures. Universal human characteristics, such as preferences, fears and dislikes, and the ability to learn some things more easily than others, have almost certainly been privileged by natural selection because they increased the likelihood of our ancestors surviving and reproducing. For example, sugar cravings are common because sweet things are an excellent source of energy, and snakes evoke fear because they are venomous. An ancestor who searched for sweet berries and assiduously avoided snakes would probably live longer than an ancestor who did the opposite. Any psychological or behavioral phenomenon that is frequently observed has probably, to a greater or lesser extent, developed through natural selection. And this includes everything from sugar cravings to recurring cultural motifs, such as Oedipal narratives. Natural selection does not select stories—but it does select the genes and associated dispositions that ultimately find expression in stories.

Almost all schools of psychotherapy acknowledge the existence of complexes, or something very similar, to explain unconscious influence. The mind is conceptualized as having a fluid upper level, in which cognitive events occur (e.g., thoughts, perceptions), and a lower level, from where more permanent features, sometimes referred to as cognitive structures or schemas, influence the nature of those cognitive events. Thus, a structure composed of interconnected beliefs about personal vulnerability will cause an individual to overestimate dangers and have more frequent anxious thoughts (e.g., "If I go out at night I'll be attacked"). The Oedipus complex is the most significant example of what has since become a widely accepted paradigm: discrete assemblies of unconscious knowledge and associated emotions can alter our relationship with reality. John Bowlby's working models are also a form of cognitive structure. Contextualized in this way, the Oedipus complex should be approached with the respect due to any early (and consequently imperfect) advance in the history of ideas.

Freud has always attracted torrents of criticism. Many of his early followers eventually rejected his conclusions (often because of his insistence on the importance of the Oedipus complex), and entire academic careers have consisted of little more than what is now generically called "Freud bashing." Among Freud bashers, one stands head and shoulders above the rest. His bashing was so well aimed that—for several decades—it looked as if the entire edifice of psychoanalysis might come crashing down.

When I was a student at what was then called the Institute of Psychiatry, in south London, I was living, somewhat inconveniently, many miles away in north London. In order to avoid the rush hour traffic I would rise early, sometimes ridiculously early, and drive across the city. I would often arrive at the institute before sunrise, when the parking lot was virtually empty. The building was silent, and the sound of my footsteps produced a pleasing echo. When I reached the psychology department it was necessary to walk down a long windowless corridor. All the doors were shut—with one exception. As I hurried past this single, open door, I would glance into a small office and see a casually dressed man (who

nevertheless always wore a tie) standing next to a desk, speaking into a handheld recording device.

His name was Hans Jürgen Eysenck. Usually, he had his back to me—like a man in a Hopper painting—but I could see his concentrated expression in the black mirror of the office window. He could dictate a whole book in a couple of weeks. Sometimes our eyes met, but he was never distracted by my fleet reflection, and his recitation continued without pause. He was in his seventies but so enthused by the prospect of discovery that he was hard at work while most of the academic staff were still in bed.

H. J. Eysenck was the leading British psychologist for much of the second half of the twentieth century. He was born in Berlin but fled Nazi Germany in 1935 and settled in London. His research interests were broad, spanning everything from genetics to astrology; his industry was exceptional. In addition to academic publications, he wrote accessible psychology books for the lay reader that sold millions of copies. By the end of the 1950s, he was relatively well-known beyond the confines of academia. His prose style was combative, and by the beginning of the 1960s he was being described as a controversial figure. A decade later, his name became strongly associated with research linking race and IQ. He was accused of being a fascist, physically attacked, and received death threats. Today, his reputation rests on an influential personality theory, and he is remembered for his refutation of Freud and psychoanalysis. In 1952, Eysenck reviewed the evidence for the efficacy of psychotherapy—including psychoanalysis—and concluded that outcomes were no better than spontaneous remission rates.

The debates that followed were heated and rancorous. Eysenck's critique created a climate of opinion that encouraged the development of alternative psychological treatments based on the laboratory experiments of Ivan Pavlov (who famously conditioned dogs to salivate in response to a bell) and B. F. Skinner (who modified the behavior of pigeons using rewards and punishments). These new "behavioral" treatments proved to be very effective—particularly for bedwetting, anxiety, and conduct disorders.

If you had asked Eysenck why he was so critical of Freud, he would have answered that the claims of psychoanalysis were not supported by the evidence. Eysenck was an empiricist, and his professional life was dedicated to the pursuit of truth. This was his primary motivation. Or, at least, his primary motivation as he understood it.

In 1990 Eysenck published his autobiography, *Rebel with a Cause*. It is a fitting monument to his very considerable achievements, but marred, perhaps, by an authorial voice that is somewhat lacking in self-awareness. There are several passages that are startlingly immodest: "'How have you managed to write so much, and to become so influential a figure?' is a question I am often asked." He shamelessly informs us that he is included among forty-two Nobel Prize winners whose names appear on the science citation index, and that his position on the list is preeminent in relation to all other living psychologists. Nevertheless, he concludes this particular paragraph with a telling afterthought: "Freud, however, came out ahead of me." It was something that bothered him.[1]

I was educated and trained as a psychologist almost exclusively by academics and clinicians who, largely because of Eysenck's hostility to psychoanalysis, dismissed "Freudianism" as dangerous, fraudulent nonsense. Over time, I began to feel uneasy when sitting in research meetings or case supervisions where simply mentioning Freud would be guaranteed to raise a laugh. It became tiresome. The antipathy seemed disproportionate, too extreme. I began to suspect that there was more going on than could be explained by an honest difference of opinion.

Freud suggested that between the ages of three and five, boys wish to possess their mothers exclusively and begin to perceive their fathers as rivals. On reaching sexual maturity, these tensions usually resolve; however, vestiges of the Oedipus complex can survive in the unconscious and might continue to influence behavior indefinitely. Institutions and authority figures, which symbolize paternal control and dominance, can easily reawaken juvenile feelings of resentment and jealousy. Because the Oedipus complex exerts its influence from the unconscious, few men connect their desire to challenge authority with the impotent rages of childhood.

Although Freud's initial formulation of the Oedipus complex gives particular emphasis to nascent sexual feelings, it can also be conceptualized in broader terms, as the first expression of a fundamental need to eliminate competition and achieve preeminence (albeit on the modest scale of power relationships within families). Freud went on to speculate, some would say rather wildly, about the evolutionary origins of Oedipal hostility. He was inspired by Darwin's suggestion that early humans probably lived together in primal hordes dominated by a senior polygamous male. Freud supposed that, under such conditions, young men would periodically band together and slay their elders in order to gain unrestricted access to females. The banding together of young males in order to attack an alpha male is in fact observed in troops of chimpanzees (although fatalities among chimps are rare).[2] An implication of Freud's proposal is that each generation is born with a "psychical disposition" to rebel against its predecessor.

When I consider Eysenck's tireless, uncompromising, and extreme assaults on psychoanalysis, I am haunted by an image of Freud, puffing on a cigar, chuckling softly, his eyes bright with knowing humor. Eysenck's transparent desire to supersede and replace Freud is curiously Oedipal in character.

Eysenck's father, a touring actor, was largely absent from the marital home, and he remarried when his son was only nine. Nevertheless, he was present enough for the boy to recognize his flaws. Eysenck described his father as a "womanizer," and one of the few things he chose to record about their relationship is their competitive arguments.

Reviewing Eysenck's last major attack on psychoanalysis, the British psychiatrist Anthony Clare urged readers to admire Eysenck's polemical talents "as he pounds his way through the flimsy foundations of Freud's theories." All that relentless "pounding"—hammer blows delivered over a lifetime. You have to ask: Where

did he find the energy? It would be naïve to suggest that his motives were pure. Indeed, it would be naïve to suggest that anyone's
motives are pure. There are always subtexts, concealed purposes,
and ulterior influences.

From the 1930s to the 1970s, Herbert Graf was a very successful
opera producer. For most of his career, he was based at the Metro-
politan opera house in New York, but he also worked in Europe.
His staging of Mozart's *Don Giovanni* was legendary. Yet, in an
altogether different role, he achieved a kind of immortality. When
he was a child, he was the subject of one of Freud's case studies:
"Analysis of a Phobia in a Five-Year-Old Boy." It is more commonly known as "the case of Little Hans," which was the moniker
Freud gave Herbert to disguise his true identity. Freud published
very few cases, so Herbert Graf was, and still is, a member of a
very select group.

Little Hans was the son of the critic and musicologist Max
Graf. Max's wife, Olga, introduced Max to Freud, and Freud
acted as an intermediary while Max and Olga were still courting.
The two men became great friends. Max and Olga were among
Freud's very earliest disciples, so much so that when their son was
born, they turned their domestic arrangements into an informal
psychoanalytic field study. They observed Little Hans closely and
reported their findings to Freud. Of all Freud's case studies, the
one on Little Hans is the most transparently Oedipal. It is also
arguably the starting point of child psychotherapy.

From the age of three, Little Hans demonstrated several
manifestations of childhood sexuality: a general preoccupation
with genitalia (he had invited his mother to touch his penis),
curiosity about his mother's body, and a desire to "sleep with" a

fourteen-year-old girl. When his mother found him touching his penis, she said she would send for a doctor to cut it off. This threat may have caused the first stirrings of "castration anxiety," the anxiety that Freud said arises when a small boy realizes that his wish to be loved exclusively by his mother might excite paternal anger and retributive violence.

A few months before his fifth birthday, Little Hans became frightened of horses. He was particularly worried by dray horses pulling wagons, which he expected to stumble and fall; his main fear, however, was that they would bite him. When this fear of horses developed, most of the boy's analysis was conducted by his father under Freud's supervision.

According to Freud, Little Hans could not cope with his powerful feelings—his desire for his mother and the anxiety surrounding his father. Consequently, his fear was transferred from his father to horses. It was easier for Little Hans to be frightened of horses, less confusing, less complicated by ambivalence. He was particularly disturbed by horses' bridles ("the black round their mouths"). Freud supposed that, from Little Hans's diminutive perspective, these bridles bore a striking resemblance to Max Graf's large black mustache, and that this similarity supplied a frictionless substitute for the transfer of fear. It is reasonable, after all, for a child to be frightened of a large, biting animal. Gentle efforts were made to reassure Little Hans that his father wasn't angry with him, and in due course the boy's phobia disappeared.

Freud died before Herbert Graf rose to prominence in the opera world. But in 1922, a young man introduced himself to Freud as "Little Hans." Freud was delighted to learn that this "strapping youth of nineteen" was perfectly well and his phobia had never returned.

Nearly forty years after that meeting, Eysenck, summarizing work previously published by two colleagues, penned a critical essay on the case of Little Hans. He noted, not without justification, that some of Freud's speculations are unmerited, and that, as the case study develops it becomes increasingly incoherent. The nub of his attack concerns an event that Freud mentions, almost in passing, which provides an alternative, non-Oedipal explanation for Little Hans's fear of horses. Just before Little Hans's troubles began, he witnessed the collapse of a horse that was pulling a bus. This experience must have been very frightening to the boy and may well have made him apprehensive.

Eysenck's explanation is appealing because it is straightforward, but it doesn't by any means constitute a fatal blow to Freudian theory. Psychoanalysts make a distinction between precipitating and ultimate causes; therefore, one might argue that the collapsing horse and Little Hans's feelings toward his parents were *both* important determinants of his phobia. It is conceivable, for example, that the accident activated underlying Oedipal anxieties.

Eysenck's critique, although admirably forensic, is somewhat misconceived. He doesn't seem to appreciate the richness of Freud's more general assertions, and it is only by considering these that the true value of the case becomes clear. It isn't easy to identify the causes of fear. In fact, it isn't easy to identify the causes of a great deal of our behavior. And Freud takes childhood very seriously. He does his best to inhabit Little Hans's skin, to look out through the boy's eyes. Naturally, the world appears very different to a child than it does to an adult. Things that an adult takes for granted—defecation, genitalia, animals—are still salient novelties to a child. We now know that early experiences are a critical determinant of development, and that memories of these experiences continue to influence our thoughts, beliefs, desires, and emotions throughout our lives, even when we are unaware of them.

The Oedipus complex remains emblematic of Freudian excesses and for many it is an insurmountable obstacle. It precludes acceptance of psychoanalysis. Much of this resistance is because of Freud's insistence on the importance of childhood sexuality, a subject that makes us uncomfortable. Typically, our discomfort becomes denial. But as Freud himself pointed out, even though his writings on the subject were greeted with alarm and incredulity, he was saying nothing that would shock most nannies and nursery school teachers. As adults, we tend to forget or repress early recollections of precocious sexuality, the examination of body parts, licensed by surreptitious games of "doctors and nurses." We prefer to think of children as being pure and innocent.

To what extent is the Oedipus complex supported by evidence? Psychoanalysts believe that case studies are proof enough, but naturally they are accused of being biased by skeptics. Evolutionary psychologists find the Oedipus complex plausible (at least as a logical possibility), and more recently, Internet search data have demonstrated that a relatively high proportion of men and women seek out incest-themed pornography.

The Oedipus complex can be viewed as a Darwinian inevitability. A mother is the first model of womanhood, and pleasurable contact with her body incentivizes what will eventually become sexual motivation—the most fundamental prerequisite for reproductive success. Also, a child will attempt to command its mother's full attention to optimize its chances of survival, which will inevitably place it in competition with its father. At a later stage, Oedipal competition provides sons with opportunities to test skills that will eventually be useful in the social arena, where they must contend with peers for a mate and resources.

When Internet users are alone and seemingly unobserved, inclinations that would ordinarily be concealed, on account of their social unacceptability, find relatively easy expression. In his 2017 book, *Everybody Lies: What the Internet Can Tell Us About Who We Really Are*, the data analyst Seth Stephens-Davidowitz cites a number of statistics that appear to support Freud's Oedipal suppositions. Sixteen out of the top one hundred searches of Porn-Hub conducted by men are incest related (e.g., "mom and son," "mom fucks son"). Nine out of the top one hundred PornHub searches by women are also incest related, although women are more likely to search for material featuring fathers and daughters. Of all the Internet searches that take the form "I want to have sex with my . . ." the most popular entry that completes the sentence is "mom." Comparable sentence structures—for example, "I am attracted to . . ."—are also dominated by incestuous completions. Stephens-Davidowitz acknowledges that his evidence is suggestive rather than conclusive. Even so, he writes, "I am absolutely certain the final verdict on adult sexuality will feature some key themes that Freud emphasized. Childhood will play a major role. So will mothers."[3]

As described so far, the Oedipus complex is a phenomenon relevant only to boys. This begs the question: What about girls? Freud proposed a complementary Elektra complex (also named after a character from Greek mythology) that is a mirror image of the Oedipus complex. Young girls, he said, are attracted to their fathers and perceive their mothers as rivals. Unfortunately, Freud's writings on female sexuality (and the subject of women in general) are less persuasive than his writings on men and boys. This was a shortcoming of which he was very much aware. Much of psychoanalytic theory was influenced by Freud's self-analysis. He couldn't see another psychoanalyst at the time because he was the only one. Therefore, his ideas about the psychosexual development of boys are better informed than his ideas about the psychosexual development of girls. Irrespective of gender asymmetries in psychoanalysis, the Oedipus complex is still a cohesive formulation when judged within the frame of its own limitations.

Freud believed that humor can sometimes be defensive, and we laugh to reduce or disguise our anxiety. In Eysenck's autobiography there is a curious incident recorded near the beginning of the first chapter. When he was nine, he went to Munich to meet his father's second wife, a dancer in a cabaret. During this trip he discovered a book about sex, which he started to read: "I began to get amused when I read about cunnilingus, I guffawed when I read about fellatio, but when I got to soixante-neuf I laughed so much I fell out of bed!"[4] His father came to investigate and took the book away. We shouldn't be surprised that Eysenck found the Oedipus complex risible.

When I was a teenager, I read Eysenck's popular psychology books avidly and was impressed by his arguments. Later, I attended his lectures and published academic articles with his son. He was a colossal figure. Perhaps, as I write these words, I'm being a little Oedipal too.

The unconscious is deep, and almost everything we do is shaped by its influence.

Freud made the unconscious the central and most consequential concept in psychoanalysis. Even some of his earliest collaborators believed that he had given it too much significance. Conscious mental activity, they argued, is just as important, and should be given equal emphasis. After Freud, psychotherapists became increasingly focused on talking to patients about remembered experiences rather than the recovery of forgotten or repressed memories. As critics formed an eager queue behind Hans Eysenck, disaffection with psychoanalysis became more widespread and the entire concept of unconscious mental life was treated with suspicion. The unconscious was freighted with too many fanciful associations to be taken seriously by a groundswell of young empiricists. It became a historical footnote, a subject of study that appealed only to mavericks. Behaviorists dispensed with the study of the mind altogether.

Yet the brain *must* be capable of processing information unconsciously, because well-practiced behaviors—driving, for example—become completely automated. We can hold conversations while performing the physical movements that are necessary to control a car without consciously initiating and monitoring those movements. William James, the father of scientific psychology in America, was aware of this fact in 1890. "Consciousness," he said, "drops out of any process where it is no longer needed." Other phenomena—for example, the so-called cocktail party effect—were puzzling and could only be explained by the unconscious appraisal of sensory information. If you are at a party and someone in a nearby group says your name, in all likelihood you will hear it, even though you heard nothing of what was being said before. This suggests that the background noise of the party was being subject to continuous analysis, and when your name was spoken, it was recognized, classified as significant, and permitted to enter awareness. The sleeping brain shows equivalent sensitivities. A person is much more likely to wake up if you say their name than if you make a sound of equivalent volume or say a neutral word. Moreover, a distinct electrical brain response to "hearing" one's name persists during sleep.[5]

Even though the unconscious was marginalized, laboratory work conducted by experimental psychologists, particularly in the area of subliminal perception, suggested that stimuli presented far too briefly to be noticed could still influence perception, choices, and mood.[6] The unconscious gained further scientific support from neurological case studies. For example, it was discovered that patients who were blind because of damage to the visual cortex (rather than the eye) could still respond to stimuli that they couldn't see.[7] These patients might be able to correctly identify letters of the alphabet even though their subjective experience was of simply making a wild guess. Once again, information was evidently being processed in the absence of awareness.

Around the same time that laboratory studies were providing proof of preconscious processing, evolutionary biologists were generating theories that necessitated the division of the mind into conscious and unconscious parts. In his 1976 foreword to Richard Dawkins's book *The Selfish Gene*, Robert Trivers wrote, "There must be strong selection to spot deception and this ought, in turn, to select for a degree of self-deception, rendering some facts and motives unconscious so as not to betray—by the subtle signs of self-knowledge—the deception being practiced." In other words, people lie to themselves so that they can lie to others with greater conviction. The psychoanalyst Heinz Hartmann once described psychoanalysis as "a theory of self-deception." Evolutionary biologists were starting to sound distinctly Freudian.

Since the arrival of brain scanning technology it has become possible to observe information being processed unconsciously in the cerebral cortex directly. For example, if words and non-words are presented subliminally to experimental subjects, it is only words (and not non-words) that will activate regions associated with the production and comprehension of language.[8] We can watch the brain analyzing a stimulus while its owner remains oblivious.

There are two dominant models of the unconscious, the Freudian (or dynamic) unconscious, and the cognitive (or new) unconscious. The former resembles a secondary personality or agency, insofar as it often seems to make "independent" decisions. It can, for instance, decide to stop particular memories from rising into consciousness. The cognitive unconscious is more mechanical, a substratum of mind where "routines" run their course in a more predetermined fashion, usually activated by specific environmental triggers. The term "new unconscious" is something of a misnomer, because figures like William James and his contemporaries had been referring to "automatisms" and "reflex functions of the brain" since the nineteenth century.[9] Victorian gentlemen scientists imagined an unconscious that could generate complex behavior from processes that resembled the workings of a clock or a combination of knee jerks.

These two models appeal to different academic constituencies and are considered mutually exclusive. But what is the fundamental difference? In 1992, Elizabeth Loftus and Mark Klinger published an article in *American Psychologist* titled "Is the Unconscious Smart or Dumb?" Psychodynamic psychologists believe the unconscious is smart, whereas cognitive psychologists believe the unconscious is dumb. The former tend to defend their position with evidence collected in clinics; the latter, laboratories. "Smart" and "dumb" are simple, everyday words that can help us to grasp the fundamental difference between dynamic and cognitive conceptions of the unconscious; however, they are practicable only up to a point. Some computer scientists, for example, maintain that a pocket calculator possesses a rudimentary form of intelligence. And according to Alan Turing, the inventor of the eponymous Turing Test, a convincing machine simulation of human intelligence *is* intelligence. Instead of thinking in terms of the presence or absence of intelligence, perhaps we should borrow a distinction made by artificial-intelligence researchers: the dynamic unconscious has *general* intelligence, and the cognitive unconscious has *narrow* intelligence.[10]

Although academics still argue about how we should conceptualize the unconscious, it should be noted that, these days, such debates take place in an increasingly harmonious context. I am old enough to remember university psychology departments where one could find tenured lecturers who didn't believe in the unconscious—in the same way that a creationist doesn't believe in evolution. Today, almost all mainstream psychologists accept that there is a stratum of mental life that proceeds below the threshold of awareness. In this sense, at least, Freud triumphed over his critics.

Neuroscientists agree that most of the choices we make are ultimately determined by unconscious processes.[11] We act on those choices and then generate convenient fictions to explain what we've just done. Most people have no idea that this is happening as they go through life deciding what to eat, what exams to take, which job to apply for, whom to marry, and whether or not to have children. Given that this is how the human mind works, it's a miracle that anyone makes any good decisions.

The young woman in Edward Hopper's *Automat* can deliberate for hours, days, even months. Could she, should she? Maybe she should, maybe she shouldn't. Most decisions are a leap in the dark, which is why we make so many wrong ones. Our complexes bend our thoughts like massive objects bend light.

In *Silent Theater*, my friend Walter Wells speculated about the young woman's deliberations, the precise reason for her melancholy. He suggested that the bannisters that edge into the frame provide a clue: "Inside this young woman's head may be the thought that there is no exit from her dilemma—only a stairway down." Despair, dashed hopes—defeat. But perhaps there's another possibility here, an alternative reading of Hopper's symbolism. Perhaps the downward stairway offers a means of escape.

Arriving at optimal solutions requires insight. We must descend into the unconscious, uncover memories, and discover how the past is influencing us. We have to understand ourselves. Like an elegant Zen paradox, the way in—and down—leads up, and out.

Making this descent isn't easy; most people find it difficult to achieve on their own. They need someone to talk to: encouragement, support, an objective opinion. Unfortunately, the memories that we need to uncover most are the ones that we least want to look at: painful memories of childhood—sexual memories—embarrassing memories—memories that make us feel ashamed—dirty secrets—unacceptable wishes—memories that expose our flaws—imperfections—damage. Freud introduced a technical term to describe this reluctance to examine the contents of the unconscious. He called it "resistance." As we probe our hidden depths, we become increasingly anxious. If we choose to withdraw, we will experience relief. Because avoidance is easier, at least in the short term, we carry on avoiding until it becomes automatic. We persuade ourselves to put everything back in the box. We close the lid and walk away. Over time, introspection becomes a meaningless exercise: raking over the topsoil, swimming in the shallows.

Hopper's young woman has her eyes lowered. She seems to be looking directly into her cup. Does she see her own face, I wonder, trembling on the surface of the coffee inside? Does she know the person she sees? And if she doesn't know the person she sees, how can she make the right decision?

We are strangers to ourselves. This is why life is frequently so difficult to negotiate.

4

DISTORTION

Warped Mirrors

We go through life acting as if our senses convey accurate impressions of the world to the brain and that these impressions are converted into faithful memories by processes similar to video recording or photography. The eye, however, is not a camera, and our memories are not like films or photographs. Vision is only possible because of educated guesswork. The brain fills in gaps based on past regularities, and what we see is determined by our expectations as well as objective reality. Remembering is more like re-creation or reconstruction than replay.

Some memories are more accessible than others, and what we remember will change over time. Before the end of the nineteenth century, Freud was referring to "screen memories," invented memories that obstruct our access to deeper and more troubling ones.[*] Many of our recollections have been modified—in much

---

[*] J. A. Underwood has suggested that the conventional translation of Freud's term *Deckerinnerungen*, screen memories, should be changed to "covering memories." For the modern reader, the term "screen" is more likely to suggest

the same way that a story changes through frequent retelling—
and some of our recollections might even belong to other people.
Childhood anecdotes about siblings are frequently converted into
"autobiographical" memories. Even recent events can be mis-
remembered. A large number of domestic arguments are driven by
differing accounts of shared experiences—who said what, when,
and where. Neither party can agree. Memories are so mutable that
simply altering the wording of a question can change the quality
of recollections. For example, a person will be more likely to report having seen shattered glass on the road if a car accident has
been described as a "smash" rather than a "collision."[1]

To paraphrase Hamlet, we hold a mirror up to life, and what
we see in the mirror will become our memories. Unfortunately,
the glass is warped. If perception and memory can't be trusted,
how much confidence can we have in our decisions? The simple
but predictable answer is very little.

Anna Freud was Sigmund Freud's youngest child, an unhappy girl
who considered herself ugly and stupid. Yet photographs of her in
early adulthood show a poised, thoughtful young woman. As she
matured, she became a tantalizing object of desire for several of
Freud's followers. Anna trained as a schoolteacher but was always
interested in her father's work. She sat with him when he met with
colleagues to discuss his ideas. Naturally, being a schoolteacher,
she developed a particular interest in child psychology.

Psychoanalytic training involves being analyzed, and Anna
was duly analyzed by her father. Today, we would regard such an
arrangement as completely inappropriate; however, at that time,

---

a surface on which images appear rather than a piece of furniture used to hide
things.

analyzing close friends and family members was a much more common occurrence. Max Graf analyzed his son, Herbert, for example. Still, Anna and Sigmund must have had some inkling that what they were doing wasn't quite right. Anna's analysis became a closely guarded secret until Ernest Jones brought it to the public's attention in the 1960s.

Anna became an extremely important child psychoanalyst. She wasn't the first child psychoanalyst (a common misconception that she made few efforts to correct). She was preceded by her father, whose Little Hans case study set a notable precedent, as well as by Hermine Hugg-Helmuth, whose psychoanalytic career came to a premature end when her mentally ill nephew strangled her (he said he'd been driven mad by her constant analyzing). Anna never married, formed several close attachments to women, and eventually became the intimate companion of Dorothy Burlingham (heiress of the Tiffany fortune), with whom she lived in Vienna and London. Anna was a prolific writer, frequently praised for her clarity of expression. In 1956, Marilyn Monroe, who was suffering from severe psychological problems during the filming of *The Prince and The Showgirl*, was sent to see Anna. Anna's intervention must have been helpful, because Monroe returned to the set and the film was successfully completed.

On Sigmund Freud's eightieth birthday, Anna handed him a copy of what is probably her most significant theoretical contribution to psychoanalysis, *The Ego and the Mechanisms of Defence*. Freud had introduced the idea of a protective response to stress in his earliest writings, although at that time he was almost exclusively interested in "repression." Disturbing impulses, ideas, or memories can be "pushed down" into the unconscious, or repressed, in order to reduce anxiety or discomfort. This creates a more acceptable notion of self, albeit a false notion, because it is incomplete. The more defensive we are, the more we become detached from reality and unavailable to others and ourselves. A certain amount of defensiveness is normal, but too much will diminish engagement with experience and limit opportunities for personal growth. Essentially, defense mechanisms are distortions that make life (in the short term) more bearable. Contemporary psychoanalysts recognize many defense mechanisms, those originally identified by Sigmund and Anna as well as others identified by their colleagues and successors.

Projection is the attribution of unattractive internal characteristics to others. For example, a person struggling to manage his own hateful thoughts might claim that he is being persecuted. *Rationalization* is the use of logical justifications for actions that were actually performed for morally suspect purposes or out of self-interest. A man who has been unfaithful, for instance, might reason that he can't tell his wife about the affair because the truth will hurt her feelings. *Splitting* is the resolution of emotional conflict by viewing oneself or others as completely good or bad, thus simplifying the world and avoiding the demands of dealing with complex and troubling ambiguities. A dependent person who is desperate to save a failing relationship might focus on a partner's lively personality, while viewing the same individual's selfishness as an occasional aberration that can be ignored. *Humor* can be employed as a release valve, in order to reduce stress, even though the situation might not be very funny. Medical professionals are notorious for using gallows humor to manage the distress caused by having to face human suffering and death on a regular basis. *Reaction formation* involves disguising unpleasant intent with behavior that suggests the very opposite. A child who wishes his baby brother dead, for example, might show exaggerated concern for his sibling's welfare. *Passive aggressiveness*—being quietly obstructive or uncooperative—can obscure more hostile intentions. The list goes on, with terms such as *acting out, disavowal, exaggeration, intellectualization, omnipotent control, projective identification*, and *somatization* all referring to specific kinds of defense mechanisms. A comprehensive list of such mechanisms would merit an entire chapter.

Once defense mechanisms have been established, they tend to operate automatically. We are largely unaware of how they systematically distort our world and sense of self. This makes us more likely to repeat our mistakes. And defense mechanisms, because they are defensive, become more noticeable when we are conflicted or under pressure. A person who does not cope well with criticism might, for example, become childish. They are defending themselves by regressing to an earlier stage of development, a time when they were not expected to be responsible and they could simply blame others for their errors.

According to classical Freudian theory, the parts of the mind that correspond roughly to the autobiographical self (i.e., the person you understand yourself to be) defend against three threats: internalized parental criticism, primitive urges, and dangers located in the real world (such as physical harm, embarrassment, or humiliation). Anna Freud maintained that it is only by analyzing defense mechanisms that we can hope to gain meaningful insights: "Without a knowledge of these we may, indeed, discover much about the contents of the repressed instinctual wishes and fantasies, but we shall learn little or nothing about the vicissitudes through which they have passed and the various ways in which they enter into the structure of personality."[2] In other words, a close examination of defense mechanisms will probably tell you more useful things about a person than their sexual and aggressive urges ever could. In a sense, we *are* our defensive distortions. When we hold a mirror up to life, the warp in the glass makes us who we are.

Defenses protect the person from threat and reduce discomfort, but an entrenched defense will almost certainly outlive its utility. *Dissociation*—in which the individual distances the self from experience—is strongly linked with a history of trauma. Affected individuals have learned to cope with stress by cutting themselves off from unpleasant feelings. Trauma such as sexual or physical abuse can be tolerated more easily if victims dissociate, if they stop identifying with the body that is being abused. "This isn't happening to me, not the *real* me." But in the long term, responding to stress by retreating into an altered state of consciousness is going to be counterproductive. The potential therapeutic benefits of love and intimacy, for example, will be mitigated if the usual disagreements that arise between couples automatically trigger numbness and emotional inaccessibility.

Anna Freud was curiously undefended herself. We know that she was capable of accepting the cruelest of realities and reaching conclusions that most of us would shrink from. On March 22, 1938, she was interrogated by the Gestapo.[3] She was carrying a lethal drug that she intended to take if she was tortured. The drug wasn't necessary, but later, when it appeared that the Freud family might not be able to escape from Vienna, she asked her father a question: "Wouldn't it be better if we all killed ourselves?" Sigmund—the hardest of hardheaded realists—still needed some defenses. Dry humor was one he frequently deployed. "Why?" he replied. "Because they would like us to?"

Most people will be able to identify with the following.

You want to get a good night's sleep because the next day you have something important to do. Perhaps you are about to embark on a long journey, make a presentation at work, or give a speech. You wake up in the middle of the night and begin to think about all the things that could go wrong. Scenarios play out in your head, with the outcomes becoming increasingly catastrophic. You find it difficult to get back to sleep and your mind is racing. You drift in and out of consciousness, disturbed by nightmarish visions. When sunlight finally filters through the curtains, you get out of bed, exhausted, and perform your usual morning rituals. You remember all the scenarios that kept you awake—your plane crashing, forgetting all your notes, or freezing in a spotlight, unable to speak—and you recognize that, in the middle of the night, you must have lost all sense of proportion. The day ahead is still going to be challenging, but the things you were worried about at two o'clock in the morning no longer seem credible (and may even seem a little ridiculous). You aren't going to drive off the edge of a cliff, trip and fall flat on your face, or faint when you get up to speak. While eating your breakfast you continue to regain perspective. You are apprehensive, but the feverish imaginings that made you toss and turn and perspire until daybreak have evaporated.

In the darkness of the night there are no reference points that will anchor us to reality, no physical spaces to remind us of objective limits, no friendly voices to check our worries. We accept anxious thoughts as if they are facts and misjudge probabilities. We become increasingly agitated and focus on potential disasters. We become *irrational*.

For thousands of years, from Zhou dynasty China to Enlightenment Europe, rationality was regarded as the defining attribute of humanity. Civilization and technological progress are only possible because human beings can think logically and solve problems. The importance of rationality becomes even more obvious when thinking is flawed or impaired. Insanity, perhaps the most extreme example of human suffering, manifests primarily as a condition of disordered thought. Other problems, such as phobias, can also be understood as reasoning failures. The threat posed by that which is feared—for example, a mouse—does not correspond with the phobic individual's reaction—leaping onto a chair and screaming. Reason has always been associated with mental health, whereas loss of reason has always been associated with mental illness.

In the early years of the twentieth century, Paul Dubois, a psychiatrist and professor of neuropathology at the University of Berne, published a book titled *Psychic Treatment of Mental Disease*. Like Freud, he preferred talking to his patients rather than giving them drugs or sending them off to recuperate in sanatoria. The kind of therapeutic conversation that Dubois advocated was very different from the free association and interpretation typical of psychoanalysis. Dubois argued that people suffering from mental illnesses functioned better if they could exercise self-control, and he supposed that odd or suboptimal patterns of behavior arose from false beliefs. If those beliefs were corrected using persuasive logic, people would become more attuned to reality, and therefore more likely to behave appropriately. Mice are not dangerous, and they do not attack humans. If one fully accepts this, then there is no need to scream and stand on a chair.

All psychotherapies make an appeal to reason, but Dubois gave reasoning special emphasis. For a short period of time, his "persuasion therapy" competed with psychoanalysis, but both Dubois and his approach were soon forgotten. It wasn't until the 1950s that anything resembling his technique was tried again (with the exception, perhaps, of Alfred Adler, who employed "Socratic questioning"—encouraging people to find their own answers by asking them questions—rather than supplying them with solutions or interpretations).

Albert Ellis, who died in 2007, was an American clinical psychologist who developed a logic-based treatment that he called rational emotive therapy (RET). It is now more commonly described as rational emotive behavior therapy (REBT). Ellis was greatly influenced by the Stoic philosophers of ancient Greece and Rome, who suggested that we only experience events as disturbing to the extent that we interpret them as threatening or malevolent. Shakespeare reiterated this view—perhaps more elegantly—when Hamlet declares, "There's nothing either good or bad, but thinking makes it so."

Before training as a psychoanalyst, Ellis worked for a clothing business that matched trousers to still-usable jackets, and as the personnel manager for a gift and novelty company. He also spent much of his spare time writing fiction, hoping, like many of his generation, to produce the Great American Novel. These occupations represented, perhaps, early indications of the nonconformity that would, at a later date, lead many academics to marginalize him.

While working at the Greystone Park State Hospital in New Jersey, Ellis became disillusioned with psychoanalysis. He developed an alternative "active-directive" method of treatment, and in 1956 he presented his first paper on RET at a psychological association conference in Chicago.

According to Ellis, human beings have two fundamental goals: survival and happiness. Being rational helps us to achieve these goals, whereas being irrational puts us at risk and generally makes us unhappy. Ellis did not make a sharp distinction between thinking and feeling. He suggested that thinking and feeling are closely connected; thoughts intensify emotions and emotions influence thoughts. A person who thinks "I have failed" is likely to feel sad, but his or her sadness will also engender more thoughts about failure. Ellis believed that human beings are prone to irrational thinking because the brain doesn't always function efficiently.

This innate vulnerability is compounded by early learning experiences. Unhelpful ways of thinking about the self and the world become established through social observation. If parents behave irrationally, then their children will inevitably imitate them and develop similar irrational tendencies.

Ellis was quite prophetic, insofar as he suggested that irrational thinking is made worse by the mass media (which favor sensational stories and "indoctrination" over nuanced argument). He made this observation long before the arrival of the Internet and the proliferation of strongly held opinions based on little or no evidence. The commonplace distortion of truth online and on our TV screens that we now call "fake news" is of course antithetical to critical thinking.

Ellis proposed a simple ABC framework within which to analyze the relationship among A, activating events; B, beliefs; and C, consequences. An activating event is an objective fact, such as another person's behavior, or a particular outcome—for example, failing to get a job after a difficult interview. Beliefs are essentially evaluative thoughts, such as, "I am utterly useless," or "Being rejected is intolerable." Consequences are the behaviors and conclusions that constitute the totality of an individual's reaction. In this example, reluctance to interview for another job, and feeling depressed or worthless. Most people assume a direct link between activating events and consequences, but Ellis said this assumption is incorrect: instead, consequences (such as self-defeating behaviors and emotional distress) are almost always more strongly associated with beliefs. The most efficient way of treating distress, therefore, is by modifying beliefs.

In reality, responses to activating events are determined by both rational and irrational beliefs; however, people are more likely to have emotional problems if an activating event resonates with early negative experiences. An intelligent child repeatedly berated by a sadistic schoolteacher for being "stupid" might become an adult full of self-doubt when given intellectually challenging tasks by his or her boss.

Irrational beliefs have particular characteristics. They tend to be personal, rigid, and demanding (insofar as they reflect high or unrealistic expectations). When competence or the behavior of others falls short of these high expectations, outcomes are perceived as catastrophic. A recurring feature of this kind of thinking is extreme and consequently unhelpful perfectionism. If outcomes are not wholly good, then they are assumed to be wholly bad. Ellis also noted that certain words, such as "must" and "should," are overrepresented in the language of irrational thinkers. If you employ sentences that incorporate unforgiving or coercive language, "I *must* do well, I *should* do better," then you are very probably thinking in a way likely to cause emotional distress. Such words rarely reflect objective assessments. There is little in life that *must* be done, and hardly anything we *should* do. The amount of freedom we have varies from situation to situation, but there is usually some scope, albeit modest, for exploring alternative possibilities. Many of the outcomes that we describe as "awful" or "intolerable" are more accurately described as "unpleasant." We would benefit greatly by resisting the use of incendiary language.

Ellis's method for combating irrationality was disputation, challenging and testing the accuracy of beliefs. His approach is perhaps best described as Socratic questioning—but practiced with focused determination. "Why is it so bad to be rejected? Is it really intolerable? Haven't you encountered a setback rather than a disaster? How can you be completely worthless? Why conclude that?" The interrogation of irrational beliefs reveals their flaws and weaknesses, making it possible to replace them with more accurate, rational substitutes.

It is difficult to change emotional states directly. Where do you begin? Although Ellis probably overestimated the degree to which cognition and emotion overlap, cognition is certainly an important aspect of emotion, and thoughts can be shared with others when converted into speech. A thought is tractable, whereas an emotion is vague and distributed (for example, as a pattern of sensations located in different parts of the body). RET is eminently practical. It focuses on the dimension of emotionality most amenable to expression and modification.

During the 1980s and 1990s, I frequently encountered mainstream practitioners who were unfamiliar with Ellis and his ideas. In retrospect, this might seem rather odd, because Ellis is a figure of unquestionable significance. Even so, his relative obscurity at that time (particularly outside of the United States) is easily explained: From 1962 to 1964, some articles containing ideas very similar to those he espoused were published by a Philadelphia-based psychiatrist, one with an inordinate fondness for wearing bow ties. It wasn't until 1963 that Ellis read one of these articles, and he immediately wrote to the author, Aaron T. Beck. This was the first of many communications that in the fullness of time became a lifelong correspondence. Thirty years later, cognitive therapy, the system of therapy that Beck devised—involving the correction of inaccurate thoughts by disputation—had become widely accepted as a powerful and effective treatment. In academic circles, Ellis's priority was either acknowledged only in passing or entirely overlooked.

Cognitive therapy, which eventually became better known as cognitive-behavioral therapy, or CBT, is now the most widely practiced psychotherapy in the world. Beck's point of departure—irrationality—was identical to Ellis's, but Beck went on to develop a more sophisticated theoretical framework, more refined therapeutic techniques, and to prove the efficacy of his treatment by organizing clinical trials. His results were impressive and he attracted many followers, who in turn developed his approach further, broadening its application considerably.

There were, however, other reasons why Beck eclipsed Ellis, and these were largely personal. Beck was tactful, diplomatic, and eschewed controversy. The same cannot be said of Ellis. He was an altogether different personality. Ellis would use expletives when conducting psychotherapy workshops; he invented the term "musturbation" to describe overuse of the word "must"; he was married three times, had a long-term open relationship, and became embroiled in a lawsuit with his own institute. And for a rational thinker, he seemed peculiarly disinterested in validating his methods empirically.

Ellis undoubtedly deserves more recognition than he has been afforded in the past; however, there are signs that an increasing number of professionals are acknowledging his originality. He was, for example, voted the second most influential psychother-apist of the twentieth century by members of the American Psy-chological Association—not after Aaron T. Beck, but after the humanistic psychotherapist Carl Rogers.

The words "belief" and "thought" are often used interchangeably, but they can be differentiated. In everyday speech, "belief" gen-erally implies some form of lasting conviction (as in a religious belief). A "thought," in contrast, is any concept, idea, or notion that enters awareness, usually as a sentence—we can also think in pictures, but when this happens, we tend to describe it as imagery rather than thought. When Ellis referred to beliefs, he was really describing evaluative thoughts (or "appraisals"); however, when Beck and his followers refer to beliefs, they are using the word to describe something much closer to the dictionary definition—deeply held convictions. Beliefs represent learning about the self and the world, stored in a permanent or at least relatively stable state. This learning is usually expressed in the form of conditional or unconditional propositions. "If people don't like me I can never be happy," or "People don't like me." Beliefs of this kind—also referred to as "dysfunctional assumptions"—are so deeply embed-ded in the psyche that we are often oblivious of their existence, even though they are very likely to influence the content of our thoughts and how we behave.

Dysfunctional assumptions cluster together. An individual with low self-esteem might have a number of deep-seated beliefs that are thematically connected: "If people got to know me bet-ter they'd discover how bad a person I am," "I am worthless," and "There is something wrong with me." Collections of dysfunc-tional assumptions are called *schemas*. They are like templates or prototypes that influence perceptions, expectations, even what we remember and forget. Schemas are like lenses through which we view the world. The more flaws there are in the lens, the more likely it is that our perception of the world will be distorted; the more dysfunctional assumptions we have, the more likely it is that our thinking and behavior will be self-defeating. Another way of understanding schemas is to imagine them as being like scripts. We follow them without question, and they tend to pre-determine outcomes. A person who has a schema composed of dysfunctional assumptions concerning inferiority will feel so-cially anxious, interpret neutral expressions as hostile, and avoid social situations. Schemas are close relatives of Freudian com-plexes and Bowlby's working models. Schemas, complexes, and working models are all forms of cognitive structure, knowledge systems that have been consolidated in memory.

Obviously, schemas are hypothetical constructs and they can-not be measured or directly observed. But at some level, schemas must correspond with material reality, because they are stored in the brain. Some ideas must, in some sense, be stored "closer" to-gether than others—otherwise we wouldn't observe associative phenomena. "Cat and mouse," for example, comes to mind more readily than "Cat and blue whale." Related dysfunctional assump-tions can be thought of as parts of the same "structure." The neu-robiologist Bruce Wexler has discussed how internal structures in the brain, once established, bias our perceptions and resist modi-fication: "We ignore, forget, or attempt to actively discredit infor-mation that is inconsistent with these structures."[4]

Cognitive therapy begins with the identification of nega-tive thoughts and proceeds in a downward direction, uncovering dysfunctional assumptions and schematically stored knowledge.

Once dysfunctional assumptions have been exposed, they can be challenged or disputed, in much the same way that irrational thoughts can be challenged. Beck has stated that dysfunctional assumptions are problematic not so much because they are irrational, but because they interfere with normal cognitive processes. In practice, however, dysfunctional assumptions are highly resistant to modification, even when therapists point out that they are discrepant with reality. As such, often their most salient feature is their irrationality.

A former student of Beck's, Jeffrey Young, has developed a form of cognitive therapy that gives special emphasis to schemas established in early life. Because some of these schemas evolved prior to the acquisition of language, they can be nonverbal. They can still serve as templates for orientation, focus, and interpretation, but their activation re-creates the raw, primal emotions of infancy—experienced largely as a strong physical reaction. Young calls unhelpful schemas established in infancy and childhood Early Maladaptive Schemas (EMSes). He also refers to them, more colloquially, as "life traps," because they tend to trap people in lifelong recurring patterns of self-defeating thought and behavior.

We find it difficult to free ourselves from these life traps because they are so much a part of who we are and so deeply entrenched. Alternatives represent not only a terrifying leap in the dark, but a fundamental threat to our sense of self. We would rather feel psychological pain than risk a form of annihilation. Another reason we repeat self-defeating patterns of behavior is that they were probably once adaptive. They may have been appropriate, or "rational," when we were children. As already suggested, emotional withdrawal might have been a rational coping strategy for a child who was frequently threatened with physical or sexual abuse. But it is not a rational coping strategy for an adult wishing to form an intimate relationship.

EMSes are activated by triggers that resemble the social situations in which they developed and were consolidated. Given that breaking free from patterns of thought and behavior associated with EMS activation produces high levels of anxiety and discomfort, it is very difficult to evolve and grow. People are inclined to produce justifications that allow them to preserve the status quo. These justifications lower levels of anxiety and discomfort, but the underlying EMS remains. The justification of self-defeating behavior necessitates a great deal of cognitive distortion—self, the world, and relationships have to be misrepresented. Here, cognitive therapy and psychoanalysis coincide. Anxiety reduction is achieved by a defensive maneuver, but on closer inspection, it turns out that the defense consists of irrational thoughts. Distortion will maintain old, unhelpful scripts and routines. For example, an individual might judge an objectively pleasant interviewer as aggressive in order to justify withdrawing a job application. The person thereby neatly avoids the risk of rejection and emotional pain, but at the cost of professional stagnation. Intolerance of prospective emotional discomfort, in this instance, has deprived the individual of an opportunity. Ultimately, distortions re-create the conditions of our childhood that caused us the most harm.

Attempting to be rational is a rational objective—yet, even when we think we are being rational, we are often still being irrational. This does not mean that we should abandon rationality, or that being rational is not a legitimate aspiration: thanks to the pursuit of reason, human beings split the atom and put men on the moon. But it does mean that being rational is much more

challenging than many imagine, particularly when we are attempting to make rational decisions of personal significance.

Symmetrical inkblots have come to represent all things psychological and may even have more symbolic currency than the psychoanalytic couch. The most famous inkblot test was created by the Swiss psychiatrist Hermann Rorschach. Rorschach didn't have an eventful life: he worked in a psychiatric hospital, married, had two children, and died relatively young. Although he "analyzed" his patients, he was never a devotee of Freud, and he recognized that psychoanalysis had limitations.

In addition to being a psychiatrist, Rorschach was a talented artist. This talent manifested early, which probably accounts for the implausibly apposite nickname he acquired at school—"Klex," the German word for "inkblot."[5] Rorschach wasn't the only person who believed that inkblots could be used to probe the mind—there were competitors—but it was *his* test that became world famous and a twentieth-century icon. Some have argued that Rorschach succeeded where others failed because of his artistic gifts. His inkblots are not merely symmetrical smears, but works of art that have depth and texture; they are carefully constructed and uncannily fit for the purpose. The balance between abstraction and suggestion is perfectly judged. There is ample scope for interpretation, but flights of fancy are restrained by the suggestiveness of the shapes. His inkblots are ambiguous—but not too ambiguous.

Unlike his predecessors, Rorschach wasn't very interested in using inkblots to measure imagination. He used his inkblots to study perception and personality, and the results of his test were intended to inform diagnosis. After his death in 1922, psychologists and psychiatrists began using Rorschach's inkblots as a "projective test." In addition to being a defense involving the displacement of undesirable or unpleasant characteristics onto others, projection can be viewed as a more general phenomenon that can be divorced from psychoanalytic theory. The brain is constantly discriminating patterns in the environment. When we are presented with ambiguous stimuli, we automatically attempt to identify what we are seeing. Interpretations are influenced by personality traits, prior experiences, and memories, so what we read into ambiguity tells us something about ourselves. We are projecting the inner world onto the outer world, seeing things that aren't really there.

By the 1940s, the Rorschach test was part of popular culture, largely because of enthusiastic American advocacy. It was even featured in a Hollywood movie, *The Dark Mirror*, starring Olivia de Havilland. After World War II, questions about human nature were asked with renewed urgency. If the Nazis were a heinous aberration, then one could be hopeful about the future; however, if they were just ordinary people, then one might expect their atrocities to be repeated. The general public looked to psychiatrists and psychologists to settle the debate.

An opportunity to study the Nazi mind presented itself at Nuremburg. Many leading Nazis were incarcerated while awaiting trial, and among them were some of Hitler's closest associates: Albert Speer, Rudolf Hess, and Hermann Göring. Testing was undertaken by two American appointees, a psychiatrist, Douglas Kelley, and a Jewish prison psychologist, Gustave Gilbert. Among the tests they administered was the Rorschach test.

Was there such a thing as a Nazi personality? Did Nazis show abnormal levels of psychopathology? The investigators discovered what they wanted to discover. Kelley found the Nazis to be sane and fundamentally no different from many ordinary Americans, whereas Gilbert found that they were murderous, evil robots—essentially inhuman—with personality traits distinct from most people. Kelley and Gilbert—who had always had a strained relationship—became enemies. Many years later, their data were reanalyzed, and still no consensus was reached; however, the most recent review of Kelley and Gilbert's Rorschach results, *The Quest for the Nazi Personality: A Psychological Investigation of Nazi War Criminals*, published by Eric Zilmer and colleagues in 1995, concluded that the Rorschach records could not be used to support Gilbert's view. The science journalist Jack El-Hai provided the following summary statement concerning current opinion: "Until someone else refutes it, the latest study suggests that the Nazi personality that eluded Kelley, seduced Gilbert, and tempted so many other researchers is a myth."[6] But note the qualification: *until someone else refutes it*. Of course, it is possible that the debate will be revived again.

The simple explanation for this uncertainty is that the Rorschach test is unreliable—which is probably true. But this is a rather shallow observation that fails to acknowledge a broader and perhaps more interesting point. Kelley and Gilbert interpreted their test results according to their own beliefs and expectations, because that is what human beings do. Although Nuremberg resulted in confusion and undermined the authority of the Rorschach test, looked at in another way, Kelley's and Gilbert's contradictory conclusions prove the principle underlying such projective tests. We see what we want to see. And for much of our lives, we view the world defensively, in ways that minimize short-term discomfort and entrench existing beliefs. A Nazi standing in a prison cell can be viewed as a man or a monster. Gilbert had very good reason to see a monster. His parents were Jewish immigrants from Austria, and he had visited Dachau before the final surrender of Nazi Germany.

If, as Kelley believed, the Nazis were just ordinary people, then tragedies comparable to World War II would happen again. Perhaps this is why, on New Year's Day, 1958, he ended his own life. We know that he was stressed and that his marriage was unhappy, but given the alarming implications of his views, one can reasonably suppose that the psychological causes of his suicide were much deeper. After a domestic argument, Kelley positioned himself on a landing and, looking down the stairs at his wife, father, and son, proclaimed, "I don't have to take this anymore! I'm going to take this potassium cyanide and I'll die in thirty seconds. I'm going to take this, and nobody will care!" His hand went to his lips and he swallowed. Not long after, he was having seizures and foam was bubbling out of his mouth.

Gilbert, untrammeled by his former colleague's criticisms, went on to testify at the Eichmann trial in Jerusalem, where his Nuremberg test results were admitted as evidence. History seems to have given the political philosopher Hannah Arendt the final say. She was sent by *The New Yorker* to report on the Eichmann trial, where she coined the phrase "the banality of evil." If there was such a thing as the Nazi personality, it was terrifying, but only because it was so terrifyingly dull.

When something is said "with feeling," we assume that the sentiment being expressed is authentic. "Gut feeling" is trustworthy, something that emanates from the core of one's being. But feelings can be just as misleading as our thoughts.

Evolutionary psychologists suggest that feelings encode judgments about the environment. They are the outcome of accelerated assessments that tell us whether things are good or bad. Feelings also incorporate physiological changes that ready us for action. As with almost every other feature of mental life, ultimately, feelings were selected and shaped by evolutionary pressures to facilitate the transfer of genes from one generation to the next. They were not selected for their accuracy. Feelings encode judgments—but not necessarily accurate judgments. They serve the primary evolutionary objective, not secondary and tertiary objectives that benefit us personally. We want to have sex because it is pleasurable, but the pleasure is simply a ploy to make us have more sex.

Ancestors who responded fearfully to hairy plants and sinuous vines—mistaking them for venomous spiders and snakes— were more likely to take flight, survive, procreate, and pass on their fearful predisposition than their more daring peers. Evolution has introduced interpretive biases into the processing system in order to favor survival and reproduction. Sometimes a sinuous form on the ground really is a snake, and running away is entirely appropriate. But as a general principle, our genes "want" us to overreact to potential dangers, not underreact. All of our feelings are subject to the same evolutionary influences. As such, they are not always correspondent or proportionate responses to specific situations. When we are trying to make decisions, they frequently misinform.

A basic tenet shared by all major schools of psychotherapy is that psychological problems arise when we become distanced or detached from reality. But in a sense, that is our default position. "Being" is always discrepant with actuality. Our perceptions, thoughts, and feelings are unreliable, and when we base our decisions on unreliable information, our purchase on reality slips further.

Figures like Dubois, Ellis, and Beck urge us to be more rational. We need to test our perceptions and beliefs. We need to be more wary of our feelings. Being reflective is not optional, something that can be postponed indefinitely or deferred until the next time we get a chance to sit on a beach and watch the sun set. It is an ongoing necessity.

As with many of the ideas that have arisen from psychotherapy, the claim that being reflective is beneficial seems obvious. And it *is* obvious. What isn't obvious is that being productively reflective is a labor of Herculean scale. When we attempt to evaluate the validity of our thoughts, we do so relying upon logic that is constantly under threat of derailment. It is as if we were trying to inspect objects in a warped mirror—reflected in a second warped mirror—which might also be reflected in a third. Under such circumstances, it is almost impossible to ascertain what we're looking at. Self-examination is complicated by infinite regresses of distortion that veer off into infinity.

"I just need to think things through."

It sounds easy. But if you believe it's easy, you are profoundly misguided. Indeed, believing that you can just "think things through" might be one of your biggest problems.

5

IDENTITY
The Divided Self

Where do we find ourselves? A good place to start looking is inside our heads. But what do we discover when we introspect? Thoughts and images that are neutral in tone or perhaps shaded by a particular mood. One idea is substituted for another, and there is a sense of flow, the so-called stream of consciousness. This stream is shallow and not very wide. Entertaining two thoughts simultaneously is almost impossible. Yet, despite this limitation, at any given point in time we are aware that our totality is much greater. St. Augustine may have been the first to comment on this peculiarity when he wrote, "I cannot grasp all that I am." Somehow, our dormant personal histories provide a resonant context. If I look at a tree, I am not only aware of its features—the texture of the bark, the shape of the leaves—I am also aware that the tree is being looked at by a person—and that person is me, myself. Unconscious memories impress upon my awareness an ongoing sense of identity. Insofar as it cannot be dissected or photographed, the self is an "ideal object," but it supplies us with the necessary philosophical proof of certain knowledge: "I think, therefore I am."

Although the self is elusive, it can be defined in terms of its properties and characteristics. It has a physical aspect. We are aware of our embodiment and identify strongly with the face we see when we look into a mirror. Selfhood is continuous and only interrupted by dreamless sleep. The memories you have of your childhood, and the memories you have of what happened yesterday, are still *your* memories. They are owned by the same person, even though your experience of the world as a child would have been qualitatively different from your experience of the world as an adult. The self is reflexive. It can examine itself. We can say, "I am feeling sad today," and consider how our mood colors our thoughts and perceptions. Everything we do is initiated by an act of will. We are self-motivated. Embodiment, continuity, reflexivity, and agency—or at least, apparent agency—are all key features of selfhood. To this list we can also add unity. We experience ourselves as a cohesive whole. Our hopes, fears, recollections, emotions, beliefs, and desires coalesce. Our past, present, and expectations for the future are melded together. The unitary nature of identity has been afforded a pivotal role in many of the theories of mind and behavior inspired by the practice of psychotherapy. Most share a common supposition that when the unity of self is disturbed, when the self is fragmented, duplicated, or divided, we become unhappy, anxious, and vulnerable.

Do selves divide along similar fault lines? What are the psychological consequences of the fragmentation of identity? Why do selves divide? And how is a divided self made whole again?

When people think of divided selves, they usually imagine extreme examples, like the sinister split personalities that appear in crime and horror novels. But not all divisions of self are quite so spectacular. We all know what it's like to feel conflicted, to feel our conscience, for example, attempting to resist temptation, and sometimes—depending on circumstances—this inner struggle seems like an argument between two different versions of ourselves. The same is true of other dilemmas. Many parents feel torn between staying at home with a new baby and returning to work. Such quandaries can be described as an identity problem: "parent" and "careerist" are suddenly pulling in different directions. Usually, this results in mood disturbance, and subsequent episodes of worrying resemble attempts to sew competing identities together again. Frequently, dilemmas expose tensions between who we really are—our true self—and an assumed or less authentic identity, a false self or idealized one. Very recently, psychologists have introduced the concept of "derailment," meaning a discontinuity between current and past selves.[1] This disconnect is a risk factor for depression. And virtually all schools of therapy agree that the repair of inner divisions is essential for well-being. Some have elevated this principle to the extent that it resembles a spiritual goal. We are all, in a sense, fragmented, and the integration of our separate parts is a lifelong project.

Zoe had short spikey hair and studs in her nose and lower lip. Her labia were also extensively pierced. "Yeah," she said, pointing in the direction of her genitals. "I've got a lot of rings down there." She was restless, heavily tattooed, and wore combat fatigues and boots. Frequent use of intravenous drugs meant that she was vulnerable to HIV infection. (This was at a time when testing HIV-positive was effectively a death sentence.) She had become a subculture celebrity, a famous name in an underworld of windowless clubs where extreme forms of sadomasochistic role-play were commonplace. "People leave you alone when you look like this," she once assured me. "They don't fuck with you."

We were talking about love, and I invited her to consider the benefits of forming a meaningful long-term relationship.

"I am in a meaningful long-term relationship," she said, justifiably annoyed that I had made an assumption. "We've been together for years. She lives in Paris."

"What's her name?"

"I don't know, she's never told me. I just call her Mistress."

Zoe's mistress lived in a spacious apartment in the 20th arrondissement. Visits were infrequent and by invitation only. As soon as Zoe was inside, she became a willing captive—a sex slave.

"I never know how it's going to be. Sometimes I arrive and we go straight to bed. And other times she takes me to an empty room and orders me to strip. Then she makes me put on manacles—so I'm like, hanging—and I can't sit or sleep or anything. She attaches weights to my rings and leaves me there. She just walks off—and she plays the cello—I can hear her playing, for hours—she plays and plays and plays. A whole weekend can pass like that. The pain gets bad, really bad, but it's like we're taking things to the limit, to a whole new level."

Zoe took unnecessary risks and on occasion her sexual practices were potentially life threatening. I was worried that some of the acts she performed would result in serious internal injuries. She oscillated between states of extreme passivity, in which she would allow herself to be tortured, and episodes of anger and rage. It was almost like she was two different people. I discussed this with her, and she surprised me by saying, "I *am* two people."

"What do you mean?" I asked.

"I'm Zoe and I'm Miss Smith."

I tilted my head to one side: "I'm sorry . . ."

"I live my life as two people. I'm Zoe now, but sometimes I wake up and decide to be Miss Smith."

"What's she like, Miss Smith?"

"Quiet, bookish, she doesn't spike her hair or wear studs. And she doesn't dress like this." She swept both hands down her body. "She has an entirely different wardrobe. Literally: a different wardrobe."

"You have two wardrobes in your flat?" I was unable to conceal my skepticism.

"Yes, one for Zoe and one for Miss Smith—and there are two CD collections, two stereos, two toothbrushes, two types of deodorant, two of everything."

Individuals with multiple personalities have been described in the medical literature since the seventeenth century, but these were preceded by instances of metamorphosis in folklore and mythology. Werewolves are a notable example. The scientific study of multiple personality flourished from the mid-nineteenth century, a development reflected in contemporary works of fiction such as Robert Louis Stevenson's *Dr. Jekyll and Mr. Hyde*. Doctors accepted that the mind can spontaneously divide, creating two or more identities with varying degrees of mutual awareness. Today, the classic split personality, in which an individual experiences a discontinuity of consciousness and has no memory of an alter ego, is termed "dissociative identity disorder."

Zoe had two distinct but mutually aware identities. The decision to make the transition from one to the other was made in a state of lucidity. Zoe selected a costume, stepped into Miss Smith's shoes, and instantly became more conventional. This element of stagecraft does not alter the fact that Zoe's sense of self was worryingly unstable.

Although Zoe's dual identity seems, at first sight, to be bizarre, it can be understood as an exaggerated form of ordinary phenomena. We frequently modify our behavior according to situational demands. Indeed, at times it might appear to others that we are acting like a different person. Mood also modulates behavior. When oscillations of mood become clinically significant—as they do when a patient is described as bipolar—the same person might be talkative and disinhibited when they are "high" and taciturn and wary when they are "low." Ordinarily, mood swings can be contained within a single identity. But sometimes, the center doesn't hold—and a unitary consciousness divides.

Some clinicians construe dissociative states (even extreme ones) as a defense. Again, it is possible to identify continuities that link the ordinary and the strange. A common strategy for dealing with pain is distraction. We shift the focus of our attention elsewhere. In other words, we try to separate the conscious aspect of self from the embodied aspect of self. A division is made in order to facilitate pain management. Multiple personalities might also function protectively. For some, life can be so overwhelming that it is simply too much for a single person to cope with, so that person's identity fragments into a team of specialized agencies. When threatened, aggressive instincts can be harnessed and channeled through a combative subpersonality.

Defenses, however, divorce us from reality—and this can have disastrous consequences. Zoe was confused, volatile, unfulfilled, and constantly entering dangerous environments. Whenever I saw her, I can remember thinking how remarkable it was that she was still alive.

Disturbances of the unity of self—or imbalances between the parts of self—have been repeatedly identified as a cause of unhappiness and confusion.

Freud divided the mind into three parts: the id, the ego, and the superego. These agencies correspond approximately with the unconscious, the conscious mind, and the conscience. The correspondence is approximate, because, although the contents of the id are entirely unconscious, the ego and the superego also have unconscious regions. They are traditionally described as "agencies," because they are not inert, but operational; they have different objectives and interact with each other. Freud's structural model should not be thought of as a diagram of the mind, but rather as something much closer to a computer simulation, something with moving parts.

Although conscientious thoughts enter the stream of consciousness, conscience is also experienced as something semi-autonomous. The voice of conscience is not entirely our own and addresses us from a slight distance. This is probably why conscience is frequently personified in fairy stories. A small animal, or maybe a supernatural creature, will appear at a critical juncture and persuade the protagonist to resist temptation—consider Jiminy Cricket in the Walt Disney version of Carlo Collodi's *The Adventures of Pinocchio*. The id is the exact opposite of conscience. It is unprincipled, a repository of primitive desires demanding instant gratification.

The ego is the conduit through which the totality of a person transacts with reality. It occupies a difficult position "between" the id and the superego—like a charioteer trying to control two unruly horses that want to pull in opposite directions. The conscious self must make decisions that satisfy both the id and the superego.

For example, the sexual needs of the id must be met, but without offending the moral strictures imposed by the superego. This balance is normally achieved by participating in the socially accepted rituals of courtship that lead to consensual sex.

If the id isn't restrained, the ego will be overwhelmed by primitive urges, and this will produce anxiety (e.g., "I'm going to lose control and do something I regret"). Similarly, the punitive reprimands of an oppressive superego can engender crushing guilt and shame (e.g., "I'm a bad person"). We function best when id, ego, and superego have reached an optimal state of mutual accommodation and balance. In this state, the individual is not frustrated and can satisfy his or her basic needs without violating the moral codes that underpin social order.

For Freud, psychological problems arise when there is a lack of balance among the parts of self. Other theoreticians, however, have emphasized the role of duplications of self comparable (to some degree) with phenomena observed in classic cases of multiple personality. We have already encountered Arthur Janov's "unreal self," the sham identity that coalesces around the seed of infant neglect, which eventually smothers the "real self." Janov's "unreal self" is just one of many kinds of false selves discussed by psychotherapists. Indeed, the idea of a struggle between authentic and inauthentic selves is a mainstay of post-Freudian psychology. Donald Winnicott believed that mothers ordinarily do what is best for their children; however, poor mothering (defined as inadequate day-to-day care) can lead to the development of a false identity. This outcome is particularly likely if infants experience poor mothering when they are completely dependent. Because the infant feels unsafe, it will adopt a defensive strategy of appeasement. It will comply with the expectations of others and relegate its own needs. In extreme cases, the true self is completely concealed behind a false self. The true self has no relationship with reality and life becomes a futile, empty experience. Carl Rogers—the American psychologist who developed person-centered therapy—also recognized divisions of self. He posited the existence of a real, fundamental self (sometimes described as an "organismic self") and several supplementary identities (for example, the self that others expect us to be). The more our various conceptions of self overlap with our true self, the more we will experience life as fulfilling. Rogers described this state as "congruence." Conversely, the more our conceptions of self and the real self are misaligned—and incongruent—the more dissatisfied we will be and the less likely we are to realize our full potential.

While some approaches attribute psychological problems to imbalances among the parts of self, others emphasize duplications or fragmentations of the self. Jung's analytical psychology incorporates both of these ideas. In his theoretical framework, a single identity has different aspects, many of which can be conceptualized as subpersonalities. The "shadow" is a kind of lesser self that is organized around unacceptable impulses; men have a feminine side called the "anima," while women have a masculine side called the "animus." The "persona"—a term taken from the name for the mask worn by actors in ancient Greece—is the outward face we present to the world. These subpersonalities influence our behavior and secure desirable outcomes. When a woman enters a situation in which she is physically threatened, her animus (which is informed by culturally determined gender stereotypes) might orchestrate a fearless, warrior-like response. Although these temporary states of submission to an alter ego can be helpful, they can also be counterproductive. A man in an irrational, violent rage has ceded too much power to his shadow.

Jung populated the mind with many personifications. Sometimes these are referred to as "archetypes" (although in reality, an archetype is an unconscious template that *predisposes* individuals to re-create particular classes of personification and symbols). At a cultural level, we observe the aggregated effect of these predispositions in the repeated appearance of particular character types and images in our myths and stories: heroes, sorcerers, virgins—interlinked circles, or a serpent eating its tail. Based on evidence derived from clinical and anthropological studies, Jung supposed that these templates are buried in a profoundly deep part of the unconscious that is heritable and common to all humanity: the *collective unconscious.*

Happiness and fulfillment are more easily achieved if all of these personifications—the shadow, anima, animus, and so on—are integrated into a harmonious community. Opposites are then reconciled, contradictions resolved, and the conscious and unconscious levels of mind are brought into closer relationship. Jung suggested that this desirable end point is assisted by a process that he called "individuation."

Individuation is initiated by a person who, usually after some midlife crisis, recognizes that the time has arrived to be more reflective, to look inward for answers. Progress is guided by an archetype, a template of wholeness that Jung called the "self." Because archetypes are stored in the collective unconscious, individuation is universal, and symbols representing the accomplishment of successful integration are found in many cultures. They are usually circular and quartered (for example, by a cross). Mandalas, colorful designs associated with Buddhist and Hindu ritual art,

are perhaps the most impressive example. In making this connection, Jung was signaling that individuation is as much a spiritual journey as it is a psychological process. The accomplishment of individuation represents a transition to a higher state of being. As such, it has affinities with the "self-realization" pursued by mystics. In practical terms, the necessary precondition for individuation is increased awareness of one's inner life: "Only the man who can consciously assent to the power of the inner voice becomes a personality."[2]

Because Jung's "analytical psychology" resembles a metaphysical system of thought, it has been much criticized by empiricists. Yet Jung began his career as an experimentalist and subsequently made great efforts to find support for his ideas by conducting anthropological fieldwork. Analytical psychology, in spite of its esotericism, is still grounded in clinical observation and a thorough inquiry into the symbolic language of culture. Jung is frequently referenced by students of comparative mythology, comparative religion, and world literatures (particularly those interested in universal aspects of narrative). Even so, many mainstream psychologists find Jung's model of the mind—in which epic battles between subpersonalities are fought in the unconscious like a Wagnerian opera—completely inconsistent with contemporary neuroscience. It is certainly true that Jung's writings on the self are infused with the numinous, but one can argue that his exoticism is relatively superficial; he is simply using colorful metaphors to aggrandize the basic idea that identity is composed of divisible elements and that, when these elements are balanced and integrated, the individual is likely to experience greater happiness and inner peace. He was one of the earliest theorists to emphasize the concept of identity, an approach that subsequently found widespread endorsement.

The modern world, and particularly the Internet, provides unprecedented opportunities for identities to split, duplicate, propagate, and disperse. Online anonymity and physical inaccessibility weaken the superego and liberate the id. The screen invites us to enter a virtual environment where the checks and balances of face-to-face contact are no longer applicable. In cyberspace, people are free to be whoever they wish. Approximately half of young people lie about their personal details on the Internet. From the age of around eleven, they become accustomed to creating false identities that, on the whole, exhibit distinctly regressive characteristics (such as excessive vanity, or a desire to incite envy in others). A 2019 study conducted by the YMCA discovered that two-thirds of young people edit photographs of themselves before posting them on social media, spending up to forty-five minutes removing spots, enhancing skin texture, and whitening teeth.[3] These ideal selves are almost always close to being perfect and hugely discrepant with real, embodied selves. They promote states of extreme incongruence: inner tension, discomfort, and dissatisfaction.

Information technology allows "digital natives" (that is, people born after the proliferation of computer technology and the Internet) to divide the self so deeply that their aspiration ideal—or ideals—achieve a kind of independent existence. The result is a fragmentation of self that resembles dissociative identity disorder, the cardinal feature of which is the splitting of consciousness into two or more distinct personalities. Digital natives sometimes create versions of themselves that completely transcend the physical limitations of a photographic image; they can invent beautiful avatars to represent their ideal selves in cyberspace, sloughing off embodiment like the skin of a snake.

I am not suggesting that editing selfies or inventing avatars will lead inexorably to a psychiatric diagnosis. But I do think the easy creation of visible, perfect versions of the self increases dissatisfaction with imperfect realities, and that strong identification with an ideal self can widen existing fault lines within the person. The brain is plastic, particularly so during infancy, childhood, and early adolescence. It is perhaps no coincidence that the digital native generation has, on the whole, proved particularly vulnerable to low mood.

Life is uncertain, and it is frequently disappointing. There are always losses and painful separations—we grow old, then we die. A coherent sense of self gives us the strength to face up to reality, whereas a self that is only loosely threaded together will rip easily and disintegrate. The efficacy of talking cures depends, at least in part, on the degree to which equilibrium is restored among parts of the self, divisions are healed, and false identities are abandoned. These are useful objectives—not only for patients in psychotherapy, but for all of us.

Our young woman is still sitting in the automat, and the reflected lights have now acquired greater significance. Perhaps the two rows projecting into the void signify that she is not merely of two minds because she is undecided. Perhaps her double consciousness is more fundamental. Is there some deeper tension underlying her dilemma? A tension between the person she is and the person she wants to be? Or a tension between an authentic self and the false self that she has been hitherto presenting to the person whose absence is emphasized by the empty chair? We have already noted some clues: the green of her coat and the red of the garment she wears beneath it, the suggestion of a conflict between innocence and desire. If

only she could be released from Hopper's deadly silence. If only she could speak, get in touch with her true feelings, and discover what she needs. No wonder she looks isolated and unhappy, no wonder the darkness behind her looks so ominous. It might seep into the automat, insinuate itself into the gaps that separate her identities, and take possession of her. How will she feel then?

The secondary school I attended was in a rough working-class neighborhood of north London strongly associated with soccer hooliganism and racially motivated assaults. Discipline during lessons broke down easily and order was usually restored with a beating. Teachers would pull hair, cane, smash children's faces into desks, rage, and kick furniture over. At times, it felt more like a correctional facility for juvenile delinquents than an educational establishment. Both inside and outside the school, the general atmosphere of free-floating aggression and threat was so pervasive that, when I was told a young man had been murdered a few minutes' walk from the playground, it felt like something we'd all been waiting for.

I was also told that the forensic team had not washed away the chalk outline of the body. Naturally, I was curious, so at the first opportunity I went with a friend to examine the crime scene. We soon reached our destination, an empty side street, and stood, transfixed, staring at the two-dimensional figure sprawled across several paving slabs. "Just think," my friend said, struggling in a boyish way to comprehend the existential implications of the situation. "Someone actually died there." He pointed downward. "You know . . . actually died." We could see our own deaths in that chalk outline. The bloodstains on the concrete brought our mortality into sharp focus.

One day, I was standing near the school gymnasium, looking through a wire mesh fence at a dismal block of public housing, when another friend came up to me and said, "Take a look at this." His furtive demeanor made me think he was about to produce some pornographic images, but instead he handed me a slim paperback book. I opened it and started to read:

Jill: I am frightened.
Jack: Don't be frightened.
Jill: I am frightened to be frightened, when you
      tell me I ought not to feel frightened.

The book was full of slippery propositions, arranged on the page like poetry. Some of the text had been embedded in what appeared to be technical diagrams. I didn't understand a single verse, but I could discern the workings of a cunning, mischievous intelligence behind every artfully constructed psychodrama. When I looked up, my friend said, "Cool, eh?" He was right. There was something really cool about this book. I examined the cover. It read "*Knots*, by R. D. Laing."

For about a decade, Laing was the most widely read psychiatrist in the world. His reach was so extensive that his books could be found in the backpacks of GIs fighting the war in Vietnam as well as in the tasseled bags of hippies trekking across India. He even reached me, a schoolboy, standing in the middle of a cultural wasteland in north London.

The nucleus of Laing's work reflects his preoccupation with identity and its fragmentation. His best-known book, published in 1960, is *The Divided Self.* Although Laing's principal clinical interest was schizophrenia, his understanding of how schizophrenia develops has much wider relevance, because—to some extent—we are all exposed to the factors that fracture the mind.

Laing's key explanatory concept is "ontological insecurity." Ontology is the philosophical study of being and coming into being. He suggested that, for the ontologically insecure person, the sense of self is so fragile, he or she will experience reality as overwhelming, paralyzing, and threatening. Under such conditions, the self contracts, shrinking inward, but leaving behind a kind of mask, a false self, to act as a protective shield. If the retreat of the self continues indefinitely, a threshold is crossed, and the individual will start reporting symptoms of psychosis. A person might journey so far inward that they become alienated from their own embodiment. The feeling of the mind being connected to the body is then attenuated, and physical movements are perceived as being independent of volition. Consequently, psychotic patients generate bizarre hypotheses to explain their bizarre experiences. They often conclude that their limbs are under the control of an external agency, such as a supernatural being or an influencing machine.[4]

Disturbed communications, especially within families, deepen ontological insecurity. Laing was particularly interested in double binds (e.g., demands to exercise a choice when all the outcomes are negative) and in forms of speech that invalidate and confuse the listener (e.g., mixed messages). Laing's poetic experiments, the ones I found fascinating as a schoolboy, were essentially explorations of the complex thought processes underlying disturbed communication. The way we think others see us is often very different from the way others *actually* see us. Sometimes, our communications are based on these "meta-perceptions," many of which will diverge significantly from the perceptions of others. When two people are talking, their language will be influenced by their meta-perceptions, and the opportunities for misinterpretation and mis-understanding multiply exponentially; they spiral away from each other in ever-widening loops. A distance can open up between selves as damaging as the distance that divides selves. There can be no authenticity or affirmation of feelings and opinions.

Laing became the most important psychiatric luminary of the 1960s and early 1970s. Photographs of him at the height of his fame show a man who appears to combine the qualities of a rock star with those of a shaman. The straitjacket of medical conservatism has been discarded and he seems to have assumed a new, darkly charismatic identity.

Laing's fame spread swiftly and widely because his radical views were consonant with the revolutionary idealism that defined his most productive decades. His account of schizophrenia as an understandable response to impossible situations found a sympathetic audience among a restless younger generation that strongly identified with schizophrenics. They, too, wanted to "drop out" of a world that was no longer making sense to them; they, too, wanted to protest, rebel, and reject traditional institutions and conformity.

In addition to good timing, Laing's fame was expedited by his considerable expressive gifts. His prose style is seductive and eminently quotable: "We are effectively destroying ourselves by violence masquerading as love," "Few books today are forgivable," "Experience is the *only* evidence." *Knots* and *The Bird of Paradise* (a short piece of writing that defies categorization) succeed as significant works of modern literature.

With the assistance of his associates, Laing established a therapeutic community at Kingsley Hall in London's East End. In this austere building, once a settlement house for impoverished children, the commonly accepted rules of social behavior were not imposed on residents. Their "madness" was allowed full and free expression. What appeared from the outside to be chaotic behavior was construed as evidence of spontaneous inner healing, a process that—Laing believed—should be permitted to run its natural course. The goal of undertaking this voyage was the recovery of the true self. Laing's thinking has several precedents, mostly in Jung's writings, but it was also foreshadowed by the ceremonial practices of some tribal cultures, many of them involving the induction of altered states of consciousness to achieve self-renewal. Kingsley Hall became a counterculture mecca, and it was visited by fashionable figures such as Timothy Leary and Sean Connery. Laing had made insanity glamorous.

The most celebrated resident of Kingsley Hall was Mary Barnes, a nursing tutor who, while staying at a convent in Wales, was advised by the prioress to seek psychological help. Barnes was treated principally by Laing's American acolyte Joseph Berke. In due course, Barnes and Berke wrote a book together, *Mary Barnes: Two Accounts of a Journey Through Madness.*

Barnes was encouraged to regress to an infantile state from which she would later reemerge as a more integrated and ontologically secure person. For a time, she stopped speaking, squealed like a baby, was fed from a bottle, and slept naked in a wooden chest. She soiled herself (a symbolic expulsion of "badness") and smeared the walls with feces. When Berke supplied her with crayons and paints, she began creating murals of artistic merit: eruptions of primal and religious imagery, incandescent landscapes animated by flowing energies. Her work was bold and vigorous, and it captured something of the unusual mental states she had experienced. Eventually, she became a successful artist, and her paintings were frequently exhibited. The repair of her fragmented identity was critical to her recovery. Berke refers to Barnes "coming together" and being reassembled like a jigsaw puzzle.

When the 1970s gave way to the 1980s, materialism and pragmatism replaced revolutionary fervor. Laing's ideas began to feel increasingly outmoded. He started drinking too much, appeared in front of a magistrate on a cannabis charge, used intemperate language when giving talks, and unnerved people by dispensing with civilities. A former patient alleged serious professional misconduct: Laing had taken him to a pub on one occasion, and on another had asked him to participate in someone else's treatment session. The General Medical Council invited Laing to withdraw his name from their register. He died of a heart attack, aged sixty-one, while playing tennis in St. Tropez. When asked if he wanted a doctor, his last words were, "Doctor, what fucking doctor?"

Laing's books, read without prejudice, are a towering monument to his sensitivity and creative genius. It is truly ironic that Ronnie Laing, the drunk, should have obscured the greatness of R. D. Laing, the existential psychotherapist whose major insights concerned the disturbing consequences of allowing divisions to widen within the self. Although Laing is still regarded as a controversial figure, his views have been slowly reabsorbed into the intellectual mainstream—often with little or no acknowledgment. Contemporary psychotherapists assume that the symptoms of psychosis are, at some level, intelligible, and there are now interesting epidemiological studies that can be interpreted as showing a relationship between ontological insecurity and schizophrenia.

Some of the most compelling evidence of this kind comes from research on the mental health of migrant and migrant ethnic minority populations, many of whom have a very high risk of developing psychotic symptoms. This elevated risk is most probably attributable to psychosocial, rather than biological, factors.[5] The experience of geographical displacement, which involves complete loss of social context, amplifies ontological stresses and weakens identity. Clearly, belonging is a central feature of selfhood. When we no longer feel that we belong, we forget who we are.

The true self, as described by psychotherapists, is a hypothetical construct, just as complexes, schemas, and working models are hypothetical constructs. It cannot be directly observed or quantified. For many brain scientists, this is a problem. What—they ask—are we actually talking about? Beyond performing its duties as a figurative abstraction, to what extent does the true self have any purchase on reality?

Many years ago, I was discussing a patient (an elderly, depressed man) with a biologically minded psychiatrist. I thought the patient's treatment was being overly influenced by the results of his brain scan, which showed significant cortical degeneration. I suggested that the patient's experience—his sadness and his grief—should be taken into consideration, and I may have referred to one or two hypothetical constructs as I argued my case. The psychiatrist, somewhat irritated, frowned and said, "Look, at least I'm basing my opinion on something that's real." I was reminded of one of Laing's most astute and quotable lines: "Who could suppose that angels move the stars, or be so superstitious as to suppose that because one cannot see one's soul at the end of a microscope it does not exist?" Ninety-six percent of the universe is invisible. But it's still there.

The neuroscientist Susan Greenfield has written, "The dynamics of environment and neuronal malleability give rise to an ever-evolving identity, one that is unique to the individual, yet an individual that is constantly transforming."[6] There must be signature patterns of neuronal activity associated with selfhood, a combination of permanent and semipermanent biological events. Ultimately, permutations of self—everything we mean by terms such as "true self" or "false self"—must be anchored in matter. Brain scans are already beginning to distinguish patterns of activity associated with authenticity from those of pretense.[7]

The default mode network (DMN), a network of regions that interact with each other in the brain, connects areas of the cerebral cortex with subcortical structures such as the hippocampal formation.[8] It was originally supposed that this system was the brain's "default"—the biological substrate of nonfocal attention and mind wandering. However, more recently, neuroscientists have been suggesting that the DMN might provide the scaffold around which we build our identities. The neuroscientist Robin Carhart-Harris, based at Imperial College London, has shown that reduced blood flow and oxygen consumption in the DMN is linked with loss of sense of self. Moreover, default regions are only sparsely connected in children between the ages of seven and nine, possibly because the scaffold of identity is still under construction.[9] Some neuroscientists are already describing the DMN as "the me network."[10] Perhaps one day we will be able to quantify the relative contributions of different cell networks as they generate iterations of self. We might even be able to see Laing's ontologically insecure self glowing like a collapsed star in its nebulous shell of falsity.

Evolutionary neuroscience supposes that the circuitry of the brain is organized in modules that determine mental states and behavior. So when the "self-protection module" is triggered by a physical threat, adrenaline is released and we experience the physical and emotional correlates of the fight-or-flight response (such as increased heart rate, perspiration, and fear). These modules are essentially systems in the brain that, when activated, regulate repertoires of behavior with specific functions relevant to successful reproduction: self-protection, mate attraction, mate retention, affiliation (i.e., social bonding), kin care, social status, and disease avoidance. Although evolutionary neuroscience and analytical psychology are generally regarded as incompatible systems of thought, modules and Jungian personifications are convergent concepts. When we need to fight, the activated self-protection module gives us the strength of a "warrior," and when we need to care for our kin, biological programming guides us, as if we were channeling a tutelary goddess, such as an "earth mother."

Terms such as "true self," "false self," and "ideal self" are extremely useful. They are concise summary terms that help us to organize large amounts of personal information. We find it relatively easy to think in this way. Even when scientists are studying rarefied aspects of cognition, they sometimes reach a point where they discover that clarity is best achieved by introducing duplications and divisions of self into their formulations. The Nobel Prize–winning psychologist Daniel Kahneman, for example, makes a distinction between the "remembering self" and the "experiencing self."[11]

The idea that fragmentation or division of the self is a major determinant of human unhappiness, anxiety, and discomfort appears in the writings of many of the key figures in the history of psychotherapy. Our sense of self accompanies all our perceptions, so when the self begins to crack and splinter, everything else begins to crack and splinter too. The world around us (and our place in it) becomes unreliable, uncertain, frightening, and in some instances untenable. We experience ourselves as a unity, and threats to this cohesion are deeply distressing. Consider, for example, gender dysphoria—feeling that one's true self and embodied self are sexually incongruent. Rates of suicide and attempted suicide are massively inflated in this group.[12]

The course of life is shaped by decisions. If we don't know who we are, we won't know what we need. And if we are of "two minds"—vacillating, uncertain—engagement in the act of living can be postponed indefinitely. We enter Edward Hopper's *Automat*. We find a table, sit down, and ask the same questions: Will I? Won't I? Should I? Dare I? The darkness on the other side of the glass is eager, and the clock is ticking.

6

NARRATIVE

Life Story

Does knowing someone's income tell you much about them? Does it matter that they drive a hatchback rather than a sedan, or live in the center of town rather than the suburbs? You might claim to know someone if they tell you about their past, but critical life events must be contextualized or they won't have meaning. Unconnected disclosures are likely to confuse us. "Why are you telling me this?" Even hearing someone's intimate secrets won't help. "Where is this going?" Attitudes change over time, and people can behave differently from one situation to the next. Aging alters how we look; fashion determines how we dress.

What is the essence of a person? When we profess to know someone, that is, *really* know someone—like a close friend, or a husband or wife—what is it that we know?

Pillow talk is one of the principal means by which newly acquainted couples bond. It is honest, confessional, and almost always expressed as a story: this is what happened to me and this is what I did. Sometimes, such revelations are also tests: now that you know what I did, can you still love me? Postcoital self-disclosure, perhaps the most intimate of all forms of communication, usually expresses what we judge to be most important about ourselves. It is also an implicit invitation for the addressed party to reciprocate. Exchanging stories brings us closer together than touching or kissing, closer than embodiment will allow.

When old friends reminisce, they repeat stories and recycle shared experiences. A friendship group is often defined by its stories, many of which, if recounted while imbibing alcohol, are exaggerated for humorous or dramatic effect. Stories are entertaining. But they are also an affirmation of identity and belonging.

Every culture has a storytelling tradition. Just like small groups of friends, countries define themselves with stories: sagas, folktales, and heroic epics that celebrate the national character. Even religious rituals are stories, insofar as they are often symbolic reenactments of something that has happened in the past. The Christian ritual of Holy Communion, for example, is a reenactment of the Last Supper. As soon as infants are able to focus on a sequence of pictures, they show a keen interest in storybooks. They can understand and appreciate a story before they have acquired language. Noisy children will be magically pacified by the words "Once upon a time." It is like casting a spell.

Adults, too, find stories more compelling than facts. This aspect of human psychology has been exploited mercilessly by politicians for millennia. A good story is always more persuasive than a well-constructed argument backed up by evidence. This is why populists and dictators favor simple narratives over nuanced discussion. During crises, people are reassured when commentators tease explanatory narratives out of breaking news.

The ease with which the attention of infants can be captured by stories and the universal popularity of storytelling demonstrate something very fundamental about the human brain and how it works. Stories help us to organize experience. The world is more navigable if we can recognize patterns of cause and effect. When we encounter a monster in a fairy tale, we know that the monster must be slayed so that the prince and the princess can live happily ever after. Narrative templates, what we think of as familiar plots, are instructive. They identify obstacles and show us how we might overcome them.

Our instinctive appreciation of stories and storytelling was probably established very early in our evolutionary history. In the 1990s, Daniel Povinelli and John Cant published a paper titled "Arboreal Clambering and the Evolution of Self-Conception."[1] Between five million and eleven million years ago, we shared a common ancestor with chimpanzees, gorillas, and orangutans: an animal called *Oreopithecus bambolii*. This was a large, tree-dwelling creature that weighed approximately ninety pounds and moved through its habitat slowly, by clambering. Unlike smaller primates, *Oreopithecus* was too heavy to swing from branch to branch. A branch might bend or break, resulting in a fatal fall, so *Oreopithecus* had to proceed with great care. It had to develop a sense of self, a sense of itself in relation to its surroundings, and planning skills. Before clambering through the tree canopy, it had to imagine itself displaced forward in time; it had to mentally simulate future situations in order to avoid making the wrong, catastrophic decision. "If I step on that rotten branch, it might snap. Therefore, I should take the long way round. I should make my way to those thicker branches. Then, if I reach out and grab that vine, I could get to the next tree—where there's plenty of fruit."* In order to survive, *Oreopithecus* had to tell itself stories about itself: cohesive narratives with beginnings, middles, and ends. Unlike most animals, for whom survival depends mostly on *real* responses to *immediate* environmental demands, *Oreopithecus* depended mostly on its capacity to *imagine* responses to *prospective* environmental demands.

Obviously, *Oreopithecus* didn't talk to itself as we do; however, it must have been able to reflect and foresee eventualities. It must have possessed, at some level, mental capacities that were equivalent to an inner monologue. Self-consciousness and rudimentary storytelling evolved together and are inextricably linked. What is now known as the "arboreal clambering hypothesis" might have relevance beyond its stated aim. It might also explain why human beings instinctively make sense of the world using stories. The special circumstances that favored the evolution of sophisticated self-awareness might have simultaneously necessitated the evolution of narrative intelligence. Consequently, self-awareness and narrative intelligence overlap to a considerable degree. We have a natural inclination to think of ourselves—our past, present, and future—as an ongoing story.

We make sense of the world by ordering events into narrative forms. We also make sense of ourselves in the same way, by ordering experiences into meaningful sequences. Just like our remote ancestor *Oreopithecus*, we are constantly telling ourselves stories about ourselves and imagining how those stories might develop.

---

* I'm paraphrasing Jesse Bering, who imagines *Oreopithecus's* stream of consciousness in *A Very Human Ending: How Suicide Haunts Our Species* (New York: Doubleday, 2018).

Psychoanalysts have always been fascinated by fairy stories, myths, and legends. Freud collected antique figurines of mythical figures, which he proudly placed on his desk, and the lakeside house that Jung had built to his own specifications was essentially a miniature fairy-tale castle. In *Wish-fulfillment and Symbolism in Fairy Tales*, published in 1909, Jung's relative and collaborator Franz Riklin argued that dreams and fairy stories are shaped by the same Freudian mechanisms. Concurrently, the German psychoanalyst Karl Abraham published an essay, titled *Dreams and Myths*, in which he suggested that myths are like the dreams of "infantile" humanity. Others elaborated these ideas in following decades. One such elaborator was Bruno Bettelheim.

Bettelheim is a controversial figure. He was born in Vienna and led a comfortable and cultured existence until he was imprisoned in the Dachau and Buchenwald concentration camps. He subsequently settled in the United States, where he became well-known as a writer and psychotherapist. After his suicide in 1990, Bettelheim's reputation went into steep decline as allegations mounted concerning the validity of his qualifications, plagiarism, and professional misconduct.

Yet one of his books, *The Uses of Enchantment*, which emphasized how exposure to fairy stories can benefit child development, is still widely read and referenced. Although Bettelheim failed to acknowledge all his sources (particularly the work of contemporary folklorists), *The Uses of Enchantment* contains enough original and insightful material to justify the plaudits it received when first published in the 1970s.

Bettelheim's ideas about the role of fairy stories and psychological development were greatly influenced by his clinical work with severely disturbed children. He concluded that healthy

maturation involves the growth and consolidation of identity, the establishment of close relationships, and the capacity to assign meanings to experience. He identified two ways by which these outcomes might be achieved: through "good enough" parenting, or cultural exposure. In most cases, both factors are simultaneously influential.

The most educational and emotionally enriching ingredients of heritage are literary, particularly those forms of literature that distill centuries of folk wisdom. Fairy stories "see" the world from a child's point of view. A child is surrounded by adult giants, and his or her parents exercise power like a king and queen. There are obvious correspondences between the daydreams of children and what happens in fairy stories. For example, inanimate objects come to life and animals talk. It should be noted, however, that children are not out of touch with reality. Familiar fairy-story openings, such as "Many years ago, in a distant land," or "Once, in a deep dark wood," declare that the real world is being exchanged for a make-believe equivalent, a world of symbols. Fairy tales might be unreal, but they contain figurative truths.

Children think in terms of polarities, because polarization simplifies experience. Humans, animals, and supernatural beings are represented in fairy stories as either good or bad, and identifying with protagonists facilitates moral development. The child is offered easy answers to important questions, such as "What kind of person do I want to be?" Bettelheim believed that fairy stories dramatize the problems and challenges associated with growing up, such as overcoming narcissistic disappointment, resolving Oedipal dilemmas, coping with sibling rivalry, relinquishing dependency, accepting moral obligations, and developing a sense of self. Many fairy stories exemplify how fundamental conflicts can be managed. Dilemmas are presented in their most essential form, and plots proceed economically in order to increase engagement and understanding.

Fairy stories often begin with the death of a parent, signaling the greatest and most fundamental challenge facing any child, the necessary accomplishment of independence. Countless plots involve a young person who is forced to leave home, setting off on a lonely road. During the course of his or her adventures, the protagonist finds someone to love—a permanent solution to the problem of separation anxiety. According to convention, the couple live "happily ever after." Children know this is impossible. No one lives forever. However, the formation of a loving relationship makes knowledge of one's own mortality tolerable.

Bettelheim, of course, appreciated the fragility of human existence more than most—having spent almost a year in Dachau and Buchenwald. Over a decade before writing *The Uses of Enchantment*, he had documented his concentration camp experiences in

The Informed Heart, a book that is simultaneously a memoir and a psychological dissection of totalitarian tendencies. On his way to Dachau, Bettelheim was struck on the head and wounded with a bayonet. He lost a lot of blood and became very groggy, but years later, he retained vivid memories of his thoughts and emotions at that time. He had wondered about the psychology of his tormentors. Why didn't the SS just murder him? Some prisoners had chosen to kill themselves by jumping out of the train windows. Bettelheim consoled himself with the thought that the SS hadn't driven him mad or to suicide—a sadly ironic reflection given his ultimate end: he killed himself on the fifty-second anniversary of the Nazis marching into his native Austria.

The abuse that prisoners had to endure was motivated by what Bettelheim called (presaging Arendt's "banality of evil") "unimaginative" sadism—whipping, kicking, slapping, shooting, stabbing; forcing prisoners to stare at glaring lights or to kneel on the floor for hours; forcing them to hit each other. These were the initiation experiences, the preamble. The most appalling acts of sadism were those that occurred after Bettelheim had settled into the routines of concentration camp life. He was given civilian clothes and told that he was about to be released. In fact, it was a cruel prank, and he was sent back to the camp. The ruse was repeated a second time, when again he was sent back to camp. The third time Bettelheim was summoned for release he refused to go. He later learned that on this occasion the call was authentic. It is difficult to imagine what that must have felt like, the sheer weight of his despair.

Bettelheim asserts in his book that modern parents have become overprotective. They much prefer to read their children anodyne stories, rather than anything potentially upsetting.

Traditional fairy stories are shunned because they can be sinister and violent. But monsters are all too real, and a wise parent must make sure that his or her child knows how to recognize one. Fairy stories are an excellent introduction. If we forewarn our children that they will inevitably experience setbacks and frustrations, injustice, hostility, perhaps even mindless brutality, they will not be surprised and crushed by adversity.

Like psychoanalysis, fairy stories give shape to formless fears and acknowledge the darker realms of desire and imagination. That which is denied or repressed is invited into consciousness, where it can be safely approached and understood. Homeopathic doses of evil will make a child grow into a giant-killer.

The story of Little Red Riding Hood, of which there are several variants, is a good example of how fairy stories encode the psychological. After the preliminary scene-setting, Little Red Riding Hood encounters a wolf disguised as her grandmother.

Superficial appearances can be deceptive. We are being told that Little Red Riding Hood's failure to perceive the wolf's true nature is placing her at risk. But at a deeper level, the story is much more about Little Red Riding Hood's true nature than that of her predatory companion. There is something about the wolf that she finds fascinating. "What a deep voice you have," she remarks. "And goodness, what big eyes you have." The dilemma here is one that all "innocent" young women must resolve. Should I? Shouldn't I? If a young woman succumbs to seduction before she is ready, there will be adverse psychological consequences.

Fairy stories are "enchanting" because they work unconsciously. The mechanisms that underlie their beneficial effects are invisible. Deep learning exerts its influence from below the awareness threshold. An adult, forewarned of the existence of fictional monsters in childhood, will *automatically* be better equipped to identify "real" monsters in later life. Fairy tales are the means by which children approach reality by stealth. This is an important point and one that Bettelheim continued to stress in his later writings, because from a child's perspective, reality has very sharp edges. In his 1987 book *A Good Enough Parent*—a title that pays homage to Donald Winnicott—Bettelheim describes a conversation that he once had with a ten-year-old girl whose mother and father were insistent realists. "I know there is no Santa," said the girl. "And no Tooth Fairy who puts a dime under my pillow." Then she broke down and burst into tears: "I hate reality."

This hatred of reality, Bettelheim suggests, was a direct consequence of the girl being forced to give up wish-fulfilling fantasies too early. The uncompromising realism of the girl's parents was not (as they had intended) instilling in their daughter a healthy, rational understanding of the world. Indeed, their inflexible logic had achieved the opposite effect. The girl had been alienated from reality. Sometimes, reality has to be diluted. "Unrelieved reality," says Bettelheim, "becomes just too unbearable for the young—and for quite a few of the not so young." Bettelheim is not advocating disengagement from what is true. Rather, he is alerting us to an interesting paradox: a permissive attitude toward magical thinking in childhood ultimately helps children to face and cope with reality.

It is summertime and we are in the Austrian Alps. A middle-aged doctor, wishing to forget medicine, turns off the beaten track and begins a strenuous climb. When he reaches the summit, he sits and contemplates the view. He hears a voice: "Are you a doctor?" He can't believe that someone has followed him. When he turns, he sees a sulky-looking eighteen-year-old. She served him his meal the previous evening. "Yes," he replies, "I'm a doctor. How did you know that?" She tells him that her nerves are bad. She needs help. Sometimes she can't breathe and there's a hammering in her head. And sometimes, something very disturbing happens. She sees things—a face that fills her with horror.

This could be the opening of an Alfred Hitchcock film, but in fact it's the opening of a case study: *Katharina*, by Sigmund Freud. It can be found in *Studies on Hysteria*. Freud knew how to tell a story. He took the case study and turned it into cutting-edge modern literature. Freud's detractors sometimes point out that he was never awarded a major scientific prize. Instead, he received the Goethe Prize, which is a prize for writing. But this doesn't discredit Freud at all. If stories and storytelling are fundamental to the human condition, then it is precisely because Freud possessed a literary sensibility that his creation, psychoanalysis, has proved to be such a rich and illuminating framework.

Arguably, Freud's most important patient was Sergei Panke-jeff, a wealthy young Russian now better known by his clinical alias, the Wolf Man, a name Freud chose because Pankejeff had reported a significant dream about wolves perched on the branches of a tree. In 1971, the Wolf Man published a memoir containing a very interesting memory of Freud. Doctor and patient were discussing books, and the fictional detective Sherlock Holmes was mentioned. The Wolf Man had assumed that Freud, renowned for his love of the classics, would be dismissive of "this type of light reading matter," and he was surprised to discover that Freud had read Sir Arthur Conan Doyle "attentively." Later, the Wolf Man concluded that perhaps it wasn't so surprising after all: "The fact that circumstantial evidence is useful in psychoanalysis when reconstructing a childhood history may explain Freud's interest in this type of literature."[2]

Crimes are like symptoms, and the psychoanalyst and the detective are very similar animals: both examine circumstantial evidence, reconstruct histories, and seek to establish an ultimate cause. Freud was perfectly aware of these correspondences. Patients tell their stories to therapists, and analysis proceeds in the manner of a "whodunit." In a way, Freud's ideas about sexual development and the origins of psychopathology were greatly influenced by detective fiction. The story of King Oedipus provides the narrative template for the Oedipus complex. It is also one of the oldest whodunits ever written. When we meet Oedipus in Greek tragedy, there is a curse on his country. He is told that this curse will not be lifted until he has discovered the identity of the man who murdered his predecessor, King Laius—the former husband of Oedipus's new wife, Jocasta. Oedipus follows clue after clue, until his investigation leads him inexorably to a terrible conclusion.

It was he, Oedipus, who killed the king: Laius was his father, and he is married to his mother.

People are like narrative Russian dolls. Their stories can be opened, and inside these stories we find more stories: stories within stories. Freud's feeling for narrative is not incidental, or something that can be consigned to the marginalia of psychoanalysis. It is central to the evolution of his thinking. Freud used narrative templates both to inform his method of inquiry and to make sense of his patients' histories and memories. Complex internal states can be made more intelligible when they are organized by a Greek myth. If treatment involves giving shape to experience by employing narrative prototypes, then the converse should also be true: distress and unhappiness must be associated with either the absence of narrative or its breakdown.

The earliest psychoanalytic patients experienced narrative breakdown. Treatment usually involved an investigative process that led, ultimately, to the revelation of a repressed and traumatic memory. The therapist could then piece together the "whole story."

Trauma interrupts personal narrative, and the underlying biological mechanisms are well understood.

Sensory information passes through a structure in the brain called the thalamus, where data streams are integrated so that memories can be retrieved holistically. The sharpness of a rose's thorns, the color of its petals, and the sweetness of its smell are stored together. But when we are overwhelmed by a traumatic experience, the thalamus stops synthesizing data streams. Information can only be stored in a fragmentary form. Memories of the trauma are inaccessible or discontinuous. There is no logical sequence of events to remember, only islands of sensation and emotion. The left hemisphere of the brain is deactivated, and experience cannot be understood as a series of causes and effects.[3] The story we tell ourselves about ourselves becomes confused and breaks down.

I have had countless conversations with people who have been traumatized: people who have been sexually abused as children or raped; people who have survived earthquakes or drowning; people who have been injured in appalling accidents, attacked in the street, or had to fight their way out of a war zone. They all described *shattering* experiences. They all felt as if they had lost the plot—not only in the narrow sense of being unable to recall the trauma as a narrative episode, with a beginning, middle, and end, but in the much broader sense of having lost the central continuities of their entire life story. They were no longer sure where their story was going or what their story meant.

To a lesser extent, all of life's problems can be conceptualized in this way. Patients frequently present chaotic accounts of their life events to therapists, who then typically order these disconnected fragments into a meaningful story. This is sometimes all it takes to make a distressed individual feel less confused and more in control. The psychologist Mary Main and colleagues, at the University of California, Berkeley, have found that a sense of emotional security is closely related to internally consistent and coherent self-narratives. You will feel more contented and less anxious if the stories you tell yourself—about yourself—are well structured. Presumably, the skill of imposing narrative structure on experience is (as Bettelheim suggested) learned by listening to stories when you are very young.

I have often found myself offering patients narrative frameworks to help them make sense of their lives. These frequently corresponded with the basic plots of fairy tales, such as "slaying the monster," "rags to riches," or "voyage and return."[4] Significant therapeutic gains usually followed, once formerly meaningless and confusing recollections were placed in a narrative context. In addition to being associated with poor mental health, a failure to develop a cohesive and emotionally meaningful personal narrative might be associated with antisocial behavior. The forensic psychologist David Canter has suggested that the inner narratives of violent criminals are impoverished, resulting in a complete loss of empathy.[5] Without having a story of your own, you won't be able to appreciate other people's stories. They will be dehumanized and their pain will mean nothing to you.

Good lives—like good books—require editing. People benefit by reflecting on their experiences and ordering episodes into chapters that proceed according to patterns of cause and effect. There is an art to thinking about your life.

Most of the reasons why we do one thing, rather than another, are not accessible. Consequently, the brain creates explanatory narratives. These are essentially confabulations, or best guesses. Neuroscientists call the inner, story-generating voice the "left-brain interpreter." We exist in a terrifying vastness of unimaginable complexity. Narrative brings order to chaos. It is reassuring and makes us feel more in control. The universe is less frightening if we have a story. It doesn't have to be a true story—most stories aren't—it just has to be a story that serves its purpose. A human being is not so much a single person as a community of selves. There is a consensus across almost all schools of psychotherapy that psychological health is strongly associated with integration. Congruence is always preferable to incongruence.

What keeps all these selves together? What links the inner child with the adult—the ego with the ego ideal—the slob we are at home with the efficient professional who arrives in the workplace? They all share the same story. The neuroscientist David Eagleman has stated that behavior is simply the final outcome of a battle between competing selves: our inner narrator "works around the clock to stitch together a pattern of logic to our daily lives: what just happened and what was my role in it?"[6]

Your story is your communicable essence—and if you can't tell your story, you are in danger of losing the plot.

What have we learned so far?

Love makes us feel safe, and security is our foundation. An individual is more like a theatrical cast than a single character, and when roles are congruent, a person is more likely to enjoy good mental health and deeper levels of fulfillment than when roles are not congruent. Selves are held together by stories—just as different actors perform together as an ensemble when they follow a script. A coherent life-story and the core elements of self constitute what we think of as the true self. Life is fulfilling when the true self can satisfy its basic and complex needs. There are always obstacles to satisfaction, and many of these are internal. Our choices are not always in our best interests. Decision-making is complicated by the influence of unconscious memories and distorted perceptions. Reflective introspection encourages insight (self-understanding), and rational thinking corrects biases. The attainment of insight and rationality is facilitated by face-to-face conversation, particularly when talk is uninhibited, exploratory, challenging, and undertaken using language that increases the accessibility of memories and emotions.

In addition to addressing questions relating to personhood, the major figures of psychotherapy have had much to say about more abstract aspects of existence, such as "being," purpose, and coming to terms with mortality. These will be discussed, along with other topics, in subsequent chapters.

7

NARCISSISM

Gazing into the Pool

In Book III of Ovid's *Metamorphoses*, Narcissus, the proud hunter, weary and thirsty, discovers a pool sheltered by a circle of trees. He attempts to quench his thirst, but when he sees his face reflected in the water he is enchanted by his own beauty and falls in love. He is tormented by his own perfection, and his attempts to kiss and embrace the object of his desire end in inevitable frustration. He cannot leave the pool: "As golden wax melts with gentle heat, as morning frosts are thawed by the warmth of the sun, so he was worn and wasted away with love, and slowly consumed by its hidden fire."[1] Only a small flower could be found by the pool after his disappearance.

The story of Narcissus is well-known. This is curious, because the famous Greek myths tend to be heroic: Theseus and the Minotaur, Perseus and the Gorgon, Jason and the Argonauts. The plot of Narcissus lacks incident. He gazes at himself in the pool and just carries on gazing until he fades away. Yet the image is haunting, a popular subject for poets, writers, and artists. When

we hear or read about Narcissus's unhappy end, we recognize that we are being told something important.

Most artists have chosen to respect Ovid's descriptive prose. Typically, their work shows a beautiful youth in a verdant landscape bathed in sunshine. There is, however, one illustrious exception, the portrait of Narcissus by the prodigiously gifted Baroque master Caravaggio. In his painting, Narcissus is depicted as a young man, dressed in the fashion of Caravaggio's time, crouched close to a pool of dark water. There are no trees or additional details. Behind Narcissus, there is only a benighted vacuum. Caravaggio's portrait is a bleak and terrifying vision of self-absorption. Narcissus is so wrapped up in himself nothing else exists. His arms and shoulders form an arch that connects with its own re-flection to form a circle. It suggests that everything that matters to him, his entire world, is contained within the circumference of his ego. We can't see much of Narcissus's body, because it is being eaten away by shadow. Caravaggio dispenses with pastoral clichés and offers us instead a penetrating metaphor. Narcissism is a form of solitary confinement, descent into a lightless dungeon.

The word "narcissism" didn't exist until the final years of the nineteenth century. In 1898, Havelock Ellis referred to some in-dividuals showing "Narcissus-like" attitudes, and in 1899, Paul Näcke described sexually objectifying one's body as *Narzissmus*— or "narcissism" in English. The word might well have fallen into disuse, however, if Freud hadn't used it in an extended 1914 essay on the subject. Narcissism is now used colloquially to emphasize preoccupation with appearance. The technical term covers all forms of self-regard and grandiosity—for example, intellectual vanity and the overestimation of personal power. Another im-portant feature of narcissism is perceived exceptionality, a feeling of being in some way special (although this is invariably without justification).

"Narcissism," used as a clinical term, has always carried with it connotations of morbidity. Yet there seems to be considerable overlap between narcissism and characteristics that, at least in the West, are considered desirable. Attractiveness, for example, is highly valued, and it is socially advantageous to be self-confident. Self-esteem is supposedly correlated with happiness. Self-belief spurs ambition, and therefore material success; self-possession commands respect; self-sufficiency and self-reliance are strengths; self-expression is encouraged. Pop psychologists repeatedly assure us that we must love ourselves. A certain amount of egocentricity is thought to be enabling. Beyond a certain point, however, being self-centered becomes self-defeating. Self-confidence can veer into arrogance; self-belief can warp into conceit; self-worth can become vanity. Absolute faith in one's self-efficacy makes one feel omnipotent. The single-minded pursuit of self-actualization can become self-obsession. Self-evaluations can become so detached from reality that they are more accurately described as self-delusions.

If Darwinism had embraced the concept of Christian morality, then the cardinal evolutionary sin would be selfishness. In the ancestral environment, social disintegration was swiftly followed by extinction. From an evolutionary perspective, a "good person" is someone whose behavior benefits others. Early humans survived by working together in cooperative groups and died when they were on their own; in a tribal context, what was advantageous for the tribe was also advantageous for the individual. Selfless acts, such as risking one's life to save others, would maintain the size of the tribe, enhance its strength, and ultimately, produce all of the benefits that followed from large, cooperative alliances, such as hunting in packs and banding together to protect the group from predators. Watch your neighbor's back today, and he will watch yours tomorrow. Societies can "carry" a few selfish individuals and still function, but if that number increases beyond a certain point, social cohesion—and its many benefits—may be lost.

Perhaps this explains why the uneventful story of Narcissus is so engaging. A real drama is implied. Somewhere, deep in the unconscious, evolutionary alarms are sounding. Narcissists are not only a threat to themselves—they are a threat to all of us.

Freud had been using the term "narcissism" for several years prior to 1914; however, after the publication of *On Narcissism: An*

Introduction, the concept became an important addition to psychoanalytic theory, and thereafter, the term was adopted more generally. Freud distinguished two forms of narcissism: primary and secondary. Primary narcissism is a universal feature of child development. Under normal circumstances, babies are born into families who love them and attend to their every need. When babies cry, they are comforted; when they are hungry, they will be fed. Simply wanting something is enough to ensure the desired outcome. The adoration of a doting mother resembles worship, and a baby has good reason to believe that it is a minor deity.

In order to be an emotionally healthy adult, infantile megalomania must be consigned to the past. When we are grandiose, we are out of touch with reality, and when we are self-centered, we can't share or give. Healthy maturation involves the gradual abandonment of primary narcissism and the formation of a more realistic worldview. The infant learns that he or she is not a fulcrum around which everything else turns. Other people are not there simply to meet needs, and there are limits to his or her powers. These humbling realizations are the harbingers of change. Eventually, infants grow out of their primary narcissism, but Freud warned that it is always possible to slip back, to regress. Even as adults, we can lose perspective and suddenly find that we are repossessed by the megalomania of infancy. This reactivation of infantile attitudes, magical thinking, and emotional volatility is termed "secondary narcissism." Individuals who have regressed don't start acting like babies, but they can become extremely egocentric.

Primary narcissism is probably a natural side effect of the bonding process. Children need a responsive primary caretaker in order to form a secure attachment and thrive. Close attention and care will inevitably encourage feelings of self-importance, which in infancy might be adaptive (at least for a limited period). A self-important child might be less vulnerable to social anxiety and more likely to initiate social interactions. He or she might be more exploratory and have increased exposure to stimulating situations that will accelerate development. Given that primary narcissism is transitional, the lasting benefits of confident social interaction will probably outweigh the costs of temporary ego-inflation.

What is it then that spurs further development? What causes the child to abandon primary narcissism before the subsidiary benefits of self-importance are mitigated by the accruing costs of immaturity?

Heinz Kohut, a psychoanalyst who died in 1981, suggested that an important catalyst is "optimal frustration," the experience of having regular disappointments that do not cause lasting harm. Optimal frustration recalibrates expectations and encourages new ways of coping. When the Oedipal drama plays out in families, the father frustrates the child's access to its mother. The child learns that some things are unattainable, and desire is subsequently transferred to more appropriate substitutes. A general principle can be distilled from this tutelary experience: accept limitations and set achievable goals.

Narcissism isn't a concept that psychotherapists working outside of the psychoanalytic tradition discuss very much. Indeed, for many years, there was a tendency to view it as another example of how Freud's extracurricular interests prejudiced his professional thinking. He was noticeably more enthusiastic about ideas that could be linked with archaeology or classical myths. Is narcissism a useful concept? Freud became convinced that narcissism, or at least our proneness to it, represented a very real threat to mental health and happiness.

Contemporary mental health statistics show that human beings (particularly young people living in Western liberal democracies) are becoming increasingly unhappy and dissatisfied. One explanation for this trend is modernity—a hypothesis that has been iterated and reiterated by numerous theorists, including Freud, from the nineteenth century onward. We did not evolve to live in the modern world, and the accelerating pace of environmental change is constantly exceeding our capacity to make healthy adaptations.

The most consequential environmental change to have occurred in recent years is the augmentation of reality with an additional dimension: cyberspace. Preliminary indications suggest that digital technology has had a detrimental effect on mental health and well-being. Much of the evidence is correlational and even some of the best large-scale studies show that screen time has only a modest influence on variables such as sleep, activity levels, social functioning, and aggression.[2] However, when it comes to narcissism, we can be more confident about potential effects. It doesn't seem quite so contentious to suggest that behaviors such as curating a gallery of photoshopped selfies might reinforce and enlarge narcissistic tendencies.

When we are connected to the Internet, there are aspects of the experience that replicate infantile omnipotence. Sophisticated, predictive algorithms can anticipate our requirements and offer us relevant products and services. Our unspoken wishes are instantly satisfied by an eerily responsive environment, just as, in loving households, our watchful parents were quick to satisfy our needs when we were children. The Internet locates us as the center of a pre-Copernican universe populated with invisible agencies that do our bidding.

Never before have there been so many opportunities, triggers, and provocations, so many incentives for self-regard and self-promotion. Why be modest and retiring when, by stepping into the metaphorical spotlight and declaring one's opinions through a digital megaphone, one can acquire fame and maybe even riches? A video-game streamer or a makeup tutorial star can easily attract thousands of followers: some become professionals. Postings that only a few years ago would have been called vain, self-obsessed, or boastful are now regarded as normal. Modesty has traditionally been counted as a virtue, and for good reason. We must protect our modesty, because our modesty protects us from ourselves. It takes very little to send the average human being into a regressive tailspin that ends in infantile megalomania and rage.

Of course, it could be argued that levels of narcissism haven't really risen at all, but rather the Internet has simply made narcissism more visible. Social scientists, however, have studied the phenomenon quite closely, and they have concluded that narcissism is not only rising, but rising at an alarming rate. In 2008, for example, Jean Twenge and colleagues published a paper in the *Journal of Personality* titled "Egos Inflating over Time: A Cross-Temporal Meta-Analysis of the Narcissistic Personality Inventory (NPI)." Narcissism was found to have increased over several generations in eighty-five samples of American college students who had completed the NPI, a measure of narcissistic traits. Almost two-thirds of recent college students scored above the mean for the period 1979–1985. The observed trend began before the appearance of the Internet. Even so, Twenge and her colleagues identify digital technology as a plausible inflationary influence: "Devices such as iPods and Tivo allow people to listen to music and watch television in their own individual ways, and websites such as MySpace and

YouTube (whose slogan is 'Broadcast yourself') permit self-promotion far beyond that allowed by traditional media. These trends motivated *Time* magazine to declare that the 2006 Person of the Year was 'You,' complete with a mirror on the cover." We can reasonably assume that older people who engage with cyberculture to the same extent as younger people—exposing themselves to equivalent provocations—would show comparable narcissistic trait scores.[*3]

Nothing is more emblematic of contemporary narcissism than the selfie. The smartphone is the modern equivalent of Caravaggio's dark reflective pool. For millennials, it has become a technologically advanced hand mirror. Around three-quarters of the photos posted on social media by young people are of themselves. According to Google statistics, around ninety-three million selfies are taken every day on Android devices and over twenty billion are uploaded on Google servers every year.[4] Tourists standing in front of famous landmarks or magnificent works of art, grinning at a smartphone attached to the end of a selfie stick, are now a familiar sight. What would once have been the subject of the picture—a palace or monument—is now of only secondary importance. The selfie stick takes the ego-expanding possibilities of lifestyle and consumption to their logical extreme. History, heritage, and works of genius become props. The *really* important thing in the picture is the person.

---

* Ideas concerning self-exploration and self-expression began circulating in Western liberal democracies in the 1960s. A few decades later, selfhood was conflated with consumption patterns and "lifestyle." Possessions came to represent extensions of self. The idealists of the 1960s had sought to make the world a better place, individual by individual, until everyone was self-actualized, but by the late twentieth century individualism was materialistic, egocentric, and sadly lacking in both integrity and substance.

There are, of course, many benign reasons why people post selfies; however, much of the posting that we see today seems to be nothing more than attention-seeking. It is regressive and infantile: "Look at me, look at me!" The audience is obliging. It looks, but unfortunately, it also judges. The fact that selfies are subject to constant peer review means that digital natives have lashed their self-esteem to the mast of appearance. The individual who links his or her self-worth to the fluctuating currencies of the Internet—"likes," "retweets," and the approval of strangers—is likely to suffer as a consequence. A disproportionately high value is assigned to youth, beauty, and sex appeal, all of which decline with the passage of time—and that decline is, of course, inevitable. Mirrors give us wise counsel. They introduce us, ever so gently— like the drip-feed of harsh realities in a fairy story—to the idea of our own mortality. For a narcissist, such counsel is interpreted as criticism. Narcissists find getting older intolerable and despair or deny what is happening to them and escape into self-deceit and self-delusion. Initially, inflated self-regard might seem relatively harmless; however, narcissism is the beginning of a journey that frequently ends in terror or unreality. One must suppose that for many digital narcissists, graying hair and wrinkles will not be experienced just as signs of aging, but as existential threats to the self.

Epistemic narcissism, the unshakable belief that one's views and outlook are correct, feeds on itself in cyberspace. Self-selected communities entrench beliefs by mutual consent, and this phenomenon has aided a revival of political extremism. Without exposure to alternative opinions, there is no cause for self-doubt.

Celebrities are renowned for expressing extreme (and often eccentric) views because, historically, they have been hermetically sealed in ecosystems of sycophancy and adulation. They are per-mitted to behave in ways that wouldn't ordinarily be tolerated: if they wish, they can trash hotel rooms, demand that their coffee is always stirred counterclockwise, and ask that their dressing rooms be filled with roses. The same mechanisms that inflated celeb-rity egos in the past—indiscriminate approbation and the absence of contradiction—now exert a pernicious influence through every smartphone, tablet, and laptop. Today, anyone can shout into the echo chambers of cyberspace and receive applause.

Narcissistic rage, the negotiating tool of dictators and infants, can be observed with increasing frequency. Many "normal" adults now respond to frustration by throwing a tantrum. Their sense of entitlement is so strong that they cannot accept denial. If they don't get what they want, immediately, they stamp their feet and shout. We have special terms to describe situation-specific in-stances: road rage, air rage, queue rage.[5] "Twitter storms"—sudden torrents of self-righteous anger and abusive language—are exam-ples of the same phenomenon.

Child psychoanalyst Melanie Klein emphasized the destruc-tive consequences of narcissism. If narcissism were simply a mix-ture of vanity, selfishness, and self-obsession, it would be bad enough, but it has the capacity to mutate into something mon-strous. Narcissistic entitlement can become so grotesque that the affected individual covets more or less everything. The narcissist becomes envious and hateful. Obstacles must be removed, unde-serving competitors must be annihilated. Only the narcissist has a right to exist.

We are back in Caravaggio's black void: It isn't a representa-tion of hell. It is, in fact, a narcissist's idea of heaven.

Society is not homogeneous, but a collection of coalitions: political parties, classes, associations, and special-interest groups. We identify ourselves as members of these "tribes" because other members share our values, because they are like us. Our closest friends are usually like us, too, but even more so. It's hardly surprising, therefore, that most marriages are a union of like-minded individuals. Successful intimate relationships are based on commonalities: enthusiasms, tastes, and activities.[6] We tend to marry people who come from a background similar to ours, subscribe to similar dress codes, and have similar qualifications. This was first established by Francis Galton in his 1870 study of English marriages, and it has been confirmed by almost all subsequent comparable research. Compatibilities of this kind are desirable, but they also tend to amplify epistemic narcissism. If the person we live with agrees with everything we say, we might be tempted to conclude that our judgments are based on flawless, irrefutable logic.

In the early days of psychoanalysis, narcissism was intellectually connected with homosexuality: it was argued that homosexuals are attracted to bodies that look the same as their own. In fact, *all* sexual awakenings, irrespective of sexual orientation, are narcissistic. Sexual awareness begins with self-exploration (often in front of a mirror) and masturbation. However, there are many other reasons why we might be disposed to find people who resemble ourselves preferentially attractive. Oedipal attraction, too, always has a narcissistic dimension, because we look like our parents. A man who chooses to marry a woman who resembles a youthful version of his mother is also marrying a woman who looks like himself. Our instinctive revulsion of prolonged Oedipal desires is rooted in biology rather than psychology: incest increases the likelihood of offspring suffering from genetic abnormalities.

Oedipal feelings, when normal, steer sexual interest in the "right" direction and then subside. They are supposed to be transitional.

Why should such a potentially dangerous method of seeding sexual curiosity have been selected by evolution? Why exploit intrafamilial attraction to inflame sexual interest when, if an Oedipus or Elektra complex is not resolved, the outcome will be genetically catastrophic? The interplay among mate choice, shared genes, and reproductive success is nuanced to the extent that selection pressures can produce counterintuitive but nevertheless functional adaptations. It has been suggested, for example, that optimal reproductive success is linked with genetic compatibility as advertised by physical similarities, such as having the same hair color or build. The ideal sexual partner isn't genetically too close, but neither is he or she genetically too distant.[7] We have sophisticated brains, and instincts can be ignored. Even so, if this speculative theory is correct, we can suppose that when we are looking for a partner, our evolutionary programming will urge us to select a mate who resembles ourselves.

Another evolutionary mechanism that favors narcissistic sexual attraction is *assortative mating*. Because everyone wants to form a relationship with the most attractive person possible—and no one wants to form a relationship with someone less attractive than themselves—the vast majority of couples sort themselves into matched pairs, where the two individuals are more likely than not to resemble each other. Thus, when we look at the person we profess to love—and admire him or her—we might also be simultaneously admiring ourselves.

Love is not a mystical force, as poets suggest. It is not boundless and infinite. You can only spend so many hours each day thinking about your beloved or performing acts of kindness.

Conversely, you can only spend so many hours each day thinking about yourself and acting selfishly. Implicit in Freud's theoretical account of narcissism is the idea that the more we love ourselves, the less love we can spare for others. Spousal love, unlike parental love, is predicated on reciprocity. When you stop loving others, you stop being loved yourself.

Zane wasn't his real name. Zane was the name he had chosen for himself because it sounded glamorous. He was twenty-six years old and spent almost all of his income on designer clothes, luxury holidays, and cocaine. He was still a schoolboy when he accepted money for the first time in exchange for sex. Prostitution became his profession, and he soon discovered that his good looks gave him a significant advantage on the streets.

He was, without doubt, striking. He had long blond hair that he was constantly repositioning, and his eyes were like moon-stones. Viewed in profile, he could easily have been mistaken for a young woman. It was only when his head turned toward me that the light from my desk lamp clarified his masculine jawline. Zane's voice was equally ambiguous. When he spoke, he repro-duced the low, husky drawl of a woman who has smoked too many cigarettes.

Zane had discovered a niche market for his androgyny. He sold his body to gay men who wanted to have sex with other gay men in drag. He told me more about his clientele. "They're mostly old guys with a lot of money. I get picked up by a car and taken to a mansion—usually somewhere just outside London. The *real* thing—you know?—paneled walls, paintings, four-poster beds. I don't have to take anything with me. I just put my face on and go. The punters have already been out to the shops—they've already bought the clothes they want me to wear—camisoles, heels, stockings . . ." He raised his foot, pointed the toe of his shoe at me, and with an upward sweep of his hands—from ankle to thigh—encouraged me to imagine how shapely his legs would look sheathed in shimmering black silk. "It's not hard work. Most of them can't even get it up. I hardly have to *do* anything."

Most of his clients were happy just to look at Zane, or alternatively, engage in a kind of ritualized, sexual worship. They would kneel, stimulate him orally, or stroke his figure-hugging dresses while they stimulated themselves. Penetrative sex wasn't requested very often. But when Zane was asked, he was perfectly happy to oblige. "They love me," he laughed. "Silly fuckers." He had nothing but contempt for them.

Zane enjoyed recreational sex, but he never became emotionally attached to any of his partners, and sexual gratification wasn't his principal motivation. If he was visiting a nightclub and a celebrity appeared, he would immediately try to seduce him. On those occasions when he was successful, which were not infrequent, the pleasure he experienced wasn't sexual but narcissistic. He was excited by the fact that a famous film star or musician had found him irresistible.

As Zane spoke to me about his life, his hands were in constant motion. He was in the habit of lifting his T-shirt and exposing his flat, faintly muscled stomach. He achieved this exposure with a movement that appeared to be unconscious, as if the hem of his T-shirt were getting accidently caught on his watch strap every time he raised his arm. I was in my thirties at the time, but I suspect that to Zane, I was just another "old guy"—another potential conquest who he might get to kneel before him in helpless adoration.

As I got to know Zane better, the extent of his narcissism became increasingly evident. He would say things that demonstrated an almost total absence of empathy. "You know, sometimes, when I'm flying I get bored, and I think about the plane coming down—the plane crashing." He found fear more tolerable than boredom. "But I don't imagine the plane coming down and bursting into flames, I imagine it causing massive explosions. I imagine buildings collapsing and thousands of people dying. Like a disaster movie—like it's the end of the world." Pain, incalculable suffering and grief, the death of countless innocents, meant nothing. These things only had meaning in relation to his fantasies. He imagined his death like "the end of the world." For narcissists, their own death is the apocalypse, because nothing else matters.

For thousands of years, religions have advocated practices that involve transcending the self. These include meditation, repetitive prayer, and chanting. Practices of this kind typically engender altered states of consciousness that are interpreted as being spiritually significant. These states also produce lasting beneficial changes, such as positivity and elevated mood.[8] It isn't necessary to be devout to profit from meditation. Atheists who meditate also report increased well-being.

The notion that transcending the self is beneficial and transformative appears in the works of many significant psychotherapists. Carl Rogers and Erich Fromm, respectively, recommend living in the "present moment" and the "here and now." If you are not caught up in thoughts about the past and worries about the future, then you will be open to experience and have a more direct relationship with reality. You will be less self-aware, but feel more alive. At first, this seems somewhat counterintuitive. If your self-awareness diminishes, there should be a corresponding reduction in your capacity to assimilate impressions. The world should shrink with you. In fact, people tend to report the exact opposite: intense pleasure, vivid experience, and optimal functioning.

When we are completely absorbed by an enjoyable task or activity, we "lose" ourselves in the process. We become engrossed, and time seems to pass quickly. Psychologist Mihaly Csikszentmihalyi has called this immersive state "flow." Athletes and musicians describe something very similar: "being in the zone." Inspired performances are achieved with effortless spontaneity. "Awakening experiences"—as defined by British psychologist Steve Taylor—are positive states, characterized by elation or serenity, intensified perception, and greater connectedness (with other human beings or nature). "Mental chatter" recedes or disappears. In other words, during awakening experiences, individuals are less self-aware.

Psychedelic drug researchers since the 1950s have found that life-changing "highs" are associated with "ego death," the total loss of the sense of self while remaining fully conscious. Documenting his vivid experiences after taking mescaline, Aldous Huxley wrote, "For the moment that interfering neurotic who, in waking hours, tries to run the show, was blessedly out of the way."[9]

What all of these states, and meditation experiences, have in common with each other is attenuated self-awareness or loss of a sense of self. They are also associated with changes in outlook and mood. These include increased confidence, greater optimism, wider interests, and the formation of new relationships. Some claim that life has acquired deeper meaning and purpose. There is some overlap here with what Maslow called "peak experiences"—states of ecstasy and wonder achieved by those who are fully self-actualized.

How can this be explained? Why do individuals who experience a temporary loss of self-awareness develop a stronger sense of identity and direction?

When you commune with nature, have an orgasm, or ski down a mountain slope, you are most definitely present. Such experiences are intensely pleasurable, not because the self is absent, but because it is completely present in the here and now. The self is fully immersed in sensation, the afferent channels of the nervous system are wide open, and you experience reality at maximum intensity. Nothing is getting in the way. Peak experiences are memorable and distinctive, because under normal circumstances, there usually *is* something that gets in the way.

The "something" that has been displaced, the "something" that is usually obstructing direct experience, is the narcissistic self, the self that is habitually attempting to distort perception in order to occupy a position of absolute centrality, the ceaseless "mental chatter" about needs, wants, desires, and how others see us. Many narcissists frequently imagine that they are in a film. They go through life imagining their day-to-day activities as they would appear on a big screen. Experience is immediately converted into a self-aggrandizing fantasy and nothing of the world "gets through." This is typical of narcissistic behavior in general. Without direct experience, there can be no personal growth and development. Narcissists constantly interpose their big egos between beauty and the experience of beauty, truth and the experience of truth. How can a narcissist have an awakening experience as the sun sets while standing with his or her back to the fiery sky holding up a

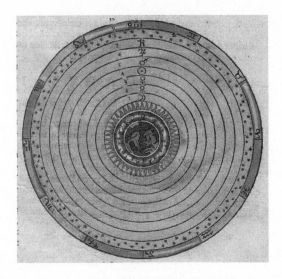

selfie stick? The true self is enriched by encounters with undiluted reality.

Freud claimed that, after Copernicus and Darwin, he had delivered the third and most damaging blow to narcissistic humanity. Copernicus demonstrated that human beings do not occupy a favored position at the very center of the universe. The stars and the planets do not revolve around Earth. Given the immensity and age of the universe, our insignificance is beyond question. Darwin proved that human beings are not the crown of creation, designed by God to reign supreme over other life-forms. On the contrary, human beings are the product of chance events and evolution. We are animals, no more divine than pigs or baboons. Freud's "third blow" was psychoanalysis, which revealed that we have little or no insight. According to Freud, the ego "is not even master in its own house, but must content itself with scanty information of what is going on unconsciously in its mind."[10] We blunder through life without knowing who we are or understanding why we choose to perform one action rather than another.

It is often observed that by aligning himself with colossal figures like Copernicus and Darwin, Freud was inadvertently revealing the extent of his own narcissism. Laying claim to primacy in such august company is, by any standard, fabulously grandiose. Freud's third blow was—in his own words—"the most wounding." He judged himself to be the heaviest hitter. But if Freud was being narcissistic, then his narcissism underscores his argument. We are all vulnerable. Our egos can expand on a cosmic scale.

The central feature of narcissism is exceptionality. When we succumb to narcissism, we believe that we are special, the beneficiary of entitlements and exemptions, and the greatest of these exemptions is from death. Other people will die—but not me. In *The Year of the Death of Ricardo Reis*, a novel by the Portuguese writer and Nobel Laureate José Saramago, a dead poet, Fernando Pessoa, returns from the grave to talk with his friend, the doctor and fellow poet Ricardo Reis. He tells Reis that the living cannot comprehend their own mortality. Reis protests—of course the living know that they will die. Pessoa responds, "You don't know, no one knows it, just as I didn't when I was alive, what we do know without a shadow of a doubt is that others die."

A narcissist is "immortal" and can spend an eternity admiring his or her own reflection. The business of living can be deferred. But remember, Narcissus was still gazing at himself even as he was dissolving into nothingness.

8

SEX

Mortal Vehicles

Sex appears twice in Abraham Maslow's hierarchy of needs. First, he placed the need for sex at the lowest level, grouping it with more substantive requirements such as air and food. A basic need, in other words. Then sex reappears at a higher level as an implicit ingredient of intimacy, subsumed under the broad heading of "love and belonging." Maslow's double counting reflects a tendency, particularly in Western societies, to be uncertain about the place of sex in the scheme of things. Sex polarizes. On the one hand, it can be seen as an animal urge that must be tightly controlled by strict laws and prohibitions; on the other, a foretaste of spiritual union.

Early psychotherapists were preoccupied with sex. As they attempted to understand the mind, and what it is to be human, it became increasingly clear to them that sex shapes us. "Anatomy is destiny," Freud acknowledged, and made efforts to elucidate the course of male and female psychosexual development by introducing ideas like the Oedipus and Elektra complexes.[1] By the late

1920s he was thinking about a big question: Is there an optimal way of managing our sex lives?

For privileged Victorians (whose outward respectability set the example less fortunate classes were expected to follow), it was difficult to accommodate sex into a cohesive view of themselves. They inhabited a world of churches, banks, offices, theaters, music, and genteel manners. Where did sex fit in? Sex seemed incongruous.

Repression, denial, and dishonesty were needed to preserve the illusion of late Victorian respectability. Professional men mouthed pious platitudes while supporting mistresses and visiting brothels. Venereal disease was rife. Perhaps the weight of so much hypocrisy exceeded the limits of social tolerance, and collective defenses began to crumble. It was no longer possible to keep sex behind closed doors or out of conversations. The private act became a topic for public inquiry, something to be discussed, written about, and analyzed. Sexology wasn't the exclusive preserve of men. Women, encouraged by proto-feminist publications and the rise of radical politics, also began to take an academic interest in reproductive physiology and sexual pleasure. (Of course, in reality, women have always been interested in sex. In 2005, a twenty-eight-thousand-year-old siltstone object was found in a cave in Germany.[2] It is eight inches long, one inch wide, and shaped like a penis. In addition to being used for knapping flints, this object may have had recreational uses. In her book *Turned On: Science, Sex and Robotics*, Kate Devlin, a lecturer at King's College London, posed an intriguing question: "So was the dildo invented 25,000 years before the wheel?")

Many of Freud's early patients couldn't satisfy their sexual needs while preserving a morally coherent sense of self. Desire conflicted with conventionality and creed. Consequently, excessive repression created hysterical and neurotic symptoms. Toward the end of his life, Freud explored the ramifications of these mechanisms in *Civilization and Its Discontents*—a title more accurately translated by Bruno Bettelheim as "The Uneasiness Inherent in Culture." Freud concluded that many psychological disturbances are a consequence of inhibitions that are necessary if society is to function in an orderly way.

Natural selection proceeds slowly, and adaptations often lag behind environmental changes. We are well adapted to satisfy our sexual needs in a primitive setting, but many human beings now live in large, technologically advanced cities where millions of people must coexist. We sit in cafés, sipping cappuccinos and working on laptops, but when we see an attractive person sitting at a nearby table, our neural circuitry returns us to the Serengeti. We cannot act on our natural impulses anymore, though, because such behavior is no longer permitted.

If, as Freud suggested, sexual inhibitions cause mental disturbances, then a solution to the problem might be to relax social mores and encourage promiscuity. This view resonated with the thinking of many fin de siècle socialists, anarchists, and Bohemians who espoused "free love" as a means of opposing bourgeois values.[3] They proposed that we should throw the bedroom doors wide open—that perhaps institutions like marriage were ultimately damaging, and a society with fewer sexual prohibitions might be liberated from guilt, inner conflict, and neuroses.

One of the earliest psychoanalysts to realize that Freudian ideas could be reinterpreted as a manifesto for social reform was Otto Gross, a young doctor who encountered Freud when Gross was still in his late twenties. Tall, blond, and charismatic, Gross was described by Ernest Jones as the personification of a "romantic genius." Gross encouraged his patients to act like libertines and to rebel against anything they found oppressive. He supposed that if human beings were allowed to satisfy all of their sexual needs, society wouldn't fall apart, but a new and more enlightened way of life would evolve. We would all be a lot happier. Gross was addicted to cocaine and morphine, kept irregular hours, and spent his nights in the company of revolutionaries. At the age of twenty-six, he married, but this didn't prevent him from living according to his heterodox principles. He seduced two sisters, one of whom would later marry the writer D. H. Lawrence, and the other he made pregnant.

Historians of psychotherapy have cast Gross as a forerunner of 1960s counterculture heroes like Timothy Leary and R. D. Laing.

There are some remarkable parallels. He advocated the use of drugs because they expanded consciousness and dissolved moral scruples; he identified tyrannical patriarchy as a cause of mental illness. The advice he gave to his patients couldn't have been very different from Timothy Leary's rallying cry: "Turn on, tune in, drop out."

Gross's lifestyle was exhausting and difficult to sustain. He began to exhibit signs of mental illness and was sent to the Burghölzli psychiatric hospital in Switzerland, to be treated by Carl Jung. Initially, Jung disapproved of Gross; however, Gross was such a pleasant and stimulating companion that Jung described his new patient in a letter to Freud as "an exceptionally decent chap."[4] Gross was cooperative and reduced the amount of drugs he was taking. Everything seemed to be proceeding smoothly, Jung thought. That is, until Gross scaled the garden wall and escaped. Jung had been seduced as easily as Gross's female admirers.

Sexual relationships are frequently deceitful. The most common pattern is serial monogamy, combined with occasional cheating, followed by marriage, procreation, and yet more opportunistic sex.[5] It would seem that the question of whether to have an affair is actually one that shadows most, if not all, relationships. In interviews conducted by the psychiatrist and pioneering sex researcher Gilbert Hamilton in the 1920s, 28 percent of men and 24 percent of women admitted to infidelity. The famous Kinsey reports of the 1940s and 1950s found that around a third of husbands in a sample of 6,427 men had strayed, and around a quarter of 6,972 married, divorced, and widowed women had chosen to have extramarital sex by the time they were forty. In spite of changing social attitudes, these figures have remained relatively stable. Although as a culture we celebrate the idea of romance, around 57 percent of men and 54 percent of women are unfaithful. When couples marry, women are less likely to transgress, but rates of adultery remain high. Around 25 to 40 percent of married men and 15 to 25 percent of married women in Western societies are adulterous. Infidelity is not—as one might expect—closely associated with marital problems. Fifty-six percent of men and 24 percent of women who engaged in extramarital affairs rated their marriages as "happy" or "very happy."[6] Such statistics suggest that Gross's critique of social conservatism is correct. The imposition of artificial constraints on sexual freedom is ineffective. We are still behaving in much the same way as our hypocritical Victorian forebears.

Is this really the best way to deal with our sexual urges?

As a means of socializing the sexual need, marriage is imperfect, but attempts to replace it with alternative arrangements have not been successful. Communal utopias, in which everyone is allowed to have sex with everyone else, have a tendency to fragment—often because of sexual jealousy—or to revert to exclusivity and commitment. After the dissolution of the Oneida community, established by John Humphrey Noyes in 1848 in Madison County, New York, a very high percentage of couples (who were former residents) immediately dispensed with ideas of "complex marriage" in favor of "traditional marriage." The fundamental problem that undermines all sexual utopias is that human beings fall in love, and when this happens, they become jealous of rivals and possessive. Even "swinging" couples and polyamorists recognize that jealousy is such a powerful emotion it cannot be eliminated.[7] Sexual utopias work only in the absence of love or if the desire for exclusivity is repressed. They function largely by replacing one set of inhibitions with another, thus negating the principal psychodynamic justification for their existence.

Our preferred solution to the problem of sexual need appears to be sham monogamy and opportunism. With the exception of psychopaths, all human beings recognize that betrayals of trust are hurtful. Infidelity will arouse guilt, and attempts to reduce discomfort by repression are associated with excessive rumination, anxiety, emotional numbing, distancing from reality, and distorted perceptions. Human beings are, on the whole, very bad liars. We give ourselves away with evasive looks and agitation, unintentional slips and blunders. Close to half of American marriages end in divorce.[8] Roughly two-thirds of marriages dissolve after the discovery of an affair, and—according to the Holmes and Rahe Stress Scale—divorce is ranked the second most stressful life event, after bereavement, for both men and women. Both parties commonly suffer an episode of mental illness after divorce, but men fare very badly.[9] Compared to married men, divorced men are more likely to develop a drinking problem, take drugs, become socially isolated, suffer from depression, and die prematurely. Human beings find commitment difficult, but the consequences of infidelity are frequently ruinous. Sex traps us between dire alternatives.

In 1924, Freud was offered $100,000 by the Hollywood magnate Samuel Goldwyn to write a movie script in his capacity as "the greatest love specialist in the world."[10] The word "love" was of course being used euphemistically. Freud turned Goldwyn down. Many of Freud's ideas arose from self-observation, which explains, perhaps, why the question of how he managed his own sexual urges has become a subject of interest. Loyal biographers have described Freud as a family man and wholly devoted to his wife, Martha. But he was also conspicuously fond of his sister-in-law, Minna.

Minna was a member of the Freud household. She took a keen interest in Freud's work and often accompanied him on his travels. In 2006, a hotel register was discovered showing that Freud and Minna had shared a double room for two nights as husband and wife. This seemed to confirm rumors that had been circulating for over a century; however, the evidence is still circumstantial. Freud and Minna had posed as husband and wife on more than one occasion, and Martha was fully aware of this. At that time, an unmarried couple requesting board and lodging would have been politely asked to leave the premises. Posing as husband and wife might have been the only way to get the last available room. The discovery of the incriminating register provided a good story. Headlines referred amusingly to Freud's first "slip," or, more crudely, to him having "bedded" his sister-in-law.

Perhaps we are consoled by the possibility that Sigmund Freud, the greatest love specialist in the world, couldn't control himself. Minna was pretty, funny, and intelligent. She had long dark hair and wore elegant dresses. When they were playing cards, it must have been tempting to steal glances, to imagine the corsetry beneath the crêpe de chine. Perhaps we want Freud to be morally weak, because his weakness offers us a kind of absolution.

Is sex really a basic need? Obviously, not in the same way that food and water are. No one ever died because they were starved of sex. But that doesn't mean that sex is less important than eating and drinking. Indeed, Freud believed that sex is *so* basic, all other needs are auxiliary to its reproductive purpose. This only becomes clear when we look beyond the interests of the individual.

In his essay *On Narcissism*, Freud wrote, "The individual himself regards sexuality as one of his own ends; whereas from another point of view he is an appendage to his germ-plasm, at whose disposal he puts his energies in return for a bonus of pleasure. He is the mortal vehicle of a (possibly) immortal substance—like the inheritor of an entailed property, who is only the temporary holder of an estate that survives him." This is an astonishingly astute observation, because it is entirely consistent with modern evolutionary biology. Richard Dawkins, in *The Selfish Gene*, also argued that a human being is nothing more than a temporary "vehicle" for carrying genes, or what Freud called "germ-plasm." (And if you are ever in doubt about the evolutionary expendability of organisms, consider the fate of the honeybee drone. Erection causes paralysis, and on ejaculating, its genitals explode. Death follows shortly after.) The "bonus of pleasure" that we receive in return for our "energies" is an orgasm. Orgasms, arguably the most pleasurable of all natural experiences, incentivize reproduction. It is precisely because sex is of supreme importance that natural selection has made the orgasm uniquely intense.

Returning to the base of Maslow's hierarchy: We need food to live, yes, but we all know that there are good foods and bad foods. Can sex be evaluated in this way too? Are some forms of sex healthier than others?

Wilhelm Reich was a lieutenant in the Austrian army and fought in the Italian campaign of World War I. After being discharged from the military, he studied law, but later he switched to medicine. He led an impecunious existence and suffered significant hardship. While still an undergraduate, he met Freud for the first time. This was a turning point. They liked each other, and Reich was swiftly assimilated into Freud's circle.

Reich accepted Freudian orthodoxy without question. Neurosis and hysteria are caused by sexual repression, Reich agreed, and when those repressions are lifted, symptoms will disappear. As Freud was expanding the compass of psychoanalysis and introducing new ideas, Reich remained attached to these earlier formulations. Indeed, his obsession with sexuality contracted until his focus was restricted to the genitals and genital gratification. He suggested that mental illness was primarily related to an impaired capacity to experience satisfactory orgasms, summarizing his ideas in a 1927 volume titled *The Function of the Orgasm*.

The physiological and largely automatic processes that ordinarily culminate in the experience of a satisfying orgasm can be disturbed by many factors: distraction by thoughts and feelings, conflict (as happens when partners no longer feel love for each other), ambivalence because of moral considerations or religious scrupulosity, self-consciousness or inhibitions. The notion of "blockage" features significantly in Reich's writing. He suggested that "dammed-up" sexual excitation causes anxiety in much the same way that too much nicotine causes nicotine poisoning. Even frequent sex can be a problem—because too much sex will reduce the strength of orgasms. A mentally healthy person is not troubled by disruptive thoughts and feelings during intercourse. He or she is able to focus on genital gratification, submit fully to the release of sexual tension, and benefit from the deep relaxation that follows. There are no discomfiting sequelae, such as heaviness, disappointment, or a sense of incompletion. Reich's recommendations concerning total surrender anticipate ideas about ego transcendence and optimal experience. Absence of mental chatter facilitates a degree of pleasurable immersion that has the potential to transform a physiological response into ecstasy.

Reich's theoretical underpinnings are questionable. But his thinking was guided by empiricism. Everything he noted was based on clinical observation. Given the evolutionary significance of orgasm, it is perfectly reasonable to suppose that the capacity to achieve satisfying orgasms qualifies as a fitness indicator. Since the 1920s, the relationship between orgasm and health has been studied more systematically. Orgasms are associated with better bonding (mediated by the release of oxytocin), reduced stress, resistance to opportunistic infection, and longevity.[11] It is also very likely that the release of endorphins (endogenous opioids) during orgasm improves mood and sleep.

The final chapter of Reich's book returns to familiar territory. How do we reconcile sexual needs with the social demands of civilization? Religion and middle-class strictures, Reich suggested, are profoundly unhelpful. We should embrace our animal natures and be more accepting of our fundamental needs. Sexual moralizing confuses us, particularly with respect to gender politics. It promotes the kind of dichotomous thinking that insists women are either prim housewives or whores. Reich's solution to the problem of tensions arising between our higher and lower selves is a combination of good sex and realism: "Polygamous wishes emerge less often the better the husband and wife recognize and satisfy each other's sensual needs and the more understanding each brings to the polygamous tendencies of the partner." Sex is something we should work at, and if a spouse strays, we should try to be philosophical.

After spending five years in Norway, and just before the outbreak of World War II, Reich fled to the United States to escape Nazi persecution. It was there that his thinking became increasingly eccentric. Freud's concept of libido had acquired mystical significance for Reich. He reimagined it as a universal life force—"orgone"—and designed laboratory experiments that would prove its existence. Defenders of Reich's legacy point out that Albert Einstein was willing to take him seriously. On January 13, 1941, Reich visited Einstein at his home in Princeton, New Jersey, where Einstein listened to Reich's theories for five hours. It is true that Einstein was welcoming, and the physicist apparently even agreed that he could see (what might be) orgone energy flickering through a magnifying tube, a device Reich had brought with him and that he called the "orgonoscope." But Einstein was probably just being polite and humoring his guest. Naturally, he was sympathetic when petitioned by fellow exiles.

Reich's aberrant thinking spiraled into absurdity. He designed boxes and cabinets in which orgone energy could supposedly be collected. He called these receptacles "orgone accumulators" and claimed they could cure cancer. He became preoccupied with atmospheric phenomena and theorized that the "effects" he was studying were caused by a negative form of orgone energy that he called "deadly orgone." When deadly orgone was present, he believed, black clouds formed in the sky, and beneath them, vegetation became limp and animals and humans lost vitality. In order to dispel these clouds, Reich invented a large device, the cloudbuster, which consisted of metal tubes mounted on a turntable. It worked by "drawing off" negative energy—and it could also, supposedly, be used to make rain. He then became convinced that aliens were preparing to invade Earth and used his cloudbuster to sap energy from passing UFOs.

Eventually, Reich was identified by the US authorities as a potentially dangerous crank. People were failing to consult oncologists for conventional cancer treatments because they had been persuaded that sitting in an orgone accumulator would achieve better results. Reich was imprisoned, diagnosed as paranoid, and all of his books and journals were burned in the Lower Manhattan incinerator. In November 1957, he died in his sleep, while still incarcerated.

According to his disciple A. S. Neill, one of Reich's sayings was "Everybody is right in some way." This could be his epitaph. His holistic approach to psychotherapy, which emphasized the close relationship between the psychological and physical, inspired a host of new treatments involving "body work" (for example, Alexander Lowen's "bioenergetic analysis"). Reich's ideas contributed to the development of what eventually became modern psychosomatic medicine, and one can even detect a prescient glimmer of environmentalism in his later writing.

Neill's memories of Reich as a conversationalist are very different from the caricature B-movie mad scientist that Reich became.[12] Neill remembers an animated soul sitting in a cabin talking late into the night, sipping Scotch or rye and smoking Chesterfields, arguing, getting overly excited, then laughing before saying, "Pass the bottle." We shouldn't let Reich's insanity define him, or exclude him from the history of ideas. He was, like all of us, right in some way.

After leaving university, Adrian had led a rather aimless existence. He was intelligent and capable, but unmotivated. His romantic relationships tended to be short-lived, and he rarely met up with his old friends. He had been diagnosed with mild depression when he was still at university and had been suffering intermittently from episodes of low mood for a decade. He was agitated and constantly fidgeting. He changed position, drummed his fingers on his thighs, and pushed his thick hair back with both hands.

We had been talking for a while when he said, "I don't fit in. I'm different." I wondered if he was being narcissistic. Did he consider himself special? As we continued our conversation, Adrian's meaning became clearer. He was using the word "different" to signify oddity or peculiarity. I asked him to elaborate. He looked at me for a long time without saying a word. His pale skin flushed and he took a deep breath. Then he said: "When I was young—very young—maybe nine or ten—I used to give my sister oral sex." His sister was a year or two older than Adrian. "We'd go upstairs and pretend we were playing. She used to want it—she'd open her legs and push me down." He twisted his torso away from me and froze in an awkward position. "That's pretty fucked up, right?"

"How long did it go on for?"

"Oh, quite a while . . ."

"Was it something you did voluntarily?"

He screwed the knuckle of a crooked finger beneath his chin. "I guess so. I mean, it's not like I was being forced. How many kids go down on their sister? Not many, I bet." He was still sitting at an angle and his eyes had narrowed. It was almost as if he wanted me to agree that his self-loathing was justified. He repeated his question: "That's pretty fucked up, right?"

Adrian was troubled by what had happened. But I couldn't accept what he was implying. I couldn't endorse his view that because he'd performed cunnilingus on his sister when they were children, we should assume that he was deeply disturbed. Whether we like it or not, children have sexual feelings, and opposite-sex siblings—whose bodies are mysteriously sleek or appended—can easily excite curiosity. Adrian's sexual experiments with his sister were not as irregular as he imagined.

Adrian's sense of being odd and freakish was symptomatic of his failure to accept his dual nature. Freud suggested that all sexual acts that don't assist reproduction are, strictly speaking, perversions. According to this definition, even kissing is perverse. Sexual inventiveness extends well beyond touching lips and exchanging saliva. Almost any object or activity can become sexualized. Many years ago, for example, a colleague of mine was treating a man who was effectively having intercourse with his car. The man's behavior seemed utterly bizarre, and the case was presented at a departmental meeting. All the psychiatrists and psychologists gathered in the lecture theater agreed that the phenomenon was exceptional. But since then, the Internet has demonstrated that we were very much mistaken. There are now several "cranking" websites. Typically, automobile fetishists masturbate while pumping the accelerator to generate engine noise.

Most people have had sexual fantasies that, when reconsidered in a calmer frame of mind, stir up feelings of guilt, shame, regret, and embarrassment. The question arises: What does this say about me? We struggle to reconcile the bedroom with the boardroom, the bestial with the angelic. Roughly a quarter of women who use Internet pornography search for scenarios that involve being overpowered or humiliated.[13] Sixty-two percent of female undergraduates have had a rape fantasy, and 14 percent report that they fantasize about rape at least once a week.[14] Our rational selves promote progressive social values like sexual equality, but atavistic impulses still command us to submit—or mount—or bite. (Needless to say, the fact that women fantasize about rape does not mean that they want to be raped.)

Sex cannot be judged according to the standards of civilized behavior. No matter how much intellect or understanding we bring to bear on anilingus or swallowing semen, these activities only make sense—if at all—on their own terms. In this respect, at least, both Gross and Reich were correct. Sex can only be assessed according to the degree to which it is satisfying. Providing the pursuit of that satisfaction does not cause harm to ourselves or others—and we can cope with the consequences—almost anything is permissible. In the bedroom, we are predominantly animals; concepts like sin or propriety do not apply. One might just as well organize Bible classes for chimpanzees.

Otto Gross and Wilhelm Reich met similarly unhappy ends. Gross was found dying on a street from pneumonia, freezing and probably still suffering from drug addiction. Reich died in a prison cell of natural causes. Their fate suggests some kind of connection. Perhaps, as outsiders, they shared a similar outlook and were well-placed to make observations from the margins. They were certainly more willing than their colleagues to think about sex not merely as a drive, or a physiological response, but as a life problem. Sex is a powerful need. How we go about achieving sexual satisfaction is an important issue. Our sex lives shouldn't just follow the path of least resistance between desire and social conformity. We have to make choices. We have to face what we are.

The young woman is still sitting in Hopper's *Automat*. The bowl of fruit evokes the sensual; the red and the green of her garments

symbolize the conflict between innocence and desire; and her low neckline and exposed legs invite speculation. What is the nature of her dilemma? Is it an affair? Is it her virginity? Is it the pursuit of forbidden pleasures?

Will she? Won't she? Should she? There is no such thing as casual sex.

9

INFERIORITY

The Consolations of Inadequacy

Even before we are born, we exist in a social environment. There are few things more "sociable" than living inside another person's body. After birth, we are embedded in expanding shells of social complexity: family, friends, intimates, acquaintances, colleagues. These expansions are nested within a culture that is part of a broader civilization. Our sense of belonging is determined by social rather than geographical factors. When we think of ourselves, we implicitly acknowledge others. I can only think of myself as shy, for example, because I have experience of people who are outgoing.

Our sense of self is distorted by its social context. We are exquisitely sensitive to appearances. Who we think we are is constantly affected by what we think other people are thinking of us. When we are in the company of others, the question that we seem to be asking ourselves most of the time is: How does this look?

The social universe is bewildering. It is so vast and complicated that it is difficult to determine which aspects of our social context (beyond the domestic domain) are most important. As social animals, what do we want most? What is the fundamental social motivation?

The desire for prestige is as deeply rooted in the human psyche as the desire to have sex. This is worth remembering the next time someone offers you the hollow consolation that "it really doesn't matter what other people think." In order to feel good about ourselves, most of us need approval. We all have what Abraham Maslow called "esteem" needs. We want to be recognized and respected; we want to get ahead, and we want our children to get ahead—identical things from a Darwinian perspective.

Given that social behavior has so many potential objectives, why is it that so much of what we do is motivated by advancement?

Our ancestors survived by working together in groups. These groups were not egalitarian communities. They were social hierarchies, probably because a group organized hierarchically performs tasks that require many participants—for example, hunting—with greater efficiency than an undisciplined mob. More can be achieved if some members give orders and others obey.

In the ancestral environment, having an elevated social position was beneficial. A dominant male had access to more food and females, he was more likely to survive, and more of his genes would accumulate in the gene pool. Desirable females, who mated with dominant males, were better protected and better nourished than the other females. Their genes would also be more likely to retain a significant presence in the gene pool. In evolutionary terms, status equates with reproductive success. Almost everything selected by evolution that favors survival and propagation is associated with pleasure: eating, orgasms, and cuddling small children are basic examples. Social advantage feels good, too.

Early humans low in the tribal hierarchy still benefited from group membership, although not as much as their superiors. If the group survived, the low-status members also survived, and so did their genetic legacy. Those who occupied lowly positions in tribal hierarchies were extremely interested in what was going on at the top. The fate of the group was determined by its leaders. This tendency to look "upward" still manifests indiscriminately in the modern world as a preoccupation with status and celebrity, even though looking "upward," in this case, no longer serves any evolutionary purpose. What a celebrity thinks or does won't affect anyone directly, but millions of people still gossip about celebrities and hang on their every tweet. Be that as it may, status is still strongly associated with satisfaction, whereas lack of status (or sufficient cause to bolster self-esteem) makes us feel bad.

The first significant psychotherapist to consider well-being in a broad social context was Alfred Adler. Many others—historians, philosophers, and sociologists—had already written extensively about the relationship between social conditions and quality of life, but Adler's emphasis was on the individual. He was an avowed socialist and an advocate of community medicine, though he understood that political reform has its limits. It doesn't solve all problems, particularly personal ones.

Adler studied medicine in Vienna and was awarded his medical degree in 1895. From the very beginning of his career, he was sensitive to the social aspects of medical practice. In an early work, *Health Book for the Tailoring Trade*, he explored the links among economic situations, occupations, and disease. He became acquainted with Freud in 1902, and shortly after, with a few other enthusiasts, began attending meetings at Freud's apartment to

discuss psychoanalysis. Adler was never an obliging disciple—his exchanges with Freud were frequently competitive and tense. Although he became president of the Viennese Psychoanalytic Society in 1910, he resigned the following year, as he had come to doubt the value of many of Freud's key ideas. By the 1920s, Adler had established his own school: "individual psychology."

According to Adler, human beings are purposeful and motivated by goals. Individual psychology is *teleological* rather than causal. Unlike Freud, who believed that we are driven by the past, Adler believed that we are attracted to the future (or at least the future as we imagine it). We are "pulled" rather than "pushed." Although progressing through life involves setting an incalculable number of short-term goals, Adler supposed that all of these serve an ultimate aim, such as becoming financially secure or a good person. "If we can understand this goal, we can understand the hidden meaning behind each separate act." Individual psychology does not seek to probe the soul. It has been described as a "pragmatic" or "concrete" system, created to enable individuals to gain practical self-knowledge.

Freud did not regard Adler as an intellectual threat, but he was concerned that his erstwhile colleague had produced a sanitized version of psychoanalysis that would appeal to the medical establishment and the general public. There was less in Adler's psychology to cause offense than in Freud's theories, less emphasis on primitive sexual urges and the darker recesses of the unconscious.

Adler became a prominent figure and his new approach proved very influential; however, individual psychology did not displace psychoanalysis as Freud had feared. In 1937, Adler collapsed on a street in Aberdeen, Scotland, and died of a heart attack at the age of sixty-seven. Freud was delighted to hear that he had outlived his rival and gleefully declared that Aberdeen was an appropriately inauspicious setting for the death of a traitor. It was, Freud suggested, "proof of how far he had come." Whether Adler deserved such a large helping of schadenfreude is debatable. Some remembered him as cantankerous and quarrelsome, whereas others insisted that he was a friendly man who was fond of telling jokes.

Adler's books aren't read very much today. Some of them are not very polished—they consist of edited collections of his lecture notes or, bizarrely, notes made by those who attended his lectures.[1] Sections do not follow on from each other in a logical progression, and the content can be rather shallow. He didn't have Freud's literary or rhetorical gifts. Although his books can be badly written, the writing isn't quite bad enough to conceal occasional flashes of brilliance. All of which brings us to a quite extraordinary fact: a general lack of familiarity with Adler's original publications has encouraged generations of psychotherapists to steal his ideas without ever acknowledging his priority.[2] I have read entire volumes of psychology that borrow extensively from Alfred Adler in which his name is never even mentioned.

It is quite common for the term "inferiority complex" to be used in newspaper articles or everyday conversations. Apart from "Oedipus complex," I can't think of a psychological term that has gained comparable popularity. Most people know that the Oedipus complex has something to do with Sigmund Freud, but I'd be surprised if the average person could as easily connect the term "inferiority complex" with Alfred Adler. (Adler also wrote about the "superiority complex," but notions of inferiority and superiority are so closely related that the distinction is somewhat redundant. We only strive for advantage if we first recognize our inferiority. Inferiority and superiority are essentially two facets of the same construct.)

Adler used "inferiority" to describe a condition that is perhaps more accurately captured by the word "inadequacy." The inferiority complex, which manifests as depression and thoughts about shortcomings, defects, and insufficiencies, only has meaning in a social context. It implicitly acknowledges disparities: the self, judged as wanting in relation to others. Adler's starting point, "organ inferiority," was biological rather than social. Organ inferiority was a medical hypothesis concerning how weak organs cause disease and how the body adapts when specific organs are compromised. A weakness in one organ can be offset by the complementary strengthening of another organ. Adler noted that compensations of this kind might result not only in good health, but also, in some cases, superior health. He also gave examples of how physical weaknesses can promote psychological strengths:

musicians with hearing problems and painters with eye disorders. Adler proposed that inferiority and compensation might underlie many aspects of psychological development. They might even be understood as engines of motivation.

We are all born helpless, and childhood is a prolonged state of dependency. The human infant is extremely vulnerable, a diminutive creature surrounded by powerful giants. The child is constantly looking up to them. They supply food, warmth, protection; they deliver punishments and show approbation. Inferiority is a universal, formative experience, an inescapable first condition. Adler asserted that an individual's response to inferiority shapes many aspects of his or her character. The way we cope with feelings of inferiority will be determined by a number of factors, such as physical constitution, gender, the parenting we receive, and our position in relation to siblings (whether first born, second born, and so on). A response to inferiority that is effective, insofar as it achieves a desired goal, is likely to become consolidated in the individual's behavioral repertoire.

Adler described three possible responses to inferiority, two of which are forms of psychological compensation. Once our responses to inferiority are established, they become our default setting. The first successful compensation is a healthy and proportionate response. Feelings of inadequacy resolve as the child overcomes challenges, builds confidence, and learns to set realistic goals. The second response is overcompensation. This is an excessive and disproportionate reaction to perceived weaknesses. The child goes beyond the requirements of successful compensation and adopts strategies and attitudes that are potentially harmful. A dramatic example of this would be a child who is bullied at school becoming a gangster as an adult. Overcompensation doesn't always have a negative outcome. A child with a speech impediment, like Winston Churchill, might become a great orator.

The third and final response to inferiority is neurotic illness. The child discovers that it cannot overcome feelings of inferiority by straightforward, conventional methods; however, it also discovers that developing an "illness" is a socially acceptable means of avoiding situations that make it feel inadequate. Even though this strategy has the outward appearance of resignation, the desire for social advantage is still present. Consequently, "illness" is often exploited to control others.

Adler offers an illustrative example. A married couple professed to believe in free love. The husband began having affairs with the wife's consent, and she subsequently developed agoraphobia. Because of her illness, the husband had to accompany her whenever she wanted to go out, and thereafter his freedom to have sexual liaisons was strictly curtailed. The wife's illness was functional. It had a purpose. In effect, she was using her "weakness" to exercise greater power. Individuals can be fully aware, partially aware, or completely unaware of their ultimate objectives, although Adler, unlike Freud, did not give special emphasis to the unconscious and understood the mind as a more balanced and integrated composite of conscious and unconscious parts.

From a theoretical perspective, Adler departed from psychoanalytic doctrine by replacing sexual motivation with social motivation, and the Oedipus complex with the inferiority complex—although one could argue that the inferiority complex is simply a social version of the Oedipus complex. The inferior child must compete with its superior father for maternal attention, a prize that within the family signifies status.

Adler was never entirely happy with the term "complex," because he thought his ideas about inferiority and compensation might have explanatory value beyond psychoanalysis. He believed that inferiority and striving for superiority affect almost every aspect of identity and behavior. "To be a man," Adler said, "means to suffer from an inferiority feeling which constantly drives him to overcome it." This grandiose summation betrays loftier ambitions, the possibility that we can observe in ourselves the operation of a principle that, like natural selection, is applicable to all living things. Even basic cellular life-forms are, in relative terms, engaged in a struggle for ascendance. With respect to compensation, it is interesting that human beings, who do not have a cheetah's speed, a rhino's armor, or an elephant's strength, are planetary overlords.

It has been suggested that Adler's thoughts on power-seeking have been misunderstood, and that, in reality, he was more interested in power as a means of improving self-control than power as a means of controlling others. But Adler's psychology cannot be made more palatable by downplaying its evolutionary origins and the personal and political power struggles that underlie much of our social reality. Adler was a committed socialist, but ironically, his account of humanity seems to legitimize capitalism. We compete with each other and want to get ahead. That's who we are. Perhaps this explains why Adler's work was particularly influential in the United States.

In spite of his preoccupation with power, which acquired darker nuances after World War II, there is much in Adler's writing that is warm, optimistic, and hopeful. He encourages us to be brave and not to worry inordinately about failure. The important thing is to try, to simply do one's best. We are weak and have flaws. We are only human. But, he assures us, that doesn't really matter. What *really* matters is how we cope with our weaknesses. He asks us to view them not as handicaps or deficiencies, but as a resource: latent potential. He argues that our vulnerabilities can provide us with vital compensatory energies that can carry us forward and help us to achieve our goals.

For two million years it was relatively easy for human beings to feel good about themselves. Living in small hunter-gatherer tribes, there wasn't much competition. You might not be the leader, but you might be able to run faster than anyone else. You might have the keenest eyesight or the most fetching smile. You might have the sweetest singing voice or make the sharpest tools. Today, with global connectivity, it's almost impossible to be the best at anything. We compete in a tribe that has seven and a half billion members. It is a world in which it is all too easy to feel inferior and overcompensate in damaging ways: steroid addiction, faddish diets, unnecessary cosmetic surgery, punishing exercise routines, mania to succeed, the exhausting pursuit of various imaginary ideals and unreachable states of perfection. We have an unprecedented number of opportunities to compare ourselves unfavorably with others who occupy elevated positions in a vast, interconnected hierarchical network, and our compensations have become as tragic as they are grotesque.

We are always being urged to broaden our horizons. It has become received wisdom. But perhaps we should broaden some horizons while we judiciously narrow others. A musician of middling talent might still shine on a local concert platform, and a competent chess player might still be hailed a prodigy by his provincial club.

Aim high, by all means. But occasionally aim low. In a world that frequently exposes our inadequacies, we must rely on small successes and achievements to sustain us.

10

WANTS

The Acquisition Trap

By the age of fourteen months, most infants have learned to point.* Infants point for a number of reasons, but the most frequently observed purpose is to draw parental attention to something that the infant wants. We start wanting things early.

Freud thought that ultimately, for most of us, life is reducible to work and love. We want to be industrious and contribute to society; we want to love and be loved. These objectives are closely allied to the superordinate benefits of life having direction and meaning. Making a contribution to society and forming intimate relationships will make us feel more rounded, more complete. These are legitimate wants and, in many respects, we actually *need* both.

We have many more supplementary desires beyond these Freudian necessities. Since industrialization and mass production, the number of things we can point at in our environment has risen

---

* Pointing was originally considered an exclusively human behavior, but actually, chimpanzees point too.

exponentially. There have never been more things to covet or buy. Yet the acquisition of possessions, irrespective of whether those possessions are physical or digital, doesn't seem to make people any happier. Worse still, it is self-evident that for a significant percentage of the population, such wants have become inflated, unrealistic, and objectively impossible: "I want to be young again—I want to be perfect—I want to live forever." Those desires are being met by the marketplace: there are several cryonic preservation facilities where you can buy eternal life (or at least the expectation of eternal life).[1]

The existential psychotherapist Irvin Yalom wrote: "So much wanting. So much longing. . . . Pain that is always there, whirring continuously just beneath the membrane of life."[2] Spiritual teachers have made the same observation for thousands of years; however, their answers, asceticism and the promise of heavenly reward, have limited appeal to many who live in the Aladdin's cave of a prosperous economy. Those promises have seemed even less appealing since the computer screen on our desk and the phone in our hand became shop windows. We think we can buy anything and everything, and, in a sense, we can. As Arthur Janov suggested, we might want so many things because we are actually trying to satisfy a more fundamental emotional need. The pursuit and acquisition of "things"—substitute gratifications—continues because such needs cannot be satisfied by shallow indulgences. We are thus engaged in a labor that is as pointless as trying to fill a hole in the ground with air instead of earth.

When we desire unnecessary things, we reinforce a set of attitudes that alter our relationship with reality. These attitudes have a surprisingly global influence on mental functioning. They even affect the way we respond to our own thoughts.

This approach to the problem of constant wanting was proposed by the German-born psychoanalyst Erich Fromm. In 1976, Fromm published a book titled *To Have or to Be?* In it, he argued that human beings would be happier if they were less preoccupied with acquiring things and more open to experience. His thesis can easily be misconstrued as a late example of counterculture idealism, but Fromm's reasoning is more nuanced. He offers us subtle insights into the workings of the mind and arrives at pragmatic recommendations for personal growth and social change.

Like many other significant twentieth-century psychoanalysts, Fromm, who was from an Orthodox Jewish family, had to leave his homeland after Hitler seized power in 1933. He lived in Switzerland and then New York, where he taught at Columbia University. Fromm didn't like self-help books. He wrote disparagingly about their fraudulence, how they might cause harm, and how they exploited people's "malaise." Ironically, self-help books—albeit self-help books of a very sophisticated kind—were his legacy. *The Art of Loving*, first published in 1956, became an international best seller, and it is still widely read. Within the first few pages, he offers a simple but helpful distinction between *falling* in love and the more permanent state of *being* in love, "or as we might better say, of 'standing' in love." This juxtaposition, which finds a new use for an otherwise unremarkable word, "standing," is typical of his expressive gifts.

According to Fromm, the core problems of the human condition are separation from nature and other people. As a consequence, we frequently experience feelings of powerlessness and anxiety. Such feelings can be overcome by self-discovery, recognition of personal uniqueness, and development of the capacity to love. These ideas, in one form or another, had already been circulating in the psychotherapeutic community for several decades. Fromm's contribution wasn't to identify what human beings could do to lead better lives, but rather to specify what stops them from leading better lives. The major obstacle, as he saw it, was the acquisitive mindset typical of postindustrial societies. Too much wanting prevents us from getting what we really need.

Fromm suggested that human mental life is characterized by two basic states, or "modes": the "having mode" and the "being mode." The "having mode" is the mode of wanting things. Of course, we must have *some* possessions in order to live comfortably. But in the West, much of what we do is motivated by acquisitiveness. Wanting and acquiring are so much a part of us that the desire to own things affects our entire worldview. The extent of this influence is more profound than most people realize, and the consequences are almost wholly negative. Indeed, the effects are so pernicious that we are frequently unable to enjoy the simple

pleasure of being alive. We get caught up in cycles of craving and disappointment. More often than not, "we are glad when we have killed the time we are trying so hard to save."

Identity and esteem have become entangled with ownership, to the extent that self-worth is calculated according to the number of possessions a person has acquired. Consumption has become an entirely inappropriate and unreliable surrogate for self-respect. Emblems of wealth, such as massively expensive watches or hand-bags, are frequently used to signal importance—but the only distinction this displays is that the owner may have more things than other people. Things are just things. A Rolls-Royce might signal prestige, but it is still only a car, a vehicle with an engine and four wheels. In some respects, people who buy a Rolls-Royce to enhance their status haven't actually acquired a car at all: they have acquired more egocentricity; they have bought an "image." This might make them feel good, at least for a while, but, as we know, an inflated ego will diminish the quality and immediacy of experience.

Desire is routinely intensified by modern advertising, which has psychoanalytic origins. Many techniques devised to influence consumer behavior were invented in the 1920s by Freud's American nephew Eddie Bernays, who realized that his uncle's theories could be used to inform marketing campaigns. The id is insatiable, human beings are narcissistic, and objects can symbolize qualities such as glamour or virility. He introduced celebrity endorsement, product placement, and the use of sex to sell automobiles. He linked merchandise with unconscious desires. His greatest public relations triumph was getting women to start buying cigarettes by associating smoking with women's suffrage. He described cigarettes as "torches of freedom"—alluding obliquely to the Statue of Liberty. When women parted with their money, they were buying freedom and independence as well as tobacco.

In 1927, the Wall Street banker Paul Mazur said, "We must shift America from a needs, to a desires, culture. People must be trained to desire, to want new things even before the old had been entirely consumed. . . . Man's desires must overshadow his needs."[3] Corporations offer us the prospect of personal transformation through ownership—an outcome as implausible as overcoming gender inequality by buying cigarettes. No one has ever "self-actualized" by acquiring a Rolex or the latest smartphone.

Natasha was an oligarch's wife. To say that she was beautiful doesn't really do justice to her appearance; it only highlights the limitations of language. Natasha was *exceptionally* beautiful. Her origins were relatively humble, and she had learned at an early age that her beauty could be exploited. She became an extremely successful model and eventually married a multibillionaire. For many years she was regarded as one of the world's most beautiful women. Even so, she still decided to have cosmetic surgery in order to approximate more closely some imaginary ideal. She also followed a strict beauty regimen devised by a team of experts in her entourage, who worked tirelessly to maintain the suppleness of her body, the purity of her complexion, and the thick, fiery, Byzantine luxuriance of her hair.

Being in the same room as Natasha could be disconcerting. It is one thing to see outstanding beauty represented on a poster or in a magazine; it is another thing entirely to be in its presence. I can remember thinking that she seemed barely human, almost alien. Her beauty was transcendent, so far above the ordinary that she aroused wonder rather than desire.

Natasha's art collection was extensive. She owned as many paintings as you might find in a modestly sized museum. She also owned fleets of cars, a super-yacht, houses and apartments in the major capitals of Europe, as well as in New York, priceless jewelry, and a plane. Natasha worried about her teenage sons, one of whom was something of a rebel, but this was her single clearly defined concern. Her husband was devoted to her, and she had a wide circle of friends and associates, many of them influential politicians and celebrities. It struck me that she was the nearest thing to a goddess I had ever encountered. She could have anything she wanted, anything at all, and I suspected that her power, if she ever chose to use it nefariously, could be exercised beyond the reach of any legal jurisdiction. She had absolute freedom.

Her expression was rarely animated. She never smiled and frequently complained of feeling miserable and lonely. Her stillness did not communicate composure, but rather indifference, paralysis, and the deadening of emotion. No matter how many Impressionists or stately homes she purchased, it made no difference to how she felt inside. Once, she fell silent and held my gaze for a long time. Her eyes, which had unusually dilated pupils, were like discs of jet. I shifted on my chair, because her fixed, intense scrutiny made me feel uncomfortable. "I want peace," she said. "All I want is peace." It was as though life had become so utterly meaningless that the idea of rest, possibly even eternal rest, was starting to look attractive.

Fromm's indictment of materialism and its false promises was hardly new in the 1970s. Nor was it unexpected coming from a left-wing intellectual. The more interesting aspects of Fromm's critique concern the cognitive repercussions of the "having mode."

Most people are not aware of how acquisitiveness alters their entire psychological landscape and orientation. The "having mode" is associated with narrow-mindedness and rigidity. Opinions become possessions, so we tend to hang on to them, even when they have been successfully challenged. We stop caring about what's actually right or wrong.

The "having mode" operates at such a deep level that its influence can be detected in language. For example, we use phrases like "I have insomnia" when we mean "I can't sleep," or "I have a wife" when we mean "I'm married." Possessive constructions objectify and alienate. They color relationships with inappropriate notions of ownership. We think of romantic love, for example, as something that we can look for, find, and possess. It is associated with immutability. But love is an ongoing process; it changes and grows. The imposition of artificial limits and boundaries, through objectification, denies the essential fluidity of love. When we talk about love, we are really talking about "loving"—a reciprocal, evolving experience.

Our sense of security is often based not on love, but on "things." This means that loss of things is experienced as a loss of self. People become extremely fearful of losing their possessions, because material loss is mistakenly felt as an existential threat. This attitude encourages mistrust and paranoia and motivates further acquisition to reduce anxiety. Our personal, defensive fortifications are made from luxury goods. "Things" simultaneously protect us and isolate us from others.

Acquisitiveness even affects the way we read books. We read to acquire cultural property, and we hurry from volume to volume in order to expand our estate. We forget that reading is pleasurable. When we treat knowledge like a possession, it loses something of its richness. Accumulating knowledge becomes mechanical, the

transfer of information from the page to the brain. Being knowledgeable is more than *having* knowledge. Like loving, knowing is
more fluid and interactive.

According to Fromm, the fundamental reason why we fear
death is that we are terrified of losing what we "have," not only
our material goods but also our bodies. We fear losing the things
that we have mistakenly construed as ourselves. Overcoming our
fear of dying does not necessitate any form of spiritual preparation. It is achieved by continual efforts, throughout life, to reduce the influence of the "having mode." The less we invest in
our possessions and the less we relate to our thoughts and feelings
as possessions, the less we will have to lose. These ideas are supported by research investigating the therapeutic benefits of ad-
ministering psychedelic drugs to cancer patients with a terminal
diagnosis.[4] The precise therapeutic mechanisms are still unclear,
but such patients frequently say that they have lost their fear of
dying, because transcendent experiences have reduced the degree
to which they can identify with their minds and bodies. Their
sense of ownership has been weakened. "The instruction on how
to die," Fromm tells us, "is the same as the instruction on how to
live."

Fromm supplied many examples of how the "having mode"
shapes our sense of self and modulates intimacy. By wanting more
we become less, and the less we are, the more we want. The phenomenon is similar to addiction. What we identify as the solution
to our problems is often the cause. Possessions will not make us
whole or more accessible to others. Wants escalate and eventually
become obscenely overblown and unrealistic. Life becomes the
breathless pursuit of impossible dreams.

The alternative to the "having mode" is the "being mode."
When we are in the "being mode," we are not motivated to acquire

things. Instead, we are in a state of readiness to engage with experience. The exact nature of experiencing cannot be defined. A person's sense of "being" is always unique, subjective, and ultimately incommunicable. Experience is open-ended, flexible, and interactive. It is a process and not a "thing." As soon as you try to *have* an experience, the limiting nature of acquisition will immediately degrade the quality of that experience. If "having" is primarily about possession, about holding on, then "being" is primarily about letting go—letting go, even, of each passing second, so that it can be replaced by the next. This lack of attachment is a prerequisite for personal growth. To find fulfillment, we must not cling to mere emblems of identity and security. We must stop "sitting on" our possessions, even our intellectual possessions, and allow ourselves to connect more directly with the world and those around us.

Digital technology makes it easier for us to acquire things, but it also provides us with a ready means of converting our experiences into possessions. Studies show that individuals who take incessant photographs and make video recordings of experiences (such as attending a concert) remember less than those who simply focus on what they can see and hear.[5] Memory, consolidated with accompanying emotions, is being supplanted by emotionally inert images on a small screen. Such images are then frequently displayed on social media to perform the same function as status-enhancing possessions. The storage of "memories" on a smartphone—instead of in the brain—is a compelling example of the objectification of experience and self-alienation.

Fromm suggested that his distinction between "having" and "being" modes is applicable beyond the lives of individuals. He argued, with prophetic zeal, that if Western societies do not shift from the "having mode" to the "being mode," ecological disasters and global conflict will be the inevitable and final fate of humanity. Some people, Fromm observed, are content to appreciate a flower, while others must pick it. The latter have the satisfaction of owning the flower, but a picked flower will soon die. Ultimately, almost all ecological problems have their beginnings in some form of appropriation. The "having mode" also drives nuclear proliferation—*We have more bombs than you*—and motivates the various territorial disputes that cause wars.

Sometimes, Fromm's visionary writing comes close to expressing metaphysical sentiments; however, his basic observations are entirely consistent with evolutionary psychology. Pleasure is usually associated with activities that increase the chances of reproductive success. It may be that natural selection has limited our capacity to experience lasting pleasure, in order to maximize the motivational potential of dissatisfaction. The more dissatisfied we are, the more likely we are to pursue pleasure, which tends, in turn, to advance our reproductive interests. If orgasms produced lasting satisfaction, then our ancestors would have been content to mate infrequently, and humans may have become extinct. This evolutionary mechanism, which precludes lasting satisfaction, resonates with Fromm. It might even be an antecedent of the "having mode." In tribal societies, a dominant male *had* allies, food, and access to females. However, if *having* all of these things didn't make him feel satisfied, he would then be motivated to form new alliances, hunt farther afield, where he could find more animals, and mate with more females from different tribes, all of which would increase his chances of survival and reproductive success.

Fromm concluded *To Have or to Be?* with a description of "the new man"—the prototype of what humanity might become. He must be willing to renounce all forms of "having" so that he can "fully be." He must define himself with reference to his interests and inclinations, his relationships, and love—rather than his possessions. He must transcend narcissism, recognize his limitations, and live in the moment. Fromm's suggestions are practical, positive, and optimistic. If we all started living according to his principles tomorrow, the world would be a safer, more peaceful, and happier place. However, when reading Fromm, it is easy to overlook the fact that he has already given us good reason to suspect that following his recommendations won't be easy. There is a catch: conceptual small-print.

Having just encountered Fromm's notion of the "having mode," it is likely you will take possession of this idea and add it to your mental furniture. It will almost immediately become inert information, intellectual property. We are so entrenched in the "having mode" that knowing about the "having mode" isn't enough to ensure change. But if you paused, reflected, and fully inhabited this moment—right here, right now—what then? What might you experience?

11

ADVERSITY

Rooted Sorrows

Adversity is inescapable. There are many different types of adversity, and it can be encountered at any point during the course of a life. It may come in the form of minor but frequent stresses (such as work problems), or in the form of major but infrequent life events (such as bereavement). Accidents, disease, rejection, bullying—war, terrorism, natural disasters—the list of potential misfortunes is indeed limitless. And for many people, life becomes challenging at an early age. A 2016 World Health Organization fact sheet summarizing the results of several international studies estimated that a quarter of all adults have been physically abused as children; moreover, one in five women, as well as one in thirteen men, have been sexually abused.[1] Romance and love are supposed to make us happy, but the Centers for Disease Control and Prevention in the United States reported in 2010 that domestic violence is a problem for a staggering one in three couples.[2] The victims of domestic abuse, mostly but not entirely women, often develop anxiety, depression, and severe mental illnesses.[3] The pernicious effects of adversity are checked by many factors, not least of which is resilience, a characteristic that varies enormously from person to person; however, even the most robust individual must expect to experience some adversity and suffer as a result.

Macbeth, in Shakespeare's eponymous play, challenges his doctor: "Canst thou not minister to a mind diseased, / Pluck from the memory a rooted sorrow?" Rooted sorrows are impediments to growth. They disturb our mood, make us apprehensive about the future, and erode our confidence. They redefine us according to our limitations rather than our potential.

Many late nineteenth-century case studies document a link between adversity and mental illness. The symptoms of hysteria were frequently attributed to "subconscious" memories of bad experiences. Today, it is assumed that most psychological problems have their ultimate provenance in historical events. The past might not provide a complete explanation of why a particular person has a particular set of symptoms, but it is usually implicated as a contributory factor. Such a relationship is explicitly acknowledged in some psychiatric diagnoses, most notably posttraumatic stress disorder (PTSD). In PTSD, emotionally charged memories cause a variety of intrusive and repetitive symptoms, such as flashbacks and nightmares. Affected individuals also experience a general state of tension and avoid situations and objects that remind them of the traumatic experience.

Bad things happen, impressions linger, and distressing memories become a fixed feature of who we are. We can't travel back in time and alter events and outcomes. We can't change the past. We can only attempt to accommodate it. The vocabulary of psychotherapy is full of terms that describe the accommodation of distressing memories. Patients "work through" and "come to terms with" problems; they achieve "closure" and "resolve" complexes. Different schools of psychotherapy advocate different approaches to treatment; however, all of them seem to be at least partially effective. What underlies successful emotional adjustment? Is it possible to identify fundamental therapeutic processes, and if so, to what extent can we make use of this knowledge when we are bruised and buffeted by the inescapable turbulence of adversity?

Ed was a man in his early twenties and somewhat boyish. It took me a while to get him to talk about what had transpired on his birthday. His speech was indirect and he had a tendency to digress.

"Tell me what happened . . ."

"There are gaps. I can't remember everything."

"Just tell me what you can."

He shifted in his chair and scratched his head. "We went to a nightclub—to celebrate."

"We . . . ?"

"Me and a couple of my friends, Jake and Wayne. There was a queue outside and the doorman didn't let us in until quite late."

The three friends had already been drinking beforehand. Even so, they headed straight for the bar. They had a few more beers, then attempted to become acquainted with a group of young women who were also celebrating a birthday. When the young women left the bar area to dance, Ed and his friends followed.

"It wasn't a very big dance floor, the club was packed—and I was quite drunk. I bumped into this guy who was wearing a glow-in-the-dark T-shirt. He was dancing with a blonde girl— very pretty—and he just turned on me and started shouting. I apologized—not that he could hear me, the music was too loud—and I kind of backed off." Ed raised his arms and positioned his palms either side of his head, reconstructing his movements. "'Okay, okay—my fault. Sorry.' And then he pushed me. I couldn't believe it. You know, it was an accident and I'd just apologized. What else did he want me to do? I suppose he was showing off in front of the girl. I squared up to him and then Jake grabbed my arm and pulled me away."

The three friends returned to the bar and carried on drinking. The altercation had been unpleasant, but they weren't going to let it spoil their night. Shortly after, the man in the glow-in-the-dark T-shirt reappeared, accompanied by three other men and the blonde woman. As the man walked past, he barged into Ed, causing Ed to spill his drink.

"I know I shouldn't have reacted, I know I should have ignored him, but it just didn't seem right. I called him a prick and he turned round and told me to fuck off. I'm not sure what happened next—there was some scuffling—and then punches were being thrown—and then the bouncers got involved. A few seconds later I was being frog-marched toward a door. The door flew open and then closed and I found myself in an alley with the guy and two of his mates. The door had locked automatically. I would have run but they were blocking my exit. I thought—right—this isn't good—I'm going to get beaten up really badly. All of a sudden the guy comes forward—lunges—and stabs me—right here." Ed touched his side, gently, as if the injury were still tender. His speech, which had been fluent until that point, stalled. The recollection of the stabbing made him shudder. He swallowed and continued, but his sentences were now short and fragmented. "The guy—he ran off with the other two—and there was a lot of blood—and I looked down—and thought—oh shit this is bad—this is really bad—so I

banged on the door—but no one let me in—and I was just panick-
ing and thinking oh shit, oh shit, what's going to happen now?—
and then Jake and Wayne came round the corner."

Ed took a deep breath, and when he released it, he produced
a faint whistle, the pitch of which descended a steep gradient. His
hands were trembling.

"I can't remember what happened next or who did what. There
was some shouting, activity, but I ended up sitting on the ground
with my back against a wall and Jake was saying, 'There's an ambulance coming. You're going to be okay.' I kept looking down
and seeing all this blood—and I was starting to feel faint—'It's all
right,' Jake kept on saying. 'It's going to be okay.' But he sounded
anxious, *really* anxious, and I thought, I don't want to die like this.
I can't die like this, not on my birthday . . . pathetic."

A police car and ambulance arrived. Ed was given first aid by
paramedics and then rushed to the nearest hospital.

"I can remember lying there in the ambulance and feeling
pretty awful. Everything went black—and I came round again—
and then it went black again. I kept on passing out. And then . . ."
he shook his head and appeared embarrassed.

"What?"

"This part—well—this part is weird."

"Okay."

"I was like . . . out of my body, floating—looking down on
myself—and then there was this tunnel and a light, this beautiful
light." He studied me to gauge my reaction. I gestured for him to
continue. "Then I was back in my body and feeling—well—I'm
not sure what I was feeling."

"Confused?"

"Yes, confused—very confused."

Earlier that evening, Ed had left his home in order to celebrate his birthday. Instead of having a good time, he'd almost died. His brush with death had been so close that he'd had a near-death experience.

Listening to patients like Ed is deeply affecting. I've heard many similar stories. Some of them ended in appalling tragedy—carnage, flames, debris, bodies on water. We are usually inured to cautionary adages concerning the fragility of life and the haphazard nature of fate through overexposure: "Live each day as if it's your last." But whenever I found myself sitting in front of a person like Ed, tired sayings recovered their poignancy and power. I always thought: *We aren't so different. That could have been me.*

Life hangs by a thread.

Individuals who are uncomfortable self-disclosing can be retraumatized if rashly encouraged to discuss negative life events. They have to feel completely safe before they can open up. Even so, it is widely accepted that talking is strongly associated with successful long-term emotional adjustment, whereas suppression tends to be associated with only short-term gains. There are many reasons why suppression isn't likely to be a very effective long-term coping strategy, but significant among them will be diminished opportunities for eliciting social support.

Talking about traumatic events isn't easy. Affected individuals frequently blame themselves when bad things happen. They are made mute by shame, guilt, or despair. Brain scanning studies show that Broca's area, a critical language center, is deactivated when traumatic events are remembered.[4] People quite literally lose their voices. The words aren't there anymore. Brain activity spreads across the nonverbal right hemisphere and the amygdala (a small, almond-shaped structure that generates fear and anxiety) glows fiercely in the right temporal lobe. Emotions seem to be locked in, dangerously confined. Meanwhile, the cortical area that allows people to express how they are feeling is reduced to a dull luminescence. Patients who can't express their emotions often experience terrible frustration, a prolonged buildup of tension that might suddenly erupt as an angry outburst.

Seneca, an ancient Roman philosopher, said that "tears ease the soul." Crying is usually accompanied by a sense of release and followed by a period of exhausted calm. I have noticed that many patients need to cry before they can proceed beyond a certain point in therapy. Crying can wash away obstacles to progress. Tears that arise because of strong emotions are chemically different from tears caused by a physical irritant. In the 1980s, the biochemist William Frey analyzed tears produced by upset and tears produced by irritation (for example, onions). He found that protein concentrations in emotional tears exceeded the protein content of irritant-induced tears by 24 percent. There are more stress hormones in emotional tears—it is almost as if they are being flushed out.[5]

Aristotle originally used the term "catharsis" to describe the effect of the dramatic arts (especially tragic plays) on the mind and body. It has a somewhat different set of connotations when used by psychotherapists and over the years has accrued multiple layers of meaning related to purification and cleansing. Psychotherapists use another term, "abreaction," when referring specifically to the outpouring of emotion previously attached to repressed memories. Catharsis and abreaction are frequently used interchangeably; they have in common the basic assumption that the release of emotion can be restorative.

The venting of feelings and the amelioration of psychological distress have been linked for centuries. Demonic possession, the first explanation of mental illness, was treated with exorcism, prompting displays of extreme emotion. Mesmerism, the precursor of hypnotism, produced mounting nervous excitement that led to convulsions, collapse, and recovery. A similar pattern of heightened emotionality and collapse is typical of Pentecostal faith healing. The curative effects of these rituals, all of which resemble forms of Aristotelian theatricality, are very probably attributable to catharsis.

At the end of the nineteenth century, Josef Breuer supposed that the purging of emotion was a key factor in the treatment of mental illness. The treatment that he pioneered (prior to his professional association with Freud) is still known as the "cathartic method." When we talk, particularly with the aim of coming to terms with a traumatic experience, words alone (even when we are able to find them) might not be enough. Many psychotherapists since Breuer have observed that talking in a cool and detached manner about distressing past events seems to be less helpful than when recollections are accompanied by emotion. By the early years of the twentieth century, the cathartic method had metamorphosed into Freudian psychoanalysis.

Interest in catharsis as a treatment method revived during the two world wars. Almost immediately after the outbreak of World War I, soldiers began developing symptoms that were not attributable to their physical injuries. These included paralysis, mutism, blindness, and loss of hearing. Others displayed signs of extreme psychological distress, such as tearfulness, anxiety, tremors, and episodes of panic. These symptoms—both the inexplicable physical problems and the more understandable psychological problems—were collectively described as shell shock, nervous shock, and war neurosis. Many doctors advised against returning shell-shocked soldiers to the front, but the military authorities were worried that mass infirmity would compromise their war efforts. The swift treatment of shell-shocked soldiers became a pressing issue. Existing treatments were experimental, theoretically weak, and at worst, barbaric. They included hunger cures, isolation in dark rooms, and painful electrical "stimulation." A more compassionate approach was advocated by Ernst Simmel, a German battalion physician who, in 1916, became the medical director of a specialist hospital. His methods were various: he employed psychoanalysis, dream interpretation, and hypnosis. His principal objective was to achieve catharsis. He supposed that recurring nightmares, a common feature of shell shock, represented failed attempts at catharsis. Within a few years, Simmel was reporting the successful treatment of very large numbers of patients. News of his success spread, and when Freud finally heard about Simmel's accomplishments, he was extremely impressed.

Interest in catharsis as a treatment method dwindled after 1918, but during World War II psychiatrists were faced with the same problem. Many traumatized soldiers were unfit for combat, and the authorities were anxious to return them to battle. Naturally, psychiatrists consulted the work of their predecessors to guide treatment practices, and therapeutic procedures that aroused strong emotional responses became popular once again. Around the time of World War II, catharsis was more likely to be described as "abreaction."

The most enthusiastic advocate of abreaction in the postwar years was a flamboyant figure whose name had become associated with the development of cutting-edge, controversial treatments.

For several decades, he was regarded as one of the most important psychiatrists in Great Britain—and at the peak of his career he was counted among the most influential psychiatrists in the world. You won't find him mentioned in any mainstream histories of psychiatry, however. Since his death in 1988, his life and work have been tactfully ignored. Why should this have happened? Clues can be found in how people remember him. He was once described by a colleague as having "a whiff of sulphur about him."[6]

William Sargant was a broadcaster and a respected author, a Royal Society of Medicine president, a founding member of the World Psychiatric Association, and the head of the department of psychological medicine at St. Thomas's Hospital in London. His writing was praised by the likes of Aldous Huxley, Robert Graves, and Bertrand Russell. Long before most of his contemporaries, he realized that the rising incidence of mental illness was a major problem and that failure to provide effective care would have serious social consequences. He sought to avert the impending catastrophe by advancing psychiatry as a biological science and a branch of physical medicine, advocating brain surgery, the induction of comas using insulin, electroconvulsive therapy (ECT), and narcosis (or deep sleep therapy).[7] All of these have now been condemned (often, but not always, for good reasons) as reckless, dangerous, or ethically questionable.

Treatment by narcosis was originally developed in the 1920s.[8] Patients were sedated so that they slept (apart from when sleep was briefly interrupted for meals and voiding) for durations of up to several months. In Sargant's "sleep room," Ward 5 of the Royal Waterloo Hospital in London, patients were given extremely high doses of chlorpromazine (a major tranquilizer) and three sessions of ECT per week. The justification for this extreme regimen was the eradication of bad memories. However, memory loss was of course global: good memories disappeared along with the bad ones. Many of Sargant's patients awoke to discover that they could remember very little about their former lives. Other patients weren't so lucky—and died in their sleep.

Sargant also developed a form of drug-assisted psychotherapy, the purpose of which was to intensify recollections of traumatic experiences and trigger a strong abreaction. Combat veterans had been encouraged to abreact while under the influence of drugs during World War I—although then, the procedure was mostly undertaken using hypnosis. Sargant had many opportunities to refine this intervention during (and after) World War II, when he was obliged to treat soldiers and civilians suffering from battle-related neuroses and nervous shock. He used ether poured on a mask, intravenous methadrine (a form of methamphetamine), and inhaled carbon dioxide to "excite" patients as they recounted their traumatic experiences. Sargant discovered that he could embellish a patient's story or even replace it with a thematically related fantasy and this would still be therapeutic. For example, he might tell a drugged patient to imagine being trapped in a burning tank, when no such event had actually happened. The crucial ingredient of the procedure was the strength of the abreaction, that is, whether or not a patient's emotional state could be raised to what Sargant described as a "grande finale of rage and terror." Collapse was followed by a period of calm, after which patients reported improvements. When they subsequently remembered their actual traumatic events, they were no longer distressed.

Immediately after abreacting, patients were often in an impressionable state, and Sargant could not resist implanting what he judged to be helpful ideas in their minds. A sinister preoccupation with indoctrination and thought control was constantly surfacing in his clinical work.

It is difficult to make an objective assessment of Sargant's contribution to psychiatry. His personality gets in the way. He has been described as overbearing, arrogant, a bully—even as a monster. Yet we should endeavor to separate the man from his work. Excitatory abreaction confirms some of Breuer's and Freud's early clinical observations—namely, that emotionally charged recollection is more therapeutic than neutral recollection. And it is one of the most dramatic demonstrations of a "cathartic method" practiced in modern times.

Sargant was right to stress the urgent need for brief, affordable treatments. We do need quick fixes—desperately. But for most people with mental illnesses, a jolt of electricity to the brain or a sedative won't make life much better. Some people are undoubtedly helped by these methods, but the treatments are not—nor have they ever been—cure-alls. Sargant was impatient to create a medical utopia, but he probably caused more suffering than he succeeded in eliminating.

Throughout his life, Sargant was dismissive of talking cures. He thought psychoanalysis was intellectually weak and took far too long. Yet the only treatment Sargant pioneered that hasn't attracted a significant amount of criticism is excitatory abreaction—a form of psychotherapy.

John Watson (the hapless dispenser of very bad child-care advice) is now regarded as the father of American behaviorism. On discovering the work of Ivan Pavlov, Watson recognized that the Russian physiologist's findings provided a firm foundation for a new form of psychopathology. Negative emotions, for example, could be understood as conditioned reflexes. Pavlov had famously demonstrated that after repeatedly pairing food with the sound of a bell, dogs could be conditioned to salivate in response to the sound of a bell alone. Watson believed that irrational fears like phobias might be the result of similar forms of associative learning.

With the assistance of another American psychologist, Rosalie Rayner, whom he later married, Watson conditioned a baby boy to fear a rat by pairing appearances of the animal with harsh, loud noises (although no subsequent efforts were made to relieve the boy of his acquired fear). Several years later, the psychologist Mary Cover Jones, also American, treated a child who was fearful of rabbits by giving him candy to eat whenever he was shown a rabbit. In the late 1950s, Joseph Wolpe, a South African psychiatrist, devised a comparable "counterconditioning" treatment, replacing food consumption with deep muscle relaxation. Patients were asked to enter a series of increasingly challenging situations while maintaining a relaxed state, the purpose of which was to inhibit fear. The final version of this treatment, "systematic desensitization," involved a combination of actual and imaginary encounters with feared objects and situations.

Systematic desensitization was an effective treatment and became the first form of behavioral psychotherapy to be widely practiced. It was radically different from previous forms of psychotherapy, because it worked even if the therapist knew nothing about the patient's mental state and memories. If fear is a conditioned response (and associations can be weakened or broken completely by counterconditioning), there is no need to probe the mind to any great depth.

Although systematic desensitization was revolutionary and influential, its theoretical rationale was vulnerable to criticism. One can dispense with the practice of deep muscle relaxation and patients will still get better. This suggests that, when successful, fear reduction is not attributable to counterconditioning, but rather to "habituation"—the tendency of the nervous system to become less reactive when exposure to a stimulus is prolonged. An everyday example of habituation would be ceasing to hear background noise when it continues for any significant length of time.

Physical reactivity is an important feature of emotion. We register the degree to which our bodies are reacting—heart rate, hyperventilation, perspiration—when we self-observe and determine how anxious we are. When we experience habituation, we adjust our judgments accordingly: "I don't feel so wound up, so perhaps there's nothing to worry about." Changes in physical reactivity are almost always accompanied by modified appraisals.

By the 1980s, only the most dogmatic behavioral therapists were still eschewing references to cognition. Many had started to explain the efficacy of their treatments with explicit reference to belief change. An anxious person might believe a particular situation to be dangerous; however, if he or she stays in that situation long enough, anxiety will diminish—demonstrating that fearful expectations must have been exaggerated. Beliefs are then spontaneously corrected or replaced by new and more accurate beliefs.

There are obvious parallels between Sargant's experiments with excitatory abreaction and exposure therapies. Both involve the arousal of emotion and the tolerance of distress. For a period of time in the 1970s, a form of behavioral therapy known as "implosion" entered mainstream practice.[9] Anxious patients were encouraged to imagine their worst fears as vividly as possible and to introduce nightmarish elements into their fantasies. Someone with a spider phobia might describe encountering a spider the size of a house.

In many respects, behavioral therapy can be construed as the provision of various frameworks within which anxious individuals can rehearse being courageous. That is certainly how Alfred Adler would have accounted for its success. The cultivation of courage is a central tenet of his individual psychology. For Adler, courage is not a thing we lack or possess, but something closer to a choice—a willingness to enter certain situations even when we know that we are taking a risk and might experience discomfort. Life, unfortunately, is full of difficult challenges that must be faced and overcome. Sometimes we must simply act, irrespective of our misgivings.

A person who has been humiliated at work by a disagreeable colleague will feel a certain amount of discomfort. He or she will think about what happened a great deal—or even dream about it.

As time passes, memories of the experience will interrupt mental activity with decreasing frequency, and the associated distress will diminish. Memories of the experience will then remain dormant unless the person chooses to think about them. Although a traumatized infantryman will possess memories that are more vivid and frightening, if he is able to adjust to his trauma, his adjustment will progress through roughly the same stages. Intrusive thoughts and nightmares, frequent at first, will become less of a problem, and over time, remembering the traumatic experience will cause him less discomfort. Memories will sink below the threshold of awareness and remain dormant until they are voluntarily retrieved.

All upsetting thoughts and memories seem to require a certain amount of "chewing over" before they can be "swallowed" and "digested." Moreover, if they are "indigestible," they will be "regurgitated."

In 1980, Stanley Rachman, originally one of Hans Eysenck's doctoral students and a leading advocate of behavioral therapy, published a theoretical paper in which he proposed that many apparently disconnected problems might be best understood as mental phenomena arising from emotional processing failures. Usually, emotional experiences are absorbed without sequelae, but if emotional processing is unsatisfactory or incomplete, then symptoms such as obsessions, disturbing dreams, intrusive thoughts, crying, and emotional volatility will persist. Stressful experiences, especially those we associate with the later development of PTSD, are so intense that the processing channels become overloaded and recollections reappear in the stream of consciousness.

Many psychological therapies probably work, to a very significant extent, by facilitating emotional processing. This is usually accomplished by regulating the intensity of reminiscences, starting with more manageable memories and building up to the most upsetting. At its simplest, this might involve having several conversations where memories are explored in great detail. Systematic desensitization and graded forms of exposure also conform to this incremental pattern. Even cathartic therapies, which can be so overwhelming they could potentially retraumatize patients, are graduated in practice. Full-blown abreaction, excitatory or otherwise, is rarely accomplished in one session. Patients often require several, each becoming more intense.

When bad things happen, people frequently try to manage their distress by avoiding things that remind them of the past, or by "cutting off" emotionally. Recreational drugs or alcohol are sometimes used to dull the pain.[10] But all forms of avoidance and denial are likely to interrupt emotional processing and delay recovery. Human beings seem to have an innate completion tendency that reworks traumatic information in "active memory" until it is reconciled with our broader understanding of the world.

It has been suggested that the critical feature of absorption is belief change—the same kind of belief change that might underpin the success of exposure therapies. Inaccurate beliefs can be corrected if a trauma is reimagined in a safe environment. The heart speeds up, nothing terrible happens, and the heart slows down again. Mind and body are reeducated. But successful belief change is probably one of many adjustments that occur simultaneously and interactively when people come to terms with any upsetting event. Other recalibrations are almost certainly taking place, and at many different levels—neurochemical, hormonal, neuroanatomical, psychological, and social.

Traumatic experiences cleave the self and trap a fragment of being—a frozen, historical incarnation—in the past. In order for a person to be whole again, in order to fully occupy the present, distressing memories must be fully reintegrated into the person's totality; they must become part of the affected individual's "story." Otherwise, the past will keep on interposing itself between the person and experience. Their story won't move on.

One day in the spring of 1987, while walking through a park, an American psychologist named Francine Shapiro* made what she subsequently described as a chance discovery.[11] She noticed that some disturbing thoughts suddenly disappeared when they occurred at the same time as spontaneous rapid eye movements. When she brought the same thoughts back to mind, they weren't quite so upsetting. Fascinated by her observation, she deliberately paired more negative thoughts and memories with rapid eye movements and found that the effect could be replicated. The eye movements involved swift oscillations between the extremities of an imaginary, diagonal line.

After a few days, Shapiro tested the technique on friends, colleagues, and workshop participants. The first thing she discovered was that most people can't maintain rapid eye movements for very long. She asked them to track hand movements instead (which is considerably easier). Her next discovery was that upsetting memories were neutralized by eye movements more effectively if they were broken down into composite parts: images, thoughts, or physical sensations. This is analogous, perhaps, to facilitating digestion by taking smaller mouthfuls. Over a period of many years, Shapiro formalized her procedure. It is now called Eye Movement Desensitization and Reprocessing (EMDR).

---

* Sadly, Francine Shapiro died on June 16, 2019.

The most distinctive feature of EMDR is the use of rapid eye movements to accelerate emotional processing. Rapid eye movements also occur during sleep when we dream. Is there a connection? Neuroscientists and psychologists now believe that one of the principal functions of dreaming is to dissolve emotions associated with unpleasant memories.[12] Individuals who have contemporaneous dreams about difficult life experiences, such as marital breakdown, are more likely to overcome depression and despair at a later date than those who do not. Rosalind Cartwright, a psychologist at Rush University in Chicago, collected dream reports from people who were going through a divorce. She then identified correspondences between emotional content in their dreams and the distressing emotional reality of their waking lives. Follow-up assessments were undertaken a year later. Cartwright found that it was only those individuals who had dreamed about their painful experiences (for example, dreams featuring their former partners as a character) when they were actually occurring who made full psychological recoveries. Their mood had improved, they had achieved greater financial stability, and they were more likely to have formed new intimate relationships. Those who had dreamed, but hadn't dreamed about their particular traumatic experiences at the time of their occurrence, did not make comparable gains. The implication of Cartwright's work is that people enjoy better mental health if they process distressing experiences more thoroughly.

When we say that "time heals," we might be mistaken. It is possible that it is not so much time that heals, but having certain kinds of dreams. If emotions were not detached from memories by dreaming, then distressing recollections would have the same emotional charge as actual events. The cumulative effect of this would be a continuous state of heightened arousal that would make everyday living intolerable. Even mild stress would make us startle and panic. Dreaming might be essential to emotional processing, facilitative—or both. For example, dreams might strip emotion from distressing memories to the extent that they become easier to talk about. Aspects of experience can then be explored at the higher levels of narrative identity and meaning.

It has been proposed that EMDR stimulates patterns of regional brain activity that overlap with those associated with dreaming.[13] Shapiro's procedure encourages the wakeful brain to perform the same operations that it normally performs while asleep. Although, interestingly, *any* oscillating shift of attention seems to achieve comparable results—tracking alternating taps on the knee or clicks played through headphones will also accelerate emotional processing. This might mean that the effects of EMDR are mediated by all forms of bilateral brain stimulation, and eye movements are simply the best-known example.

One of Shapiro's clinical observations bears interesting comparison with the work of William Sargant (who planted positive thoughts in his patients' minds after abreaction). Shapiro noticed that if EMDR was successful, her patients started having positive thoughts automatically. She described the case of a man who had served as an infantryman in Vietnam. One of his duties had been to unload dead soldiers from a rescue helicopter. Prior to treatment, whenever he'd thought of Vietnam he'd also thought of bodies. After receiving a relatively brief course of Eye Movement Desensitization, he was able to describe Vietnam as looking like "a garden paradise." It was the first time he'd had such a thought in over twenty years.

An incalculable number of words have been written about overcoming adversity, but the wisdom of saints and sages, scholars and intellectuals, philosophers and gurus, can be exchanged for a single valuable insight. The ultimate solution to a history of parental criticism, sexual abuse, divorce—or even being the victim of torture—is the assimilation of painful memories. Different people do different things to achieve this, but the assimilation of painful memories is what underlies the conquest of adversity. Psychotherapy has arrived at an extremely parsimonious and practicable answer, one well supported by neuroscience.[14]

Traumatic experiences are recollected not only by the mind, but by the muscles and viscera, the palpitating heart—by the bowels and the bladder. This is why when we process emotions they must be felt again: it is important to process embodied memories as well as mental residues.

Psychotherapy has always respected the body. Freud, from the very beginning, was more willing than any of his associates to acknowledge the blood-and-guts reality of being human—the anal and the phallic, viscous fluids and evacuations. This ruthless honesty can be contrasted with loftier conceptions of humanity. The spiritual response to adversity is transcendence: rise above it all, focus on the divine. For psychotherapists, this kind of transcendence is merely another form of evasion, like drinking whiskey or smoking cannabis to numb psychological pain. The work that needs to be done *must* be done. Otherwise the affected person will never be fully present. A part of the individual will remain trapped in the past, and the person's body will continue to remember terrors, even when his or her mind is seemingly unencumbered.

When we are able to process difficult emotions, we become whole again; the mind accommodates the body, and the body accommodates the mind. Past and present become ordered chapters in a meaningful narrative. Fragments of memory, shattered by adversity, can be pieced together again and slotted into place. Breuer and Freud knew this as early as 1893. On the very same page that they discussed the concepts of abreaction and catharsis for the first time, they also wrote about a mechanism that they believed might underlie healthy adjustment. A traumatic memory, they suggested, "enters the great complex of associations, it comes alongside other experiences, which may contradict it." The memory is "rectified by other ideas." They went on to say that "in this way a normal person is able to bring about the disappearance of the accompanying affect through the process of association."

Catharsis is probably as much about acknowledging our emotions as it is about release. When we allow ourselves to express our feelings, we are able to name them more accurately. Facing our fears gives the body an opportunity to habituate: the nervous system recalibrates, the amygdala dims, and we begin to see the world differently. Painful memories become less painful, and gradually they are integrated with more general memories.

The extent to which we are fully alive is largely determined by our capacity to absorb misfortune. We are, in a very real sense, made from adversity, and we should never be tempted to "pluck from the memory a rooted sorrow." That would be self-mutilation, or at best, another form of denial. As William Sargant so ably demonstrated in his sleep room, if you erase bad memories, you are also erasing a person.

Two years after finishing *Automat*, Edward Hopper painted *Chop Suey*. Like *Automat*, *Chop Suey* shows a young woman sitting at a restaurant table in New York; however, there's something familiar about her. Have we seen her before? My friend Walter Wells thought it was probably the same woman. He noted the same figure and the same somewhat bland beauty.

Although the young woman might be the same, her context is entirely different. There is no black void outside, and light is streaming through the windows. Through one of them we can see the lower half of the sign that gives the painting its name. We can read "Suey." The "Chop" is out of view.

Our young woman is no longer alone.

A couple are seated behind her, and more significantly, the chair opposite her is occupied. We can only see her companion's back, but the woman's general appearance suggests a doppelgänger. They are two of a kind. The young woman's expression is attentive; her head is tilted slightly to one side, as if listening. Her companion must be saying something.

The fact that the two women are almost identical has fueled speculation among art critics. It has been suggested that the second figure represents the young woman's repressed self. She has accepted aspects of her identity that she previously denied; inner divisions have been healed. She has, in effect, made friends with herself. She is wearing green, but there is no red this time, nothing to suggest inner conflict.

Has the problem been resolved? Has she come to terms with her past? Her hat has lost its drooping brim—Hopper's deftly executed allusion to the tragedian's mask—and the cloud of gloom has dissipated. She looks more confident. If she was inclined to judge herself badly before, she is now more at ease; she's telling herself a different story.

Walter wasn't convinced that *Chop Suey* merited this amount of deconstruction. He viewed the painting as a candid "urban pastoral." Even so, he was intrigued by the title.

In Hopper's time, chop suey was served only in American Chinese restaurants, a concoction thrown together from leftovers. Its name comes from the Cantonese phrase *tsap sui*, meaning odds and ends, or miscellaneous pieces. Walter, noting that there is no food in the bowl on the table between the two women, suggested that Hopper is using "chop suey" to signify not what the women are eating, but what they are saying. This could be read as casual, careless misogyny—but chitchat is an essential part of psychological development. A conversation made from leftovers, odds and ends and miscellaneous pieces, is a reasonable description of free association, Freud's principal therapeutic technique. The young woman has talked things through, as she might have done with a psychotherapist, and the void has gone. Back in the automat, she was caught up in her thoughts, ruminating about the past, and fearful of the future. Should she? Could she? Now she is living in the moment, connected to the present by conversation.

When she's finished, she'll walk out of the restaurant, onto the bustling street, and into sunlight. She will be ready to get on with her life. She will be ready to embody Fromm's dictum that if you look too hard for fulfillment, you won't find it. Fulfillment isn't something you seek and take possession of. It's an emergent property. There is only one answer to the problem of living, the act of living itself.

12

MEANING
Reasons to Exist

The small village of Struthof became an increasingly popular tourist destination in the early years of the twentieth century. Many who traveled there came from nearby Strasbourg, one of the great cultural and mercantile centers of northern Europe. The surrounding slopes were ideal for winter sports, and a new hotel-restaurant was built in 1906. Postcards show a snowy landscape teeming with men and women on skis. Some of the holidaymakers have noticed the presence of a photographer and look directly at the camera. The fresh mountain air was reputed to be curative, and the pleasant summer weather was perfect for walking.

By 1941, Struthof was no longer a tourist destination. It became a Nazi concentration camp. I'd never heard of Struthof—but the guidebook I was carrying recommended a detour. As promised, the route was scenic.

I have visited many places associated with violence and human degradation, places where people were massacred, tortured, or sacrificed, but none of them have saddened me more than

Struthof. The relics of cruelty that remain overlook a panorama of outstanding natural beauty. It was almost impossible to reconcile the warmth of the sun, the vista of the Donon massif, and the chill of history.

Beyond the perimeter fence, which was festooned with barbed wire, I saw a densely wooded ridge, and beyond this, more lush green hills that became gray and featureless as they receded into the distance. I was standing next to the gallows, where deportees had been forced to watch floodlit executions while the commandant and SS officers smoked cigars. My youngest son, then about seven years old, was at my side. Is it wise to take a child to a concentration camp? I agree with Bruno Bettelheim: you are never too young to learn about monsters.

I could feel tension in my chest, an accumulation of confusion and grief. I pictured hundreds of tourists skiing down the slope in front of me and then I gazed at the watchtowers and imagined the sweep of searchlights and the rattle of machine-gun fire.

Much of the concentration camp has been demolished, but enough survives to memorialize its dreadful past. In the "guinea pig room," medical experiments were conducted on Jews and gypsies. Subjects were sterilized, exposed to toxic gases, and cut to expedite infection with typhus. Most died after a period of protracted suffering. The autopsy table is still there: a solid block, the surface of which is covered with cracked white tiles. Medical testing was undertaken to prove misguided race theories; nothing of scientific value was discovered. There are hooks for impromptu hangings, and a slatted rack on which prisoners were tied and beaten to death. The execution room was designed with slanting floors so that blood would flow directly into a central drain. This feature prevented flooding and made cleaning easier. The small furnace in which bodies were burned also served as a boiler. It heated a hot water tank. In 1942, a professor of medicine decided that he wanted to create a collection of Jewish-Bolshevik skeletons. It was important to him that the specimens remain undamaged. Consequently, a community hall that had been used for festival gatherings was requisitioned and converted into a gas chamber.

An enormous subterranean structure code-named "the potato cellar" resembles a nuclear bunker. It contains twenty-two cells spaced over a distance of about four hundred feet. The cellar's intended purpose is unknown. What could be *so* deranged that even the SS might think it best to hide such activities beneath the ground?

Concentration camps have played a significant role in the history of psychotherapy. The threat of extermination scattered the first psychoanalysts (most of whom were Jewish) all over the world. Freud settled in London, and many of his disciples traveled to America. The Holocaust is uniquely disturbing. Germany and Austria were highly civilized nations, at the forefront of art, design, music, literature, science, medicine, architecture, and philosophy. Furthermore, the Holocaust is disconcertingly close. It happened in living memory. The mass exterminations force us to ask deep questions about what it is to be a human being—not as an intellectual exercise, but as an emotional necessity. Several Jewish psychiatrists and psychotherapists were survivors of concentration camps, and their experiences afforded them new perspectives on mental life and the nature of suffering. (Curiously, the "library" at Auschwitz—which held only eight real books—included a volume by Sigmund Freud.[1])

While standing next to the gallows with my son, I was conscious of having a choice. I could look at the noose, the watchtowers, and the barbed wire, or I could look at the mountains and the blue sky. Almost seventy years earlier, a psychiatrist in another concentration camp, one of the Dachau satellites, was curious about the behavior of his fellow captives. Some stayed in their bunks, while others chose to get up and observe the beauty of the setting sun. Human beings are constantly making choices. This, he concluded, is what defines us.

As soon as Viktor Frankl emerged from the crowded transportation train, he found himself approaching a senior SS officer. The man was directing people to either the left or the right with a movement of his finger. Frankl had a haversack hidden under his coat, and he straightened his back to compensate for the heavy load. The officer, who was tall and wearing an immaculate uniform, studied Frankl for a moment. Then he landed both of his hands on Frankl's shoulders and twisted him to the right.

That evening, Frankl was looking for a friend who had been on the train. "Was he sent to the left side?" someone asked. "Yes,"

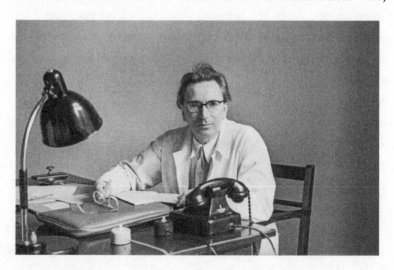

Frankl replied. "Then you can see him there," the prisoner said, pointing at a chimney belching flame and smoke a few hundred yards away. "That's where your friend is, floating up to heaven."[2] About 90 percent of those who were sent to Auschwitz were directed to the left, and within a few hours they had all become smoke and ashes.

During his six months of incarceration in several camps, Frankl occupied himself by making observations. Some people, he noticed, fought to stay alive, while others simply gave up and died. What, Frankl wondered, was the difference? He scribbled words on scraps of paper and ordered his thoughts into imaginary lectures.

When the war ended Frankl returned to Vienna and his observations became the basis of a new approach to psychotherapy. For someone who had witnessed slaughter undertaken on an industrial scale, who had been beaten, enslaved, and had lost everything, including his wife and almost all of his immediate family, Frankl reached a surprising conclusion concerning the importance of situational stress. He didn't think it mattered very much. The degree to which we rally or despair depends, ultimately, not on objective events, but on the meaning we ascribe to them. Events and their consequences are less significant than how they are experienced. Survivors, he suggested, are people who choose to distinguish their suffering with meaning: "Everything can be taken from a man but one thing: the last of the human freedoms—to choose one's attitude in any given circumstances."[3]

On arriving at Auschwitz, if Frankl hadn't straightened his back (which he only did because he was concealing a haversack), he might have been judged unfit for strenuous labor and directed to the left. Two hours later he would have been dead, whatever attitude he'd chosen to adopt. However, the majority of situations encountered over a lifetime have less conclusive outcomes, and when outcomes can vary, what Frankl termed "the will to meaning" becomes a significant protective factor.

When he was still a prisoner, Frankl had many conversations with would-be suicides. He describes two individuals in particular who had come to the conclusion that they could expect nothing more from existence. The question they should be asking, he suggested, was not "What more can I expect from life?" but rather "What more can life expect from me?" One of them had a child who had escaped to safety; the other had been incarcerated before he could finish a writing project. The prospect of reunion with a child or completing a series of books was what gave each man's life renewed purpose. Frankl had reduced the broad question of the meaning of life to a specific and tangible objective. Having a sense of why we exist (and a personal narrative that proceeds toward a desired future) can make even the most extreme forms of adversity bearable.

Frankl believed that his observations of despairing prisoners were relevant to clinical practice, insofar as many psychiatric patients complain that life has no meaning, and when bad things happen, they find it impossible to construe such events as opportunities for growth. In order to treat the conditions arising from the frustration of the "will to meaning," he developed "logotherapy"—which has become one of the most respected forms of existential psychotherapy.

Frankl was once consulted by an elderly, depressed doctor whose wife had died two years earlier. He asked the grief-stricken man how his wife would have reacted had it been he, the doctor, who had predeceased her. The doctor said his wife would have suffered terribly. Frankl commented, "Such suffering has been spared her, and it was you who have spared her this suffering—to be sure, at the price that now you have to survive and mourn her." The satisfied doctor shook Frankl's hand and departed in silence. His suffering was no longer pointless. It had been given meaning.[4]

Many people become acutely aware of the sterility of their lives when they are deprived of distractions. Meaninglessness can be ignored by immersion in work and day-to-day activities, but only up to a point. When the busy week comes to an end, people become prone to an ailment that Frankl called "Sunday neurosis," in essence, awareness of the "existential vacuum." It is a state associated with low mood, listlessness, and feeling somewhat lost. Sunday indulgences, such as excessive drinking and shopping, represent attempts to fill the existential vacuum. But compensations of this kind can never succeed because they are fundamentally meaningless. They are similar to Janov's substitute gratifications and Fromm's unnecessary acquisitions.

By the 1980s, Frankl had begun to consider the pursuit of meaning in a broader cultural context. He concluded that industrialization and its consequences were antithetical to the process. He noted that people in the developed world have usually been uprooted from their place of origin, disconnected from traditions, and alienated from value systems. He was particularly concerned about the effect of discontinuities on the young. Without reliable reference points, how can you plot a course through life? Finding meaning and purpose is made considerably more difficult when there is constant and rapid change. If conditions were unfavorable in the 1980s, they surely must have become much worse in the intervening decades. The discontinuities that Frankl was worried about forty years ago are nothing compared to the discontinuities of the digital age. Today, young people spend extended periods of time in an entirely novel environment that is almost completely disconnected from history and geography. Cyberspace is the ultimate displacement—a rootless frontier offering unlimited opportunities for superficial distraction.

The Internet also offers endless possibilities for solipsism. Frankl was curiously wary of self-reflection. He believed that the natural state of a human being is in the world. Therefore, we should endeavor to be outward looking. Too much self-reflection can be unhealthy. It is certainly possible to identify many psychological problems that are caused by "hyper-reflection." Sexual impotence, for example, is usually the result of performance anxiety. The affected individual is preoccupied with erectile functioning, rather than connecting with another human being. This aspect of Frankl's thinking shares common ground with schools of psychology that associate optimal experience with overcoming self-obsession.

It is important to recognize that when Frankl talks about "meaning" and "life," he is not claiming to know the meaning of life. His prescription for fulfillment is more modest. We do not need to find *the* meaning of life to keep existential angst at bay—rather, we need to find *a* meaning. This substitution of the definite article with the indefinite reduces the scale of the task from the cosmic to the personal. Frankl makes everything more manageable.

Personal meaning is not something fabricated, but discovered. What is meaningful to one person might not be meaningful to another. It is theoretically possible, therefore, for a particular individual to find meaning in something relatively mundane or hedonistic. However, all things being equal, the average human is more likely to discover meaning where there is also depth, substance, and opportunity for continuous development—for example, through relationships, activities beneficial to the wider community, creativity, and vocation. Our choices with respect to meaning are not fixed. The discovery of meaning is an ongoing process, and every moment of life is potentially meaningful, even, according to Frankl, "up to our last breath."[5]

He offers a helpful analogy. A film is composed of thousands of images, and each of these images has meaning, but the greater, overarching meaning cannot be grasped until the film has been watched from start to finish. Old age and the approach of death, viewed in this way, are essential ingredients of life. They complete our story and reveal who we are. The final moments of a meaningful life are closer to a consummation than an ending.[6]

The term "existential psychotherapy" is somewhat misleading, since it suggests a unitary school of thought. There are, in fact, several forms of this approach, but all of them are concerned with existence *as it is lived*. They understand depression and anxiety not as symptoms of disturbed brain chemistry or underlying psychological "mechanisms" but as experiences. No distinction is made between the person and the problem.* The problem is an aspect of the person's existence at a given point in time—and the only aspects of being that really matter are experience and choice.

---

* Almost all forms of psychotherapy are "essentialist." That is, they assume that clinical phenomena are caused by "things" or "essences" that are located at a deeper level. Thus, in psychoanalysis or cognitive therapy, distressing thoughts and emotions occur because of complexes or schemas. The mind is divisible into agencies—id, ego, and superego—or sets of connected beliefs. Existential psychotherapists maintain that a person is an indivisible totality and experience is irreducible. There are no abstract "essences" to be uncovered.

Existential psychotherapists tend to be more willing than the proponents of other approaches to engage with big questions, the most significant of which relate to our own mortality. Emphasizing the inevitability of death might seem somewhat morbid; however, in practice, existential approaches confront hard truths in order to promote optimal living. The fact that we might die at any moment should be galvanizing, an incentive for action and engagement. We should not allow ourselves to be worn down by disappointments and accept a life of comfortable but fundamentally unsatisfying routines. We should not postpone important life decisions. We should make efforts to avoid finding ourselves, at the end of life, agreeing with Shakespeare's Richard II: "I have wasted time, and now doth time waste me."

As existential psychotherapy was developing, so, too, was humanistic psychotherapy. There is a considerable degree of overlap between these approaches, which is why they are often referred to using a compound term: humanistic-existential. Both utilized concepts borrowed from philosophy, and in the postwar era, humanists and existentialists enjoyed a fruitful dialogue. The most famous humanistic psychotherapist is Carl Rogers, whose ideas about congruent and incongruent selves were discussed earlier in this book. He was born in the American Midwest into a prosperous family and raised on a farm. His Congregationalist upbringing was strict, so much so that he later wrote: "Even carbonated beverages had a faintly sinful aroma." Initially, he was attracted to religious work and attended a seminary, but he began to have doubts about his faith and turned to psychology instead. With the publication of *Counseling and Psychotherapy* in 1942, he established himself as a major figure in the field. Indeed, some argue that

no single volume influenced the practice of psychotherapy in the United States more.

Rogers asserted that fulfillment, like Frankl's "meaning," should not be conceptualized as an end point or a fixed goal. It is a spontaneous, ongoing process that evolves over time. Just as what is meaningful differs from person to person, what is fulfilling will also vary according to the dispositions and preferences of different individuals. Describing the general conditions that favor fulfillment is therefore more helpful than offering specific prescriptions. Singing in a choir is strongly associated with elevated mood and improved health.[7] But if you aren't very musical and can't sing, then you probably won't join a choir.

The Rogerian conditions for fulfillment are surprisingly few and straightforward: openness to experience, fully inhabiting the present moment, trusting one's feelings and judgments, taking responsibility for one's choices, and viewing one's self and others with unconditional positivity. We have encountered several of these recommendations before. For example, living in the here and now is a feature of Erich Fromm's "being mode." Rogers was developing what he called "client-centered" or "person-centered" therapy at a time when many practitioners who had abandoned traditional psychoanalysis were arriving at a new consensus. This was characterized by a shift of emphasis from unconscious to conscious mental life. Therapists were talking less about repressed memories and more about relationships, values, and personal goals.

An effective therapist, Rogers suggested, has particular qualities. The qualities that he identified are ones that anyone wishing to form meaningful relationships might benefit from cultivating: honesty, respect for others, and empathetic understanding.

Rogers's language is simple and conversational. He is happy to use the first-person pronoun, and he makes no attempt to assume the commanding voice of scientific authority. His tone is neighborly, community spirited. Numerous figureheads in the history of psychotherapy have concealed their flaws behind a mask, an adopted persona that convinced disciples they were in the presence of wisdom and infallibility. Rogers, however, was completely transparent. He wrote about his own sexual problems, making therapeutic blunders, and becoming more emotionally volatile with age. He had supreme faith in authenticity. The facts, he maintained, are always friendly. We should never fear truth. The more authentic you are, the more you will be able to trust your feelings and judgments.

What connects Rogers most strongly with his existential contemporaries is an unshakable belief in freedom. A lazy contrast can be made between the positivity of person-centered therapy and the dark determinism of psychoanalysis. But in reality, psycho-analysis is also about increasing personal freedom. The primary objective of psychoanalysis is to free individuals from unhelpful unconscious and historical influences.

The existential writer Albert Camus famously described suicide as "the only truly serious philosophical issue." This bold assertion is frequently quoted because of its clarity. The human animal is the only animal on earth that kills itself. Like Hamlet, we all have to choose whether we want to be—or not to be. Before we decide to do anything, we first have to decide that we want to exist. We have to exercise the freedom that Rogers cherished. Every breath you take is a choice. From a humanistic-existential perspective, you are the sum of your choices.

All day, Sarah would sit in her room on a locked ward, and then she would sleep. She hadn't spoken a word in months. Although she could manage basic self-care, such as washing and getting dressed, she could do very little else. She spent most of her time alone on her bed. The woman inhabiting her body was entirely inaccessible.

Sarah's room was small and spare—a bed, a lamp, a cabinet—and its single window offered a disappointing view: adjacent buildings and the desolate gullies of a large, rambling psychiatric institution. A square of glass in the door allowed passing doctors and nurses to check that Sarah wasn't harming herself. She had received a double diagnosis, depression and anorexia, but these sober and precise medical terms conveyed nothing of the extremity of her terror and despair.

Depression suggests sadness and anorexia suggests a preoc-cupation with body weight, mental phenomena that we can all understand. Sarah's condition was of a different order, a different magnitude. She had retreated from the world and was in so much psychological pain that labels like "depression" and "anorexia" were hopelessly inadequate. Neither antidepressant medication nor electroconvulsive therapy had had an effect on Sarah's mental state, and her consultant wasn't sure how to proceed. A team of health practitioners and her family agreed that she should stay on the ward, provisionally, because at least she would be safe there, and her body weight could be monitored. No one had troubled to ask Sarah to express an opinion, because she couldn't (or wouldn't) speak.

"You can't give her psychotherapy," said a nurse. "She won't talk, won't make eye contact. She's completely unresponsive. What are you going to do?"

As Viktor Frankl suggested, there are latent possibilities even in the most unpromising circumstances.

When I entered Sarah's room for the first time, I found her sitting on her bed with her back against the wall. She was wearing a sweater and a pair of jeans; her bare feet were exposed, and her toes tightly curled. Just having another human being standing close to her was enough to make her flinch and shrivel into a fetal ball. Her hair was unwashed and hung down in front of her face like a curtain, the last barrier behind which she could shield herself from reality.

I had read her notes and learned that Sarah was a first-class mathematician and a very competent classical pianist. This frail, mute, trembling figure had once demonstrated impressive gifts. The trolley I was pushing was loaded with a stereo system and a pile of cassettes (this was long before digital downloads and streaming). I introduced myself and told Sarah that I was going to play her some music. I supposed that music might be my way in— or her way out: a catalyst, a connection, a means of stirring memories, balm, solace, something. I slotted a cassette into the machine, closed the see-through plastic cover, and pressed a key. Miniature spools began to rotate and the room filled with Mozart—luminous harmonies and elegant ornamentation. Sarah remained in the same fixed position, her knees beneath her chin, her fists clenched, and her wrists crossed against her left shoulder. She started sobbing, and she continued sobbing for the complete duration of several piano sonatas. When the music stopped, her chest was still heaving and I felt a pang of guilt. Had I made her worse?

"I know that you find talking difficult," I said softly. "And perhaps you don't want to talk. But I think it would be helpful if we were able to communicate."

Severe depression can produce a kind of paralysis. Uttering a single syllable can require monumental effort.

I explained to Sarah that if she allowed me to hold her hand, then one squeeze could mean yes, and two squeezes no. She could then answer questions and express preferences. I got up from my chair, crossed the floor, sat next to her, and took her hand in mine. "Is it all right for me to hold your hand like this?" I was rewarded by a single squeeze.

It was difficult to believe that someone who had once spent hours practicing the piano would be completely immune to the therapeutic effects of music. Therefore, I chose to persevere. We would sit listening to Mozart and Bach for hours, Sarah always hunched on her bed, her face obscured by her curtain of hair, while I sat by the stereo. Sometimes she would cry, but not always.

When the music came to an end, I would take her hand, ask her undemanding questions, and occasionally get responses—one squeeze or two.

What was I hoping to achieve?

Music, in addition to being at least theoretically pleasurable, provided me with a reason for being in Sarah's room. Prolonged exposure is associated with anxiety reduction, and over time I expected her to feel more comfortable in my presence. Moreover, I wanted to coax Sarah out of her psychological burrow in order to facilitate reengagement with the outside world. Listening to music would draw her attention outward—a necessary first step.

When with friends, or just walking along a London street, I frequently found my mind drifting back to Sarah's room. She was like the gnomon of a sundial, and her shadow followed me. Recollecting her mental and physical confinement made me value all the ordinary freedoms I usually took for granted. Even mundane aspects of existence started to feel vivid. The fragrance of coffee was enough to make me feel totally alive.

Progress was slow, but eventually we were able to have short and rudimentary conversations using hand squeezes. On days when she wasn't sobbing, I encouraged Sarah to speak. In order to hear her, I had to place my ear close to her mouth, because she was only capable of articulating a few barely audible words. When I asked her if she wanted me to continue making my visits, she whispered, "I don't know." This was a genuine answer. Experience had become so confusing, so overwhelming, she couldn't think clearly.

Even though our methods of communication were primitive, I learned that Sarah had traveled to other countries, and that several years earlier she had enjoyed the company of her friends and gone skiing. Her history was relatively benign. She was proof that events are less significant than how we interpret them.

Due to her mutism and detachment, Sarah had been a passive recipient of care. I urged her to consider whether this was desirable. Although it might be effortful for her to make decisions, she should still try to express opinions concerning her treatment and take some responsibility for her life. Sarah was certainly listening, because thereafter she became noticeably more decisive. For example, when I asked her (as I often did) whether she wanted me to continue visiting her, she now whispered "yes."

Sarah still found the mere presence of another human being stressful, so I began to leave her questionnaires with multiple-choice answers. I supposed that she would find it easier to make decisions without the implicit pressure of me sitting next to her. I also invited her to write down her thoughts in my absence. She was only able to write a few words, but they were enough to give me a flavor of how she experienced the world: "It's all so unreal." The only substantive reality, for her, was internal.

One unexpected consequence of leaving these questionnaires was that she started to draw on the blank, reverse sides. I left paper and pencils on her bedside cabinet and told her to draw whenever she wanted. What she produced was quite extraordinary. Her sketches were highly stylized and symbolic representations of her pain: barred windows, barbed wire, hooks. They were dark and troubling and resembled the images associated with concentration camps. Many years later, when I was standing in the former concentration camp of Struthof, I took several photographs that were almost identical to Sarah's drawings.

She had been living like a prisoner. I asked her if she'd like to go for a walk, and she surprised me by consenting to the idea.

It was necessary to support her physically, because she was weak and infirm. She was like an astronaut unable to cope with gravity after protracted weightlessness. We left the secure ward, made an uncertain, precarious descent down several flights of stairs, and then emerged into sunlight. She was shaking as we made painfully slow progress between the hospital buildings. It was only a short walk, and she kept her head bowed from start to finish. She couldn't have seen very much more than her feet and the paving stones. Nevertheless, her achievement had required great courage. She had chosen to venture out into a universe of fiery brilliance and vertiginous confusion. She had exposed herself to strangers, the noise of airplanes, and the heat of the sun. She had endured her pounding heart racing toward blind panic.

In due course, her speech became more fluent and we were able to have longer conversations. She never spoke louder than a whisper, and I still had to position my ear close to her mouth to hear what she was saying, but gradually, I began to piece together her story.

Sarah had always been highly sensitive to injustice and cruelty. Her sympathies were deep—profoundly deep. The more she looked at the world—not only the everyday, directly observable world, but the world as seen through a television screen—the more she became increasingly uneasy and disturbed. Abuse, tyranny, torture, endless and repeated instances of mindless violence and brutality: the entire human race seemed to be participating in some dreadful black comedy. How could the world be like this? And more importantly, how could people carry on with their lives knowing that atrocities were taking place elsewhere?

She wanted to make a difference, help others, campaign and raise money for worthy causes. But whatever she did fell short of her exacting standards. She could never do enough.

Her eating disorder was rooted in guilt. She found herself thinking that it was obscene to eat three meals a day while others starved. It was excessive, gluttonous—greedy. And she began to question her own intentions. Was she really a good person, or simply acting like a good person to make herself feel better? Even worse, perhaps she was assuming a saintly demeanor to enjoy the dubious pleasure of feeling morally superior to others. What if her compassion was tokenistic? What if her crusades were just self-serving displays? Perhaps she was really a fraud, insincere, a liar, a bad person.

She began a process of intellectual self-dissection, which she undertook with ruthless scrupulosity, and once she had taken herself apart, she couldn't put herself back together again. By the time external scars begin to appear on the body of a self-harmer, you can be sure that they have already cut themselves to shreds inside. She could sense her own disintegration—tatters of her former self flapping in the wind—and she was no longer strong enough to endure reality: the cruelty, the absurdity, the meaninglessness of existence. The world had become a whirling vortex, an incomprehensible chaos that she had to shelter from by retreating deeper and deeper into herself. The shattering of identity is usually associated with a specific trauma. Sarah hadn't experienced a specific traumatic event. Existence itself—in its entirety—had become traumatic.

Sarah didn't want to be discharged from the hospital, because she was certain that she would kill herself as soon as she had the opportunity to do so. She just wanted the pain to end. What had prevented her from attempting suicide in the past was the paralysis that arises from a classic double bind. Living was intolerable, but so was dying. If she killed herself, she would cause her family to grieve and suffer, which to her was also intolerable. It was extremely difficult for her to talk about the subject of suicide. She would become distressed, hyperventilate, and I would have to wait for successive waves of panic to subside before we could continue.

These conversations were, I think, helpful, because the imagery in her drawings began to change. Occasionally, shafts of light angled through darkness, tangles of barbed wire metamorphosed into rosebushes, and wildflowers sprouted around the edges—usually in the lower corners of the sheets of paper. She was able to go for more walks, although always with her head bowed, and she no longer sobbed for hours at a time. Sometimes, she appeared relatively relaxed and calm. I dared to hope that she might also be experiencing periods of respite from her pain.

She was still too fragile to make eye contact. I conducted all of our sessions addressing vertical strands of lank hair. She wasn't strong enough to cope with being looked at, which I supposed must feel to her like being lanced with red-hot skewers. The most challenging aspect of reality is always other people. People are where reality is found in its highest concentrations.

The scrutiny of others was excruciating for Sarah, but looking at another human being in the same room was like looking directly into the sun. I devised a simple exercise. I would turn away, and she would look at me for a few seconds, and when she was finished, she would squeeze my hand, and I would turn back. She could become accustomed to the reality of my presence without having to worry about finding herself trapped in the blaze of my regard.

Three months after my first visit, she whispered, "I feel different."

"In what way?" I asked.

Her voice shook: "I think I'm getting better."

It seems unlikely that human beings were created by a benign intelligence for a specific reason. Cosmologists predict that space will continue expanding, the stars will go out, and all that will remain is darkness—an unimaginably vast, dead, frozen expanse. Yet human beings are always searching for the meaning of life. This is probably because of our evolutionary programming. Purposive behaviors (for example, hunting or mating) ensured personal survival and the transmission of genes. Unfortunately, the programming that makes us pursue meaningful goals also exerts a continuous pressure. We pursue goals beyond those that satisfy our material needs, and the most alluring and sublime of these goals is the discovery of an ultimate answer. We are compelled to demand more from the universe than it is prepared to give.

For many, this profitless endeavor is the cause of anxiety, sleepless nights, disappointment, and, in some cases, despair. Religions tell us that if we search, then we will find. But for thousands of years, people have searched, and still there is no consensus regarding the meaning of life. There are no incontrovertible proofs.

Providing we don't ask the universe for things it cannot give us, we will not be crushed by reality. We don't need a single, definitive reason to live. Any number of smaller reasons will do.

13

ACCEPTANCE

A Flower That Blossoms Only for a Single Night

After Hitler's rise to power, Freud and his family left Vienna and resettled in London. Although Freud was occasionally critical of Vienna, he had lived there from early childhood. He loved walking around the Ring Road and sitting in coffeehouses; he loved the German language, playing cards with friends, telling jokes. He was typically Viennese, and his name was strongly associated with the former Habsburg capital, when it was at its cultural and intellectual apogee. Vienna is often referred to as the city of dreams, because Freud, the interpreter of dreams, once lived there. Leaving Vienna must have felt like deracination—and involuntary displacement was made more challenging by age and illness. Freud was in his eighties and suffering from mouth cancer.

Freud received many distinguished visitors after his arrival in London. These included the visionary writer H. G. Wells and the surrealist painter Salvador Dalí. Dalí surreptitiously produced a sketch of his host from which he later made a pen-and-ink drawing. It's a rather sad little picture, because it shows a human being

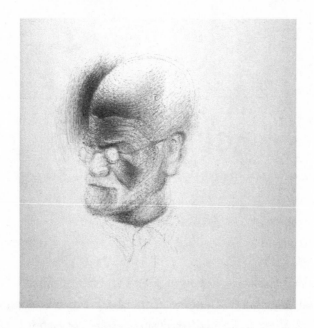

in a state of dissolution. The portrait lacks definition—Freud's stern visage is fading away, the back of his head already dissolving into nothingness. Freud is so close to death that he is no longer fully alive. He is depicted in a state of eerie transition. Neither Dalí's sketch nor his pen-and-ink drawing was shown to Freud, because they were thought to be too disturbing. Paradoxically, the artist's diffuse execution brings mortality into sharp focus.

On January 28, 1939, Leonard Woolf, the journalist and political theorist, and his wife Virginia—arguably the greatest novelist of her generation—had tea with Freud. Recollecting this auspicious occasion in his memoir, Leonard reflected that meetings with famous men are almost always disappointing, boring, or both. Freud was the exception. He was surrounded by an aura not of celebrity, but of greatness. Leonard was reminded of a half-extinct volcano. This sense of latent, brooding power was mitigated by impeccable manners. Freud was courteous in a way that recalled the chivalry of a bygone age. He presented Virginia with a flower. (Virginia was less impressed by Freud than her husband.[1] She recalled a screwed-up codger with the eyes of a monkey. Her social observations were rarely generous.)

Leonard, no doubt aware of Freud's pointed sense of humor, recounted a funny story. Apparently, in London, a man had stolen a number of books from Foyles, the largest bookshop in the world, and among the purloined volumes was a title by Freud. The magistrate fined the thief and said that he should be punished further by being made to read Freud's complete works. Freud was amused.

During the Nazi rallies of 1933, Freud's books were thrown into fires with others designated as decadent, pornographic, or politically dangerous. The presiding officer had proclaimed that Freud's writings promoted soul-destroying, instinctual gratification and undermined human nobility. When Freud was informed that his books were being burned, he made a sarcastic quip about the excellent progress humanity was making: "In the Middle Ages they would have burnt me." He obviously didn't foresee what was coming.

Freud owned a large number of books. His collection, or at least what remains of it today, contains around 4,500 volumes, most of which can be found in Freud's London house (now The Freud Museum). Around 500 books that appeared in earlier listings are missing. Freud was always giving books away, and his wife did the same after his death. A book that isn't mentioned in the most recent catalog is Freud's copy of his own anthologized cases, *Four Psychoanalytic Case Studies*, published in Vienna in 1932. It's one of the books that disappeared without a trace. I know where it is—because I can see it from where I'm sitting. For the past eleven years it has been on my desk.

When I hold Freud's former possession in my hands, a well-used edition with faded green cloth covers, I experience a curious connection. I become like a clairvoyant, releasing memories from an object. The book was once on a shelf in Freud's apartment in Vienna, and it was almost certainly in the room when Leonard and Virginia Woolf were having tea with Freud. If Freud hadn't escaped to London, it would have been tossed onto a fire and burned by the Nazis. But it survived. I can flick through the pages and persuade myself that the paper still exudes a hint of Freud's cigars. The fact of the book's existence is joyously affirmative.

Freud's cancer was at an advanced stage. A lesion in his mouth produced such a foul odor that his dog would shrink into the far corner of the room. The physical fabric of his body was rotting away. Soon, he could take very little food. He refused to take any painkillers, apart from aspirin, because he didn't want to take soporifics that would impair his ability to think. He had been advised to give up smoking years earlier, but it was advice he hadn't followed. Parts of his mouth had been surgically removed and replaced with a denture-like prosthetic. This restricted jaw movement and caused sores. Sometimes he would use a clothespin to keep his mouth open wide enough to insert a cigar. For Freud, life without smoking cigars was inconceivable. The richness of existence had been reduced to an "island of pain floating on a sea of indifference." And a few cigars.

One of his last visitors was an old psychoanalytic friend named Hanns Sachs. Sachs was amazed by Freud's resilience. In spite of being very weak and in terrible pain, Freud didn't complain and showed no signs of irritability. He wanted to know what was going on in psychoanalytic circles. His interest was undiminished right up to the end.

The single word that best summarizes Freud's mental attitude to the approach of death is "acceptance." It appears and reappears in the accounts of those who visited him. His disciple and biographer Ernest Jones wrote that "the philosophy of resignation and the acceptance of unalterable reality triumphed throughout."[2] Freud didn't rail against fate, the injustice of his predicament, or the awfulness of his undignified end. He wasn't shaking his fist at the sky. Old animals get sick and expire. His death was part of the natural order of things. Freud was staring into the void like a true Freudian—and he wasn't going to blink.

The cancer ate through his cheek and the sepsis spread. His condition was now agonizing.

Freud had spoken to his doctor about this eventuality and they had reached an "understanding." What was the point of enduring prolonged and senseless torment? The doctor pressed his hand and agreed to give him "sedation." The next morning, Freud gratefully accepted a lethal dose of "morphia." He died just before midnight on September 23, 1939. Ernest Jones wrote, "Freud died as he had lived—a realist."[3]

The poet W. H. Auden, who wrote "In Memory of Sigmund Freud," described the extent of Freud's global influence with a few well-chosen words: "no more a person / now but a whole climate of opinion." In spite of repeated attempts by scholars to discredit Freud, he remains a pivotal figure. The climate of opinion referred to by W. H. Auden hasn't changed very much in the intervening decades. Freud's books continue to reach a wide readership. He arouses our curiosity, stimulates debate, and articulates uncomfortable truths. Critics come and go, but Freud retains his position, a permanent, craggy feature in our cultural landscape.

Being Jewish, Freud attracted Jewish followers, who, after fleeing Nazi persecution, offered psychoanalysis to members of both new and established Jewish communities. The spread of psychoanalysis (and its subsequent fragmentation into other forms of psychotherapy) can be traced along diverging lines of least cultural resistance. A number of academics, mostly Jews themselves, have suggested that the relationship between Judaism and psychotherapy might actually be somewhat deeper. Jews were not only the first people to embrace psychoanalysis, but also a people with a common heritage conducive to the development of Freudianism and its later variants. Some have gone further, suggesting that Freud's ideas were greatly influenced by Jewish scripture.

Freud was hardly an observant Jew. He opposed his wife's desire to establish a Jewish home, and his son, Martin, wrote that the Freud children were raised without any instruction relating to Jewish ritual.[4] None of them, as far as Martin could remember, ever attended synagogue, and the Freud family, being very Germanic, thoroughly enjoyed celebrating Christmas. Freud dismissed religion as an illusion, published a critical work on Judaism at a time when thousands of Jews were being transported to concentration camps, and in the first decade of the twentieth century was concerned that psychoanalysis might become a parochial branch of medicine practiced by only Austrian Jews. He didn't want psychoanalysis to become, as he put it, "a Jewish national affair."

Yet Freud had another, rather different side. He was an active member of a Jewish lodge, B'nai B'rith, played cards with Jews every Saturday night, and collected Jewish jokes.

In biographies of Freud, it is often said that he was ambivalent about his religion, but this is not correct. His position was very clear: he thought all religion was nonsense, including Judaism, but at the same time he enjoyed and maintained many Jewish attachments. These attachments were initially encouraged and strengthened by the anti-Semitism that had become so widespread in Vienna. Freud once remarked that Jews had "no choice but to band together." This statement suggests that his Jewishness was expedient rather than devotional.

It is impossible to think of Freud without registering, at some level, that he was a Jew. But why does this fact merit consideration? It opens up some interesting possibilities with respect to the ultimate provenance of his ideas. Although Freud was a rational man, he was fascinated by different religions and mythologies. His consulting room was crammed with ancient figurines and statuettes—little gods and goddesses. Leonard Woolf said it looked like a museum.

In *Sigmund Freud and the Jewish Mystical Tradition*, first published in 1958, the psychologist David Bakan pointed out that psychoanalysis and Kabbalah, a body of Jewish esoteric teachings dating back to the twelfth century, have a great deal in common: dream interpretation, symbolism, an interest in sexuality, and close attention to language. Kabbalists study the texts of holy books in much the same way that psychoanalysts study people. In both cases, small things, minute details, are considered significant. There was little actual evidence to suggest that Freud was acquainted with Kabbalistic writings in 1958; however, Bakan was subsequently contacted by Chaim Bloch, an eminent student of Judaism, Kabbalah, and Hasidism, and onetime acquaintance of Freud. Bloch recalled visiting Freud and examining the great man's library. He noticed several volumes of Kabbalah and a French translation of *The Zohar* (perhaps the most important work of Jewish mysticism)—all of them absent from official registers. We are invited to imagine Freud poring over secret books, combining Jewish occultism with French psychopathology, German psychophysics, and sexology—inventing psychoanalysis. It is a romantic image, although perhaps too romantic and fanciful to be wholly credible. And yet it is tempting to entertain the possibility. The acceptance with which Freud faced his final days and the realism of psychoanalysis are both typical of Jewish mysticism.

There are Kabbalistic teachings, for example, that explain the existence of evil and suffering by accepting that the universe is the flawed creation of an imperfect God.[5] These teachings can be contrasted with the sometimes desperate arguments Christian theologians have employed to reconcile the idea of an all-loving God with phenomena such as mouth cancer and mass exterminations. The stock answer to the question of evil and suffering is that they arise because God gave humanity the gift of freedom. Responsibility is displaced from God to His creation. But this defense is untenable if God is omniscient. If God has knowledge of all causes, then He also has knowledge of all effects. Some 13.8 billion years ago, before the first stars had ignited, He would have known that Freud was going to exist and develop mouth cancer. He would have known that six million Jews would be murdered in the Holocaust. An omniscient God cannot be exculpated by a weak argument. The Kabbalists of the sixteenth century made no attempt to explain away the horrors of the world. They accepted that the world was imperfect and acknowledged that this meant the creator must also be imperfect. We must make the world a better place ourselves.

I have no idea whether Freud possessed books of Jewish mysticism and it doesn't really matter. He would almost certainly have had some exposure to Kabbalistic thinking. The celebrated Jewish folk hero Rabbi Loew was a sixteenth-century Kabbalist who lived in Prague, which is a relatively short distance from Vienna. Loew was so well-known that he became a staple of Jewish bedtime stories.

If Freud borrowed anything from Jewish mysticism, then it was realism and acceptance: Look at the world, accept what you see, and do not attempt to reduce your discomfort by misrepresentation. Accept your limitations and accept that a time will come when you must let go. If Freudianism were a religion, this could be one of its prayers.

Contemporary psychotherapists have become increasingly interested in acceptance as a means of coping with distressing mental phenomena. Advocates of this view tend to practice "third-wave" therapies. These are approaches that represent a third stage of evolution following, first, behavioral, and second, cognitive-behavioral, therapies. Behavioral and cognitive treatments, delivered separately or combined, have in common strategies devised to directly modify habitual behavior and patterns of thoughts. In cognitive therapy, for example, negative thoughts are challenged and replaced with more accurate thoughts. Third-wave therapies do not seek to alter thinking patterns or feelings directly. Instead, they seek to modify the way people *relate* to their thoughts and feelings. They do not attempt to change what is in a person's head, but what is *going on* in a person's head. In this respect, mental processes are judged to be more important than mental content. The way you think about thinking is more consequential than what you are actually thinking. Paradoxically, being less focused on achieving change often results in significant incidental gains.

Acceptance and commitment therapy (ACT), developed by the American clinical psychologist Steven C. Hayes, is a good example of a third-wave therapy. It assumes that a certain amount of psychological distress is inevitable. The very nature of thinking and the properties of language make us vulnerable to mental illness. We have a tendency to make unfavorable comparisons, to reach arbitrary conclusions, and to confuse verbal evaluations with reality (even when those evaluations are contradicted by facts). Matters are usually made worse by avoidance. We cannot face certain challenges because of anxiety or fear of failure. Opportunities to acquire new skills and demonstrate competence are reduced. Avoidance is likely to disempower, erode confidence, and inflate existing emotional problems.

ACT is predicated on acceptance. The individual's interests are best served by a willingness to accept the inevitability of distress. There are very few meaningful goals in life that can be pursued without attendant anxieties, self-doubt, and setbacks. An ACT therapist therefore makes no attempt to challenge or modify a person's negative thoughts or emotions. The individual is simply urged to alter his or her relationship with those thoughts and feelings by means of a subtle shift of perspective.

A distinction is made between the self and the thoughts and emotions that are experienced by the self. Consciousness is a medium in which mental events occur. You are not your thoughts. Indeed, you can study your own thoughts. When we adopt the perspective of an inner observer, our thoughts become more like "objects." This approach establishes a helpful distance between a person and his or her mental events. Thoughts become more like words floating around in one's head, and they become less threatening—they stop feeling like absolute truths. The thought "I am a failure," for example, loses its power to trap the person in a linguistic cage. The observer is positioned outside the cage, and it soon becomes apparent that the cage is impermanent. Thoughts, impressions, memories, sensations, and feelings flow in and out of awareness. ACT encourages the individual to acknowledge mental events and then to move on.

Adopting the perspective of an inner observer is also recommended by practitioners of certain forms of meditation. Mindfulness, a Buddhist meditation technique that involves inner monitoring, has achieved extraordinary popularity in recent years. Since the 1960s many academic publications have demonstrated an association between meditation and well-being.[6] Meditation appears to promote physical health (everything from the correction of cardiac arrhythmias to reduced constipation) and mental health (most notably, reduced anxiety, depression, insomnia, and rumination). Mindfulness practice also changes gray-matter concentrations in brain regions associated with learning, memory, emotional regulation, self-referential processing, and perspective taking.[7]

ACT employs mindfulness to help encourage nonjudgmental acceptance of mental events and to increase connectedness with the present moment. We are constantly reliving the past or inhabiting imaginary futures; however, we should strive to exist in the present moment, because this is where life is actually lived.

The idea of living in the present moment is by now probably beginning to sound familiar, perhaps even overfamiliar. It is one of the most common recommendations to be found in mid- to late twentieth-century psychotherapy. When the mind drifts away from the present, one should gently bring it back, so that consciousness and reality are more closely aligned. As noted above, ACT encourages the individual to acknowledge mental events and then to move on. But in what sense does the individual move on? In what direction is the individual traveling?

ACT practitioners seek to clarify values in order to set value-based goals and devise action plans. We all have aspirations, hopes, and dreams. We all have ideas about who we want to be and what kind of life we want to live. These aspirations are almost invariably connected with our fundamental values. But many individuals never get to realize their full potential or live the life they want to live because of anxiety, depression, and disappointment. They become avoidant. Mindfulness and acceptance processes allow individuals to cope with distressing mental states while pursuing valued goals. We should not suspend our ambitions until we resolve all our psychological problems. Indeed, the complete resolution of psychological problems is unrealistic. This does not, however, preclude the possibility of incidental and beneficial emotional adjustment. Acceptance and commitment therapy offers expanding rather than narrowing horizons. The person becomes more flexible and this can be equated with improved mental health.

Western cultures are triumphalist. Almost all our stories idealize battle, perseverance, and conquest. We are inculcated with martial virtues from an early age. Fighting is good, and surrender is bad. We are urged to be heroic, to fight doggedly until we win. Third-wave therapies are interesting because they question this set of basic assumptions.

Steve Hayes offers an instructive metaphor. Imagine that you are engaged in a tug-of-war with a deadly monster, which represents whatever it is you might be struggling with (mood disturbance, addiction, pain). Between you and the monster is a bottomless pit. The monster is trying to pull you into the pit, and you are trying to do the same to the monster. Why not let go of the rope? That is by far the simplest and most effective solution.

When Freud was dying, he dropped the rope. This is why he still had enough energy left to be interested in what was going on in the world of psychoanalysis. He wasn't struggling to defeat a monster that couldn't be defeated.

You can't face death like Freud without having lived like Freud. You can't decide to be accepting and expect to be instantly transformed. You can't listen to an uplifting song lyric and expect to be reborn. As with everything discussed in this book, philosophical equanimity arises from how you choose to live. You have to practice being the person you want to be.

Acceptance and letting go might seem to contradict the precept that self-reflection and emotional processing are necessary and beneficial. How can you process a traumatic memory if you are observing it from a distance? The dichotomy is false. One doesn't have to choose one or the other strategy. Self-reflection *and* acceptance are both important. Optimal living involves balancing the two. Sometimes, self-reflection is desirable—for example, when attempting to "work through" distressing recollections. At other times, mental health is assisted by letting go.

In popular culture, "never give up" is an inspirational catchphrase. It is repeated with the regularity of a mantra, and can usually be found in the company of "all you need is love" and "follow your dreams." Love is immensely important, but human beings have many other needs. You can follow your dreams, but there is no guarantee that you will ever live them—and heroic perseverance can result in abject failure.

Letting go and giving up are not necessarily negative. Evolutionary psychologists have suggested that depression has been selected because it expedites "giving up" and creates opportunities for productive change.[8] For an ancestral human surviving by foraging for berries, perseverance would have been beneficial, but only up to a point. After the local bushes were stripped of their fruit, energy expenditure would have exceeded energy consumption. Loss of motivation in this case would have been adaptive, insofar as it would have reduced unprofitable foraging, encouraged disengagement, and increased the likelihood of the forager moving on to discover new bushes full of ripe, delicious berries. Once the forager accepted that the first clump of bushes was depleted, and found a new clump, he or she would have once again been able to ingest lots of berries, achieving the maximum number of calories for the energy expended. A well-fed ancestor disposed to transitory but functional episodes of depression would have survived, procreated, and passed on his or her adaptive motivational deficits to progeny.

Giving up and letting go are expressions that have acquired a patina of defeatism. But, as Alfred Adler maintained, sometimes our weaknesses are also our strengths. There are junctures in life when acts of concession, resignation, and surrender are more appropriate than profitless strife.

Freud is often characterized as a pessimist. We see images of a man whose intensity of expression is constantly approximating a frown. He felt uncomfortable being photographed. Freud's acerbic comments, recorded by his admirers, frequently reinforce the caricature. When asked if he ever hankered after eternal life, he replied that any such sentiments were quickly remedied by a head cold.[9] This is very revealing. Freud could only imagine eternal life as prolonged embodiment.

We often make the mistake of associating youth with physicality and old age with intellectualism. But the body is curiously unobtrusive in youth. It carries the mind without complaint. In fact, the experience of being young, healthy, and strong is, somewhat counterintuitively, a little like being disembodied. As bones and muscles age, however, aches and pains accumulate, until existence is punctuated by constant reminders of corporeality.

In the summer before World War I, when Freud was in his late fifties, he was vacationing in the Dolomites. In an essay titled *On Transience*, he recounts going for a walk with two companions: a taciturn friend and a young poet. Unfortunately, the younger man was prone to dark thoughts. With the arrival of winter, the "smiling countryside" would become cold and bare. Nothing that is beautiful is permanent. Human beauty fades and all things must pass. Eventually, all civilizations become dust. His despondency edged toward cosmic horror, a vision of universal desolation—nothingness. How is it possible to enjoy fresh air and sunlight when everything is transient? A towering doom loomed over the horizon.

Freud was a man whose account of humanity was unflattering in the extreme, an account that was about to be confirmed with the outbreak of war. He should have agreed with his young companion. It is difficult to enjoy beauty, knowing that it will decay. Transience renders everything meaningless. Life is overshadowed by destruction, desolation, death.

Yet Freud said nothing of the sort. Although he acknowledged that truth is often painful and everything we value will eventually disappear, he felt obliged to challenge the poet. The transience of beauty doesn't make it less valuable. Quite the contrary, the very fact that beauty is transient makes it precious. And to extrapolate further, the brevity of life makes living incalculably precious.

Freud's lyrical justification deserves extended quotation: "The beauty of the human form and face vanish for ever in the course of our own lives, but their evanescence only lends them a fresh charm. A flower that blossoms only for a single night does not seem to us on that account less lovely. Nor can I understand any better why the beauty and perfection of a work of art or an intellectual achievement should lose its worth because of its temporal limitation."[10]

We feel the comforting weight of his hand on our shoulder and the tightening of his grip communicating authority and assurance.

"A time may indeed come when . . . all animate life upon the earth ceases; but since the value of all this beauty and perfection is determined only by its significance for our emotional lives, it has no need to survive us and is therefore independent of absolute duration."[11] When Freud says that beauty and perfection have no need to survive us, he is not failing to acknowledge future generations. He is speaking about *all* of humanity. Our descendants will experience beauty and perfection, and its significance will be determined by its impact on their emotional lives, too. Just like us. Life is worth living even up to the point where all life ceases.

Freud's pessimism, on close inspection, often resolves into realism: a constructive, benign realism that does not balk at difficult truths, does not seek to gloss over the pity of the human condition, does not offer trite words of comfort and empty platitudes, but nevertheless encourages us to celebrate the fact of our own existence in a universe of transient but affecting delights.

CONCLUSION

Edward Hopper's *Nighthawks* is probably his best-known painting. It is certainly among his most widely reproduced images. Many art lovers agree that the compositional elements and distinctive palette of *Nighthawks* coalesce to create what is possibly the purest and most complete expression of his art. His principal theme, the melancholy of urban alienation, is given its definitive treatment. Three patrons (a couple who face us and a man who sits with his back to us) are leaning on the counter of a diner, and a uniformed waiter, standing behind the counter, bends to attend to some chore or other. We view this group through a large rectangular window that resembles the glass panel of an aquarium. It is late, maybe even the early hours of the morning, and the shops behind the diner are closed. Hopper's diner is minimal, there is no evidence of food apart from salt and pepper shakers. Everything is so stripped down that the interior looks like an imaginary prototype or a reconstructed dream. This impression of abstracted reality belies the fact that Hopper's diner is actually modeled on a smaller original that once existed on a corner of Greenwich Street in Lower Manhattan. The prose equivalent of this painting would be authenticated by the caption "Based on a true story."

Nighthawks was completed in January 1942, a significant juncture in world history. Only a month earlier, the Japanese had bombed the American fleet at Pearl Harbor. German U-boats were already in the waters around New York City. Beyond the proximal darkness that envelops the diner is the distal darkness of global conflict, concentration camps, and the threat of conquest and totalitarian rule.

Hopper's diner has no exit. Most people don't notice this omission because the eye is so strongly attracted to the central group. How did the quartet get into the diner? And how will they get out? Are they trapped inside? Hopper was fond of incorporating impossibilities into his paintings. Even though they are often missed, such anomalies seem to register in the unconscious and create ripples of unease that pass through the conscious mind. We sense that something isn't quite right, but we can't say what it is exactly.

The sidewalk outside the diner is illuminated by green light that spills out from within and casts tinted shadows. In her book *The Lonely City*, Olivia Laing comments on this detail: "There is no colour in existence that so powerfully communicates urban alienation, the atomisation of human beings inside the edifices they create, as this noxious pallid green, which only came into being with the advent of electricity, and which is inextricably associated with the nocturnal sky, the city of glass towers, of empty illuminated offices and neon signs." Laing also likens this shade of green to the color of an iceberg, stirring intimations of frigidity and desolation. The reputation that *Nighthawks* has earned as being the most representative of all Hopper's paintings is verified by its deadly silence. Hopper has sealed off his quartet from the rest of the world. They exist in what Laing describes as a "bubble of greenish glass." We can't even avail ourselves of the theoretical possibility of opening a door to hear what they're saying—because there isn't one. The diner has been effectively soundproofed.[1]

Nighthawks is everything we have come to expect from Hopper, a disturbing foray into the twilight zone where anomalies gnaw away at the fringes of consciousness, where lonely people encircled by shadows await the arrival of existential threats: social disintegration, calamity, loss of liberty, perhaps even the apocalypse.

But is this an accurate reading of *Nighthawks*? Or are we simply jumping to conclusions, because this interpretation is consistent with what we already know about Hopper and his work? Has overfamiliarity turned the painting into a kind of Rorschach test, the ambiguities of which resolve all too conveniently in accordance with our expectations?

Walter Wells willingly conceded that pessimism is probably the strongest undercurrent of Hopper's work, but he also believed that many of Hopper's paintings, if revisited without prejudice, yield far more optimistic interpretations than art criticism usually allows. If we stand in front of Hopper's canvases with an open mind, we will discover not only men and women who are isolated and threatened by blocks of predatory darkness, but also others who have found "ways to defy, or at least forestall, the coming of ultimate night." Wells counted (somewhat surprisingly) *Nighthawks* among Hopper's more uplifting studies of the human condition.

Wells approached *Nighthawks* obliquely through the writings of Ernest Hemingway. We know that Hopper was impressed by Hemingway's fiction (especially his early short stories), because when "The Killers" was first published in *Scribner's Magazine*, Hopper wrote to the editor praising the power and honesty of Hemingway's style. The art historian Gail Levin has written about commonalities (especially with regard to mood and setting) that connect "The Killers" with *Nighthawks*. Wells, however, was of the opinion that an entirely different Hemingway short story could supply us with more penetrating insights into the genesis and meaning of Hopper's iconic painting.

In Hemingway's "A Clean, Well-Lighted Place," published in 1933, two café waiters (one young, the other more senior) discuss a suicidally depressed old man who lingers long after the other customers have departed. The younger waiter, eager to close the café and get home to his wife, refuses to serve the old man, who is then obliged to leave. The senior waiter is more compassionate. He understands that, for the old man, the café is more than just somewhere to eat and drink. It is a haven, an asylum, a place of safety. Wells reinforced this point: "The café is his only stay against the night. It provides him with sanctuary against the ultimate night in a world without God or spiritual solace."

Like Hemingway's sad old man, the patrons of *Nighthawks* have also found sanctuary in a clean, well-lighted place. There is a black opaqueness behind them—not quite as black and feature-less as the void in *Automat*, but it means much the same thing. There are, however, several differences. The light in the diner is repelling the night more successfully; the darkness isn't total, and, calculated as a proportion of the total surface area, the rectangle of darkness in *Nighthawks* takes up much less space than the square of oblivion that dominates *Automat*. So perhaps this isn't an existential departure lounge after all. Perhaps Hopper has painted a refuge—and perhaps the absence of a door doesn't carry the implication that the diner patrons are trapped inside, but instead suggests that they are shielded from harm.

Perhaps we should take another look at Hopper's noxious and sickly light. Wells was warmed, rather than chilled, by its viridescence: "To see this light in the painting as intimidating, alienating, or dehumanizing, as some have, is to miss the point: that this light is artificial. It is a light of man's own devising—not God's—to overcome the existential darkness. Its artificiality is evident in the greenish glow suffusing the sidewalk outside: green, but unnaturally so, a man made green." Fluorescent lighting, a relatively new development in the 1940s, had more positive connotations for Hopper than it has for us today. It was modern and forward-looking. It added more metaphorical candlepower to the light in "enlightenment."

The problems of living require rational solutions. Praying won't repel darkness anywhere near as efficiently as mercury vapor excited by electricity in a tube.

Art critics assert that the *Nighthawks* couple are lost in separate reveries. Yet they are sitting close together, and Hopper's symbolism is emphatically sexual. Their fingers are touching, or at least overlapping, and the man is holding a phallic cigar in his right hand. The woman is a redhead—the color of desire—a signal that Hopper chose to amplify with a red dress and lipstick. She is contemplating matches that she could use to light the man's cigar. This couple are not lost in separate reveries. They are not drifting off in opposite directions. Their thoughts seem to be converging on the prospect of intimacy.

Wells concluded that *Nighthawks* "represents a small but profoundly important victory: a holding action against the void. It has, for good reason, become one of the most resonant pictorial icons of our times."

Why should we privilege Wells's reading over bleaker alternatives?

In the 1950s, the art historian Katharine Kuh interviewed Hopper for a book titled *The Artist's Voice*. She asked him to nominate a favorite work of his own and he named three, one of which was *Nighthawks*. Kuh pressed Hopper for more information. She wanted him to clarify the painting's themes, to confirm that his work was about loneliness. Hopper's immediate response was a blunt denial: "I didn't see it as particularly lonely."

Nighthawks re-creates a primal situation that has been a feature of human existence for millennia: men and women coming together to find comfort in spheres of illumination (the campfire, the hearth) that hold back the night, in order to talk and tell stories, stories about themselves, stories about others, stories that define who they are—who *we* are—and that make sense of the world. We cannot hear the people in *Nighthawks*, but we can be certain that they have been talking (the waiter's mouth is open) or are about to talk. The late hour will very probably encourage them to speak plainly and freely, and their unguarded trains of association might lead them toward adventitious discoveries. Perhaps they will make connections between their past and their present, gain insights, and see new ways of negotiating the future. Perhaps their self-disclosures will be accompanied by feelings of relief.

My most vivid recollections of clinical practice are all autumnal: sitting in hospitals, clinics, and consulting rooms, well-lighted places, deep in conversation with patients who occupy chairs in front of tall windows that have transitioned from blue to black. The patient and I are companions in a tiny bubble of man-made light that has been plunged by a rotating world into shadow. Those recollected windows are not simply panes of glass in wooden frames, but apertures offering a universal prospect: the emptiness between worlds, the infinite, a reminder of the pitiful fragility of the human animal. Even so, lamplight and conversation,

seemingly modest bulwarks against existential dread, are enough to create a serviceable refuge, a temporary place of safety in which disclosures might lead to better self-understanding and inform the search for love, fulfillment, or meaning.

I have already mentioned my secondary school. My primary school wasn't much better, although for different reasons. I attended a convent school where I was taught by nuns and priests. Even at that impressionable age I found it almost impossible to accept what I was being told because it was so discrepant with my everyday experience of the world. The habits and cassocks, the rituals and incense, the bleeding effigies of Jesus and incessant talk of transubstantiation and miracles seemed, at best, absurd, and at worse, vaguely disturbing. In one of the convent corridors was a framed photograph of a galaxy beneath which was a quotation about God's handiwork. The image filled me with awe, not because it proved that the Book of Genesis was true, but because the swirl of stars suspended in darkness was strikingly beautiful. The sacramental pantomime of Christianity didn't close off my mind to spiritual possibilities. As soon as I reached adulthood, I started following a guru, and I spent three years absorbing "ancient wisdom" in ashrams, meditating almost every day. I had been promised an experience of cosmic consciousness. But I experienced nothing.

At several points in this book I have contrasted religious thinking with the thinking of psychotherapists like Freud. The purpose of these comparisons has been to emphasize the high value many psychotherapists place on accepting embodiment, facing reality, and employing reason. This may have led some readers to conclude that I am antireligious—which would be quite wrong.

I find the militancy and intolerance of many atheists almost indistinguishable from the self-righteous zealotry that I associate with all forms of fundamentalism. Religions provide answers to big questions, and membership in a congregation has many benefits. If you truly believe that when you die you go to heaven, then it is unlikely that you will be greatly troubled by existential angst.

But what if you can't accept religious answers? What if you can't see God's handwork in a swirl of stars—only a manifestation of the laws of physics? What if you engage in devotional activities and still don't feel any connection with the divine? You'll have to look elsewhere for your truths.

Freud suggested that religious faith is a defense erected to protect us from existential terrors. If the defense is secure, then we can be happy, but this kind of happiness is really a form of self-deception. A probable outcome is that the defense will weaken and eventually collapse when tested. The religious individual will then be assailed by doubts. Many claim that their faith is strengthened by adversity, but from a Freudian perspective, this simply shows the extent to which defenses can distort perception and logic. In such instances, reality is twisted so far out of shape that an atrocity like the Holocaust can be reconciled with notions of divine love. Of course, it is conceivable that there *is* a divine plan—and at some elevated level the Holocaust and divine love can be reconciled—but if such a plan exists (and such reconciliations are possible) it is a plan completely beyond human understanding. Men and women of faith readily accept that God works in mysterious ways. Unfortunately, this isn't very helpful for those of us who have no personal experience of the numinous and cannot accept the authority of scripture. We cannot base life decisions on beliefs rooted in obscurity. Life decisions must be based on plausible theories, observations, and demonstrable cause-and-effect relationships.

Although Freud set a precedent, biasing psychotherapy toward materialism, spirituality and psychotherapy are not mutually exclusive. In *Memories, Dreams, Reflections*, Jung described a curious incident. He was visiting Freud in 1909 and the two men were discussing the paranormal. Freud was being so dismissive that Jung became very annoyed. So much so that he started to feel hot and his diaphragm became "a glowing vault." At that moment there was "a loud report in the bookcase." Jung proclaimed, "There, that is an example of a so-called catalytic exteriorisation phenomenon." Freud told him he was talking "sheer bosh." Jung defended himself by predicting another detonation, and sure enough, another followed. Freud wasn't convinced that anything extraordinary had happened. Thereafter, relations between the two men became increasingly strained. Jung was a profoundly spiritual person. He claimed to have foreknowledge of his death, and when someone said to him, "Whatever shall I do when you go and leave me?" Jung replied, "I'll do my very best to welcome you to the other side."

Religious people still have minds and bodies. The fact that they also believe in the soul does not mean that they cannot make use of psychotherapeutic knowledge, which is still pertinent to the material and psychological aspects of their being. Spiritual feelings didn't stop Jung from being a psychologist—nor many others. Oskar Pfister, one of the earliest psychoanalysts and the founder of the Swiss Society for Psychoanalysis, was also a Lutheran minister. He embraced Freud's theories and wrote one of the first psychoanalytic textbooks. The devout, when exploring psychotherapy, are likely to encounter some ideas (particularly to do with sexuality) that are incompatible with religious teaching, but psychotherapy is much more than an account of human sexual development.

Today, people are more unhappy, stressed, and anxious than ever before. Economists warn that Western liberal democracy is at risk as a result. I have suggested that the formulations, frameworks, and ideas associated with psychotherapy should be consulted more frequently as a potential remedy. I would never claim that psychotherapy is a panacea, but I do believe that it has more to offer than most people seem to realize. As a sustained inquiry into the nature of human unhappiness, it transcends the clichés of pop psychology, psychobabble, and cartoon representations of the psychoanalyst's couch.

Many would disagree. Some political theorists, for example, assert that psychotherapy serves capitalist interests.[2] In their view, it postpones indefinitely the implementation of radical and enlightened social policies by diverting attention away from the pernicious effects of inequality, and focusing instead on the individual. We are preoccupied with psychiatric conditions and their treatment and we have failed to give due consideration to more important social causes of distress: inadequate housing, poverty, and lack of opportunity. Political change is what we need now, not more talking cures and meditation classes.

There is certainly some truth in this assertion, but it is only a partial truth.

The reasons why people become mentally ill are many and various: there are evolutionary, biological, psychodynamic, cognitive, and interpersonal causes. The brain is a network composed of one hundred trillion synapses, connecting one hundred billion neurons, that changes its configuration between ten and one hundred times per second. An individual's mental state is determined by environmental contingencies interacting with an unimaginably complex and unpredictable electrochemical information-processing system. To suggest that redistribution of wealth is the solution to all our mental health woes is naïve. After all, rich people get depressed too. A more equal society would almost certainly be a happier society, but people would still experience the uneasiness inherent in culture. They would still be troubled by the same questions that humanity has probably been asking for the past ten thousand years: Who am I? Why am I here? How should I live?

So how can the current mental health crisis be addressed?

Making psychotherapy more widely available is desirable, but this isn't likely to happen anytime soon. An enormous number of therapists would have to be trained to meet the demand, and services would have to be massively expanded at significant cost. Such drastic measures represent an extreme. People in need of psychological help don't have to enter psychotherapy to benefit from the ideas that have arisen out of the practice of psychotherapy. Some do—but not all. Many might be prevented from making the transition from general states of dissatisfaction and worry to clinical depression and anxiety if they were better acquainted with psychoanalytic, humanistic-existential, and cognitive-behavioral thinking.

Psychotherapy, viewed as a cohesive intellectual tradition, is an undervalued and underexploited resource. It is a body of knowledge that is rarely (if ever) perceived as cumulative, interconnected, and broadly applicable to everyday situations (as opposed to narrowly applicable in clinical settings). If mental health professionals were more willing to acknowledge commonalities, instead of always emphasizing differences, then the strengths of this tradition would be more readily appreciated. People would be less confused about what psychotherapy has to offer, not only as a form of treatment, but as an outlook, an orientation, or a worldview.

The dissemination of these ideas could start early. In schools, children are introduced to a number of topics pertinent to the problems of living. Moral instruction, garnished with a little philosophy, is usually provided under the banner of religious education. Practical advice—for example, sex education—often complements the teaching of biology. Courses that present the principal findings of the psychotherapeutic tradition as life lessons might leave a lasting impression on developing minds. A more psychologically and emotionally literate population would be more resilient, and prevention is invariably preferable to cure. I suspect that adolescents, who are already grappling with issues germane to psychotherapy— identity, needs, wants—would be particularly receptive.

Optimal living can be construed as an outcome that results from completing a particular set of tasks. The more of these tasks an individual accomplishes, the less unease he or she will experience, and the more able he or she will be to make beneficial life choices. In the final instance, these choices are always personal. As Victor Frankl said, the individual should search for meaning— not *the* meaning.

If life is a lifetime's work, then there's much work to be done. We are advised by the great psychologists to be reflective so that we can discover who we are; to tell our stories, not least of all to ourselves; to satisfy our basic needs, without harming others, and while avoiding the traps and snares of substitute gratification; to seek safety, so that we can love and be loved; to be a valued member of a social group, even if what we bring to the group is modest and the group is small; to resist excessive acquisitiveness; to combat irrationality; to come to terms with our histories and assimilate adversity; to strive to live in the present moment and fully engage with reality, even when reality makes us uncomfortable; to guard against narcissism, because narcissism cuts us off from others and impoverishes experience; to find our own meaning and purpose; and to cultivate an attitude of acceptance when opportunities to exercise choice are restricted.

These are the things that psychotherapy is concerned with. They overlap with the concerns of other disciplines, such as philosophy and neuroscience, but nevertheless represent a unique perspective.

The principal recommendations of psychotherapy appear to be quite straightforward. But this appearance is deceptive. We are asked, for example, to be more insightful—but psychological insight is extremely difficult to achieve. Our thinking is constantly subject to unconscious influence, and defenses distort reality. Evolutionary psychologists maintain that the brain is designed to delude us.[3] We think we have agency, but in reality this agency is relatively superficial. Ultimately, we are being manipulated by our genes.

Although the truths of psychotherapy are easily reduced to soundbites, they are, in fact, subtle and elusive. They are only partial truths when expressed as words on a page. Their value becomes fully apparent only when they are lived.

Beethoven's *Moonlight Sonata* exists as musical notation. Nothing is missing on the score, but at the same time, everything is missing. Unless the symbols, the semibreves and triplets, are used to guide the movement of fingers on a keyboard, there will be nothing to hear. The *Moonlight Sonata* only exists in the way that it was intended to exist when it is played. The same principle applies to the truths of psychotherapy. They don't really exist unless you act on them. They are only vindicated by the act of living.

You've finished this book. You are now familiar with the score.
Are you ready to start playing?

PICTURE CREDITS

p 179 Geocentric universe, Ullstein bild via Getty Images

p 182 Victorian lady, Shelley Still / Alamy Stock Photo

p 185 Otto Gross, Historic Images / Alamy Stock Photo

p 193 Wilhelm Reich, Chronicle / Alamy Stock Photo

p 202 Alfred Adler, AKG Images / Imagno

p 212 Erich Fromm, Wellcome Images

p 230 William Sargent, Christie's Images / Bridgeman Images

p 243 *Chop Suey* (Hopper), AKG Images / Imagno

p 250 Viktor Frankl, Bettmann / Getty Images

p 257 Carl Rogers, Bridgeman Images

p 270 Sigmund Freud sketch, Science Photo Library

p 285 *Nighthawks* (Hopper), Friends of American Art Collection / Bridgeman Images

p 291 Galaxy, Bridgeman Images

p 299 Sonata, Public Domain

ACKNOWLEDGMENTS

I would like to thank my excellent editors in London and New York—Richard Beswick, Claire Potter, and Lara Heimert; copy editors Katherine Streckfus and Dan Balado; Nithya Rae; my agent Clare Alexander; and Nicola Fox for reading and rereading earlier drafts.

NOTES AND REFERENCES

Major references are cited in the text. Selected supplementary references are provided below.

INTRODUCTION

1. Jesse Bering, *A Very Human Ending: How Suicide Haunts Our Species* (London: Doubleday, 2018).

2. Graham Davey, *The Anxiety Epidemic: The Causes of Our Modern Day Anxieties* (London: Robinson, 2018).

3. A. Przybylski, "Screen Time Debunked," *The Psychologist*, June 2019, 16.

4. J. M. Twenge, G. N. Martin, and W. K. Campbell, "Decreases in Psychological Well-Being Among American Adolescents After 2012 and Links to Screen Time During the Rise of Smartphone Technology," *Emotion* 18, no. 6 (2018): 765–780.

5. Berners-Lee speech at Web Summit, Lisbon, quoted in Ian Sample, "Tim Berners-Lee Launches a Campaign to Save the Web from Abuse," *The Guardian*, November 5, 2018, https://www.theguardian.com/technology/2018/nov/05/tim-berners-lee-launches-campaign-to-save-the-web-from-abuse.

6. "Spirit of the Age," *The Week*, March 23, 2019.

7. Eric R. Kandel, *The Age of Insight: The Quest to Understand the Unconscious in Art, Mind, and Brain, from Vienna 1900 to the Present* (New York: Random House, 2012), 47.

8. Catharine Arnold, *Bedlam: London and Its Mad* (London: Simon and Schuster, 2008).

9. Lisa Appignanesi and John Forrester, *Freud's Women* (London: Weidenfeld and Nicolson, 1992).

CHAPTER 1. TALKING: LEAVING THE SILENT THEATER

1. E. Becker, *The Denial of Death* (New York: Free Press, 1973).

2. Steven Pinker, *The Language Instinct: How the Mind Creates Language* (New York: William Morrow, 1994).

3. M. Mikulciner and P. Shaver, "Special Article: An Attachment Perspective on Psychopathology," *World Psychiatry* 11 (2013): 11–15.

4. Mary Aitken, *The Cyber Effect: A Pioneering Cyber Psychologist Explains How Human Behaviour Changes Online* (London: John Murray, 2016).

5. K. Wellings, M. J. Palmer, K. Machiyama, and E. Slaymaker, "Changes in, and Factors Associated with, Frequency of Sex in Britain: Evidence from Three National Surveys of Sexual Attitudes and Lifestyles (Natsal)," *British Medical Journal*, May 7, 2019, 365.

6. Anthony Stevens, *Private Myths: Dreams and Dreaming* (London: Hamish Hamilton, 1995); Alice Robb, *Why We Dream: The Science, Creativity and Transformative Power of Dreams* (New York: Houghton Mifflin Harcourt, 2018).

7. Matthew Walker, *Why We Sleep: Unlocking the Power of Sleep and Dreams* (New York: Scribner, 2017).

8. John McCrone, *Going Inside: A Tour Round a Single Moment of Consciousness* (London: Faber and Faber, 1999).

9. S. Lacey, R. Stilla, and K. Sathian, "Metaphorical Feeling: Comprehending Textural Metaphors Activates Somatosensory Cortex," *Brain and Language* 120, no. 3 (2012): 416–421.

10. Stephen Farber and Marc Green, *Hollywood on the Couch* (New York: William Morrow, 1993).

11. Fritz Perls, *In and Out of the Garbage Pail* (New York: Bantam, 1972).

12. James W. Pennebaker, *Opening Up: The Healing Power of Expressing Emotions* (New York: Guilford Press, 1990), 19.

13. D. Wegner, *White Bears and Other Unwanted Thoughts: Suppression, Obsession, and the Psychology of Mental Control* (New York: Viking Penguin, 1989).

14. M. L. Slepian, J. S. Chun, and M. F. Mason, "The Experience of Secrecy," *Journal of Personality and Social Psychology* 113, no. 1 (2017): 1–33.

15. R. A. Bryant, M. Wyzenbeek, and J. Weinstein, "Dream Rebound of Suppressed Emotional Thoughts: The Influence of Cognitive Load," *Consciousness and Cognition* 20, no. 3 (2011): 515–522.

16. M. Slepian, E. Masicampo, N. Toosi, and N. Ambady, "The Physical Burdens of Secrecy," *Journal of Experimental Psychology: General* 141, no. 4 (2012): 619–624.

17. Peter Wohlleben, *The Hidden Life of Trees: What They Feel, How They Communicate* (London: William Collins, 2017).

18. R. S. Weiss, *Loneliness: The Experience of Emotional and Social Isolation* (Cambridge, MA: MIT Press, 1973).

19. S. Cacioppo, J. Capitanio, and J. Cacioppo, "Toward a Neurology of Loneliness," *Psychological Bulletin* 140, no. 6 (2014): 1464–1504.

20. Olivia Laing, *The Lonely City: Adventures in the Art of Being Alone* (Edinburgh: Canongate, 2017), 31, 38.

CHAPTER 2. SECURITY: PRIMAL NEEDS

1. M. Huttunen and P. Niskanen, "Prenatal Loss of Father and Psychiatric Disorders," *Archives of General Psychiatry* 35 (1978): 429–431.

2. J. Parnas, F. Schulsinger, T. W. Teasdale, and H. Schulsinger, "Perinatal Complications and Clinical Outcome Within the Schizophrenia Spectrum," *British Journal of Psychiatry* 140, no. 4 (1982): 416–420.

3. Stanislav Grof, *LSD: Doorway to the Numinous. The Groundbreaking Psychedelic Research into Realms of the Human Unconscious* (Rochester, VT: Park Street Press, 2009).

4. M. Mendonça, A. Bilgin, and D. Wolke, "Association of Preterm Birth and Low Birth Weight with Romantic Partnership, Sexual Intercourse, and Parenthood in Adulthood: A Systematic Review and Meta-Analysis," *JAMA Network. Original Investigation: Pediatrics*, July 12, 2019.

5. John Bowlby, *A Secure Base: Clinical Applications of Attachment Theory* (London: Routledge, 1988).

6. Sue Gerhardt, *Why Love Matters: How Affection Shapes a Baby's Brain* (Hove, UK: Routledge, 2004).

7. M. Brower and B. Price, "Neuropsychiatry of Frontal Lobe Dysfunction in Violent and Criminal Behaviour: A Critical Review," *Journal of Neurology, Neurosurgery and Psychiatry* 71 (2001): 720–726.

8. Arthur Janov, *The Primal Scream: Primal Therapy, the Cure for Neurosis* (New York: Putnam, 1970).

9. Jerry Hopkins, "The Primal Doctor," *Rolling Stone*, February 18, 1971.

CHAPTER 3. INSIGHT: THE HEART HAS ITS REASONS

1. Hans Eysenck, *Rebel with a Cause*, rev. ed. (London: Routledge, 2017), 302, 287.

2. S. Kaburu, S. Inque, and N. Newton-Fisher, "Death of the Alpha: Within-Community Lethal Violence Among Chimpanzees of the Mahale Mountains National Park," *American Journal of Primatology* 75 (2013): 789–797; J. Pruetz, K. Boyer Ontl, E. Cleaveland, S. Lindshield, J. Marshack, and E.

Wessling, "Intragroup Lethal Aggression in West African Chimpanzees (*Pan troglodytes verus*): Inferred Killing of a Former Alpha Male at Fongli, Senegal," *International Journal of Primatology* 38, no. 1 (2017): 31–57.

3. Seth Stephens-Davidowitz, *Everybody Lies: What the Internet Can Tell Us About Who We Really Are* (New York: HarperCollins, 2017).

4. Eysenck, *Rebel with a Cause*, 13.

5. F. Perrin, L. Garcia-Larrea, F. Mauguière, and H. Bastuji, "A Differential Brain Response to the Subject's Own Name Persists During Sleep," *Clinical Neurophysiology* 110, no. 12 (1999): 2153–2164.

6. Norman Dixon, *Preconscious Processing* (Chichester, UK: John Wiley and Sons, 1981).

7. L. Weiskrantz, E. K. Warrington, M. D. Sanders, and J. Marshall, "Visual Capacity in the Hemianopic Field Following a Restricted Occipital Ablation," *Brain* 97 (1974): 709–728.

8. M. T. Diaz and G. McCarthy, "Unconscious Word Processing Engages a Distributed Network of Brain Regions," *Journal of Cognitive Neuroscience* 19, no. 11 (2007): 1768–1775.

9. Jonathan Miller, "Going Unconscious," in *Hidden Histories of Science*, ed. Robert B. Silvers (London: Granta, 1997).

10. Nello Christiani, "In Our Image: The Challenge of Creating Intelligent Machines," in *Machines That Think*, ed. Douglas Heaven (London: John Murray, 2017).

11. M. S. Gazzaniga, "The Split Brain Revisited," *Scientific American* 279, no. 1 (1998): 50–55.

CHAPTER 4. DISTORTION: WARPED MIRRORS

1. E. F. Loftus and J. C. Palmer, "Reconstruction of Automobile Destruction: An Example of the Interaction Between Language and Memory," *Journal of Verbal Learning and Verbal Behavior* 13 (1974): 585–589.

2. Anna Freud, *The Ego and the Mechanisms of Defence* (London: Routledge, 1992), 26.

3. Robert Coles, *Anna Freud: The Dream of Psychoanalysis* (Cambridge, MA: Perseus, 1992).

4. Bruce Wexler, *Brain and Culture* (Cambridge, MA: MIT Press, 2008).

5. Damion Searls, *The Inkblots: Hermann Rorschach, His Iconic Test and the Power of Seeing* (London: Simon and Schuster, 2017).

6. Jack El-Hai, *The Nazi and the Psychiatrist: Hermann Göring, Dr. Douglas M. Kelley, and a Fatal Meeting of Minds at the End of WWII* (New York: Public Affairs, 2013).

CHAPTER 5. IDENTITY: THE DIVIDED SELF

1. K. Ratner, J. Mendle, and A. Burrow, "Depression and Derailment: A Cyclical Model of Mental Illness and Perceived Identity Change," *Clinical Psychological Science*, April 2019.

2. C. G. Jung, "The Development of Personality" (1934), in *The Essential Jung: Selected and Introduced by Anthony Storr* (Princeton, NJ: Princeton University Press, 1983), 203.

3. "Young People Edit Social Media Photos," *Sunday Times*, May 12, 2019.

4. V. Tausk, "On the Origin of the 'Influencing Machine' in Schizophrenia" (1919), reproduced in *Journal of Psychotherapy Practice and Research* 1, no. 2 (Spring 1992).

5. C. Morgan, M. Charalambides, G. Hutchinson, and R. M. Murray, "Migration, Ethnicity, and Psychosis: Toward a Sociodevelopmental Model," *Schizophrenia Bulletin* 36, no. 4 (July 2010): 655–664.

6. Susan Greenfield, *I.D.: The Quest for Identity in the 21st Century* (London: Sceptre, 2008).

7. D. Langleben, J. Hakun, D. Seelig, A. Wang, K. Ruparel, W. Bilker, and R. Gur, "Polygraphy and Functional Magnetic Resonance Imaging in Lie Detection," *Journal of Clinical Psychiatry* 77, no. 10 (2016): 1372–1380.

8. R. Bucker, J. Andrews-Hanna, and D. Schacter, "The Brain's Default Network," *Annals of the New York Academy of Sciences* 1124, no. 1 (2008).

9. D. Fair, A. Cohen, N. Dosenbach, J. Church, F. Miezin, D. Barch, M. Raichle, S. Petersen, and B. Schlagger, "The Maturing Architecture of the Brain's Default Network," *Proceedings of the National Academy of Sciences of the United States of America* 105, no. 10 (2008): 4028–4032.

10. Quoted in Michael Pollan, *How to Change Your Mind: The New Science of Psychedelics* (New York: Penguin Press, 2018).

11. Daniel Kahneman, *Thinking, Fast and Slow* (New York: Farrar, Straus and Giroux, 2011).

12. R. Toomey, A. Syvertsen, and M. Shramko, "Transgender Adolescent Suicide Behaviour," *Pediatrics* 142 (2018): 4.

CHAPTER 6. NARRATIVE: LIFE STORY

1. Daniel J. Povinelli and John G.H. Cant, "Arboreal Clambering and the Evolution of Self-Conception," *Quarterly Review of Biology* 70, no. 4 (1996): 393–421.

2. Sigmund Freud, *The Wolf Man by the Wolf Man: The Double Story of Freud's Most Famous Patient*, ed. Muriel Gardiner (New York: Basic Books, 1971).

3. Bessel van der Kolk, *The Body Keeps the Score: Mind, Brain and Body in the Transformation of Trauma* (New York: Viking Penguin, 2014).

4. Christopher Booker, *The Seven Basic Plots: Why We Tell Stories* (London: Continuum, 2004).

5. David Canter, *Mapping Murder: The Secrets of Geographical Profiling* (London: Virgin Books, 2003).

6. David Eagleman, *Incognito: The Secret Lives of the Brain* (New York: Doubleday, 2011).

CHAPTER 7. NARCISSISM: GAZING INTO THE POOL

1. Ovid, *Metamorphoses*, trans. Mary M. Innes (Harmondsworth, UK: Penguin, 1955), 87.

2. J. Sutton, "Seeing Screen Time Differently," *The Psychologist* 31 (March 2018): 18–21.

3. J. M. Twenge, S. Konrath, J. D. Foster, W. K. Campbell, and B. J. Bushman, "Egos Inflating over Time: A Cross-Temporal Meta-Analysis of the Narcissistic Personality Inventory," *Journal of Personality* 76, no. 4 (2008): 875–902.

4. Minda Zetlin, "Taking Selfies Destroys Your Confidence and Raises Anxiety, a Study Shows. Why Are You Still Doing It?" *Inc.*, https://www.inc .com/minda-zetlin/taking-selfies-anxiety-confidence-loss-feeling-unattractive .html; Richard Gray, "What a Vain Bunch We Really Are! 24 Billion Selfies Were Uploaded to Google Last Year," *Daily Mail*, June 1, 2016, https://www .dailymail.co.uk/sciencetech/article-3619679/What-vain-bunch-really-24 -billion-selfies-uploaded-Google-year.html.

5. R. Sansone and L. Sansone, "Road Rage. What's Driving It?" *Psychiatry* 7, no. 7 (2010): 14–18; K. DeCelles and M. Norton, "Physical and Situational Inequality on Airplanes Predicts Air Rage," *Proceedings of the National Academy of Sciences of the United States of America* 113, no. 20 (2016): 5588–5591.

6. D. Byrne and K. Murnen, "Maintaining Loving Relationships," in *The Psychology of Love*, ed. R. Sternberg and L. Barnes (New Haven, CT: Yale University Press, 1988).

7. S. Jacob, M. K. McClintock, B. Zelano, and C. Ober, "Paternally Inherited HLA Alleles Are Associated with Women's Choice of Male Odor," *Nature Genetics* 30, no. 2 (February 2002): 175–179.

8. Rupert Sheldrake, *Science and Spiritual Practices: Reconnecting Through Direct Experience* (London: Coronet, 2017).

9. Aldous Huxley, *The Doors of Perception* (New York: HarperCollins, 2009 [1956]), 52–53.

10. Sigmund Freud, "Lecture 18: Fixation to Traumas—The Unconscious," in Freud, *Introductory Lectures on Psychoanalysis*, trans. James Strachey,

ed. Angela Richards, Pelican Freud Library, vol. 1 (London: Penguin, 1987 [1973]).

CHAPTER 8. SEX: MORTAL VEHICLES

1. Sigmund Freud, "On the Universal Tendency to Debasement in the Sphere of Love," in Freud, *On Sexuality: Three Essays on the Theory of Sexuality and Other Works*, trans. James Strachey, ed. Angela Richards, Pelican Freud Library, vol. 7 (London: Penguin, 1991 [1953]).

2. Jonathan Amos, "Ancient Phallus Unearthed in Cave," BBC, July 2005, http://news.bbc.co.uk/1/hi/sci/tech/4713323.stm.

3. Alex Butterworth, *The World That Never Was: A True Story of Dreamers, Schemers, Anarchists and Secret Agents* (London: Bodley Head, 2010).

4. Ronald Hayman, *A Life of Jung* (London: Bloomsbury, 1999).

5. Helen Fisher, *Anatomy of Love: A Natural History of Mating, Marriage, and Why We Stray* (New York: W. W. Norton, 2016).

6. S. Glass and T. Wright, "Sex Differences in Type of Extramarital Involvement and Marital Dissatisfaction," *Sex Roles* 12 (1985): 1101–1120.

7. R. de Visser and D. McDonald, "Swings and Roundabouts: Management of Jealousy in Heterosexual Swinging Couples," *British Journal of Social Psychology* 46, Part 2 (2007): 459–476.

8. A. J. Cherlin, *The Marriage Go-Round: The State of Marriage and the Family in America Today* (New York: Knopf, 2009).

9. E. Shor, D. Roelfs, P. Bugyi, and J. Schwartz, "Meta-Analysis of Marital Dissolution and Mortality: Reevaluating the Intersection of Gender and Age," *Social Science and Medicine* 75, no. 1 (2012): 46–59.

10. Peter Gay, *Freud: A Life for Our Time* (London: J. M. Dent and Sons, 1988).

11. D. Scheele, N. Striepens, O. Gunturkun, S. Deutschlander, W. Maier, K. M. Kendrick, and R. Hurlemann, "Oxytocin Modulates Social Distance Between Males and Females," *Journal of Neuroscience* 32, no. 46 (November 14, 2012): 16074–16079; A. Burri and A. Carvalheira, "Masturbatory Behavior in a Population Sample of German Women," *Journal of Sexual Medicine* 16, no. 7 (July 2019): 963–974; P. Haake, T. H. Krueger, M. U. Goebel, K. M. Heberling, U. Hartmann, and M. Schedlowski, "Effects of Sexual Arousal on Lymphocyte Subset Circulation and Cytokine Production in Man," *Neuroimmunomodulation* 11, no. 5 (2004): 293–298; G. Davey Smith, S. Frankel, and J. Yarnell, "Sex and Death: Are They Related? Findings from the Caerphilly Cohort Study," *British Medical Journal* 315, no. 7123 (December 1997): 1641.

12. A. S. Neill, "The Man Reich" (1958), reproduced in David Boadella, *Wilhelm Reich: The Evolution of His Work* (London: Vision Press, 1973).

13. Seth Stephens-Davidowitz, *Everybody Lies: What the Internet Tells Us About Who We Really Are* (New York: HarperCollins, 2017).

14. J. Bivona and J. Critelli, "The Nature of Women's Rape Fantasies: An Analysis of Prevalence, Frequency, and Contents," *Journal of Sex Research* 46, no. 1 (January 2009): 33–45.

CHAPTER 9. INFERIORITY: THE CONSOLATIONS OF INADEQUACY

1. Colin Brett, Introduction to *Understanding Life: An Introduction to the Psychology of Alfred Adler* (Oxford: Oneworld Publications, 1997), originally published as Alfred Adler, *The Science of Living* (1927).

2. H. Ellenberger, *The Discovery of the Unconscious: The History and Evolution of Dynamic Psychiatry* (New York: Basic Books, 1970).

CHAPTER 10. WANTS: THE ACQUISITION TRAP

1. Mark O'Connell, *To Be a Machine: Adventures Among Cyborgs, Utopians, Hackers, and the Futurists Solving the Modest Problem of Death* (London: Granta, 2017).

2. Irvin D. Yalom, *Love's Executioner and Other Tales of Psychotherapy* (London: Bloomsbury, 1989).

3. Paul Mazur's words, first published in a 1927 issue of the *Harvard Business Review*, are often quoted. See, for example, Gus Lubin, "There's a Staggering Conspiracy Behind the Rise of Consumer Culture," *Business Insider*, February 23, 2013, https://www.businessinsider.com/birth-of-consumer-culture-2013-2.

4. S. Ross, "Therapeutic Use of Classic Psychedelics to Treat Cancer-Related Psychiatric Distress," *International Review of Psychiatry* 30, no. 4 (August 13, 2018): 1–14.

5. D. Tamir, E. Templeton, A. Ward, and J. Zaki, "Media Usage Diminishes Memory for Experiences," *Journal of Experimental Social Psychology* 76 (May 2018): 161–168.

CHAPTER 11. ADVERSITY: ROOTED SORROWS

1. "Child Maltreatment," World Health Organization, September 30, 2016, https://www.who.int/news-room/fact-sheets/detail/child-maltreatment.

2. M. C. Black, K. C. Basile, M. J. Breiding, S. G. Smith, M. L. Walters, M. T. Merrick, J. Chen, and M. R. Stevens, *National Intimate Partner and Sexual Violence Survey: 2010 Summary Report*, National Center for Injury Prevention and Control, Division of Violence Prevention, and Centers for Disease

Control and Prevention, 2011, https://www.cdc.gov/ViolencePrevention/pdf
/NISVS_Report2010-a.pdf, 2.

3. J. S. Chandan, T. Thomas, C. Bradbury-Jones, and R. Russell, "Female Survivors of Intimate Partner Violence and Risk of Depression, Anxiety and Serious Mental Illness," *British Journal of Psychiatry* (June 7, 2019) (Epub ahead of print).

4. Bessel van der Kolk, *The Body Keeps the Score: Mind, Brain and Body in the Transformation of Trauma* (New York: Viking Penguin, 2014).

5. William H. Frey, with Muriel Lanseth, *Crying: The Mystery of Tears* (Minneapolis: Winston, 1985).

6. Dominic Streatfeild, *Brainwash: The Secret History of Mind Control* (London: Hodder and Stoughton, 2006).

7. William Sargant, *The Unquiet Mind* (London: Heinemann, 1967).

8. J. Kläsi, "Uber die therapeutische Anwendung der 'Dauernarkose' mittels Somnifen bei Schizophrenen," *Zeitschrift für die gesamte Neurologie und Psychiatrie* 74 (1922): 557.

9. T. G. Stampfl and D. J. Levis, "Essentials of Implosive Therapy: A Learning-Theory-Based Psychodynamic Behavioral Therapy," *Journal of Abnormal Psychology* 72, no. 6 (1967): 496–503.

10. H. Chilcoat and N. Breslau, "Posttraumatic Stress Disorder and Drug Disorders: Testing Causal Pathways," *Archives of General Psychiatry* 55 (1998): 913–917.

11. Francine Shapiro, *Eye Movement Desensitization and Reprocessing (EMDR) Therapy: Basic Principles, Protocols, and Procedures*, 3rd ed. (New York: Guilford Press, 2018).

12. Matthew Walker, *Why We Sleep: The New Science of Sleep and Dreams* (London: Allen Lane, 2017).

13. R. Stickgold, "EMDR: A Putative Neurobiological Mechanism of Action," *Journal of Clinical Psychology* 58, no. 1 (2002): 61–75.

14. J. Laugharne, C. Kullack, C. W. Lee, T. McGuire, S. Brockman, P. D. Drummond, and S. Starkstein, "Amygdala Volumetric Change Following Psychotherapy for Posttraumatic Stress Disorder," *Journal of Neuropsychiatry and Clinical Neurosciences* 28, no. 4 (2016): 312–318; L. Bossini, E. Santarnecchi, I. Casolaro, D. Koukouna, C. Caterini, F. Cechini, V. Fortini, et al., "Morphovolumetric Changes After EMDR Treatment in Drug-Naïve PTSD Patients," *Rivista di Psichiatria* 52, no. 1 (2017): 24–31; K. Lansing, D. Amen, C. Hanks, and L. Rudy, "High Resolution Brain SPECT Imaging and EMDR in Police Officers with PTSD," *Journal of Neuropsychiatry and Clinical Neurosciences* 17 (2005): 526–532.

CHAPTER 12. MEANING: REASONS TO EXIST

1. Nadine Wajakovski, "Dita Kraus: The Librarian of Auschwitz," *Jewish Chronicle*, January 26, 2018.

2. Viktor E. Frankl, *Man's Search for Meaning*, trans. Ilse Lasch (Boston: Beacon Press, 2015), 12.

3. Ibid., 62.

4. Ibid., 105.

5. Viktor E. Frankl, *Man's Search for Ultimate Meaning* (New York: Basic Books, 2000), 141.

6. Ibid., 143.

7. S. Clift, G. Hancox, I. Morrison, B. Hess, G. Kreutz, and D. Stewart, "Choral Singing and Psychological Wellbeing: Quantitative and Qualitative Findings from English Choirs in a Cross-National Survey," *Journal of Applied Arts and Health* 1(2010): 19–34.

CHAPTER 13. ACCEPTANCE: A FLOWER THAT BLOSSOMS ONLY FOR A SINGLE NIGHT

1. Mark Edmundson, *The Death of Sigmund Freud: Fascism, Psychoanalysis and the Rise of Fundamentalism* (London: Bloomsbury, 2007).

2. Ernest Jones, *The Life and Work of Sigmund Freud* (Lexington, MA: Plunkett Lake Press).

3. Ibid.

4. Martin Freud, *Glory Reflected: Sigmund Freud—Man and Father* (London: Angus and Robertson, 1957).

5. Lawrence Fine, *Physician of the Soul, Healer of the Cosmos: Isaac Luria and His Kabbalistic Fellowship* (Stanford, CA: Stanford University Press, 2003).

6. P. Grossman, L. Neimann, S. Schmidt, and H. Walach, "Mindfulness-Based Stress Reduction and Health Benefits: A Meta-Analysis," *Journal of Psychosomatic Research* 57, no. 1 (2004): 35–43.

7. B. Hölzel, J. Carmody, M. Vangel, C. Congleton, S. Yerramsetti, T. Gar, and S. Lazar, "Mindfulness Practice Leads to Increases in Regional Gray Matter Density," *Psychiatry Research* 19, no. 1 (2011): 36–43.

8. Randolph M. Nesse, *Good Reasons for Bad Feelings* (New York: Dutton, 2019).

9. Lou Andreas-Salomé, *The Freud Journal of Lou Andreas-Salomé*, trans. Stanley A. Leavy (New York: Basic Books, 1964).

10. Sigmund Freud, "On Transience," in Freud, *Art and Literature*, ed. Albert Dickson, Pelican Freud Library, vol. 14 (London: Penguin, 1990), 288.

11. Ibid.

CONCLUSION

1. Olivia Laing, *The Lonely City: Adventures in the Art of Being Alone* (Edinburgh: Canongate, 2017).

2. Mark Fisher, *Capitalist Realism: Is There No Alternative?* (Winchester, UK: Zero Books, 2009).

3. Robert Wright, *Why Buddhism Is True: The Science and Philosophy of Mediation and Enlightenment* (New York: Simon and Schuster, 2017).

INDEX

Credit: ©Alexander Tallis

Frank Tallis is a clinical psychologist and the critically acclaimed author of over fifteen fiction and nonfiction titles. He previously taught clinical psychology at the Institute of Psychiatry, Psychology, and Neuroscience at King's College, London. He splits his time between London and Bonnieux, France.

http://www.franktallis.com

@FrankTallis